Women and Islam in Bangladesh

Women and Islam in Bangladesh

Beyond Subjection and Tyranny

Taj I. Hashmi
Professor and Director
School of Liberal Arts and Science
Independent University
Bangladesh

Published by PALGRAVE MACMILLAN
Houndmills, Basingstoke, Hampshire RG21 6XS and
175 Fifth Avenue, New York, N. Y. 10010
Companies and representatives throughout the world

PALGRAVE MACMILLAN is the global academic imprint of the Palgrave
Macmillan division of St. Martin's Press, LLC and of Palgrave Macmillan Ltd.
Macmillan® is a registered trademark in the United States, United Kingdom
and other countries. Palgrave is a registered trademark in the European
Union and other countries.

Outside North America
ISBN 0–333–74959–6

In North America
ISBN 0–312–22219–X

This book is printed on paper suitable for recycling and
made from fully managed and sustained forest sources.

A catalogue record for this book is available from the British Library.

Library of Congress Catalog Card Number: 99–44913

Transferred to digital printing 2002

Printed and bound in Great Britain by
Antony Rowe Ltd, Chippenham and Eastbourne

To the memory of my great grandfather, Maulana Karamat Ali Jaunpuri (1800–73), who wrote Miftah ul-Jannat *for 'virtuous' Muslim women and advocated female literacy*

Contents

Preface and Acknowledgements   vii

1 Introduction   1

2 Women in Islam: a Reappraisal   12

3 Mullas, Popular Islam and Misogyny   61

4 Women as Victims of the Salish: Fatwas, Mullas and
   the Village Community   96

5 NGOs and Empowerment of Women: Some Problematic
   Prognoses   134

6 Militant Feminism, Islam and Patriarchy: Taslima
   Nasreen, Ulama and the Polity   180

7 Conclusions   205

Notes   210

Bibliography   231

Index   242

Preface and Acknowledgements

*The Great Question that has never been answered and which I have
not yet been able to answer, despite my thirty years of research into
the feminine soul is 'What does a woman want?'*
                                                    Sigmund Freud

While my book-project on Islam in Bangladesh society and politics
was in contemplation in 1993, Taslima Nasreen, the bold and controversial feminist writer of Bangladesh, entered the limelight. Local
and international media, human rights groups and individuals expressed their solidarity with her, condemning the so-called Islamic
fundamentalists for issuing the 'fatwa to kill' against her. Many of
them condemned the people in general and the Bangladesh government in particular for their failure to protect the freedom of expression
and the lives and property of free thinkers. Some Western media
even portrayed Bangladesh as an obscurantist polity run by fanatics
having no respect for women, minorities and other under-privileged
groups.

In mid-1994, while I was a research-fellow at the National Centre
for South Asian Studies in Melbourne, working on Women and Islam
in Bangladesh with special reference to the writings of Taslima
Nasreen, she again emerged as yet another victim of Islamic 'fundamentalists' who demanded her execution for her alleged blasphemous
comments suggesting the 'rewriting' of the Quran. Finally, she had
to seek political asylum in Sweden and leave Bangladesh in early
August of 1994.

The Taslima Nasreen episode is a watershed in the contemporary
history of Bangladesh. She has not only drawn world attention to
Bangladesh, this time not as one of the poorest in the economic
sense but with regard to the status of women and respect for human rights. However, despite the so-called Islamists' opposition to
the writer, the average Bangladeshi Muslim remained perplexed and
annoyed with the promoters of Nasreen. By 1994 Bangladesh society had become sharply polarized between the pro- and anti-Nasreen
groups, the latter outnumbering and overwhelming the former.
Consequently some liberal and 'progressive' writers and intellectuals

with pro-Nasreen sympathies encountered serious opposition and even death-threats from various 'Islamic' groups. Many liberal democrats and 'secular' Bangladeshis also condemned Nasreen for her 'counter-productive' writings and activities.

Although members of both the 'Islamic' and 'secular' groups cast aside her writings for various reasons, I have found a substantial part of Nasreen's work both interesting and thought-provoking. Her writings, on the one hand, are reflective of the truth in relation to the abuse of women and gender discrimination in the name of Islam and on the other, of her lack of knowledge and understanding of Islam and the intricacies of human relationships, civilizations and social sciences. Notwithstanding this, the controversy about her writings and statements reveals that there has been a wide gap between the understanding of Islamists and feminists *vis-à-vis* the rights and status of women in general and those of Bangladesh in particular. Since the gulf has not been bridged (but rather widened), they remain in two antagonistic camps divided by mutual prejudice and lack of understanding about each other.

This work is an attempt to bridge the gap between the Islamists and feminists, particularly in Bangladesh, so that women may attain equal rights and opportunities in every sphere of life without stirring up the whole society. While it is essential for the Islamists to reappraise Islam in the light of the Quran and the knowledge of history, anthropology and sociology in order to understand the rights and status of women in Islam, liberal, secular and feminist groups also need an understanding of Islam as well as of the 'new world order'. They need to recognize that: (a) anyone championing the cause of women is not necessarily a friend of the women; and (b) women can be exploited by the so-called liberal advocates of human rights and empowerment of women, as is evident in countries like Bangladesh. The subjection and persecution of women in such Muslim countries are due to various socio-economic factors other than to Islam, although Islam as understood and practised in Bangladesh has accentuated the suffering of women.

This work would not have been possible without the support and encouragement of various individuals and institutions in different parts of the world. First of all, I am indebted to Professor Marika Vicziany, Director of the Melbourne-based National Centre for South Asian Studies for her constant encouragement and support. In fact, I shifted the focus of my work from the intricacies of 'Islamic politics' to those of gender and Islam in Bangladesh in accordance with

Marika's advice. Other friends and colleagues who have been supportive of this project include Professors Peter Reeves, John McGuire, Ian Copland, S. Arasaratnam, Howard Brasted, Drs Denis Wright, Habib Zafrullah, Bruce Watson, Qamrul Alam, Abu Siddique, Meher Manzur and Asim Roy in Australia, Professors Francis Robinson and Tapan Raychaudhuri and Drs Gopal Krishna, Iftikhar Malik, Nandini Gooptu and Sarah Ansari in Britain, Professor Willem van Schendel in Holland, Professors Barbara and Thomas Metcalf, M. Rashiduzzaman and Shelly Feldman in the US, Professors Harbans Mukhia, Mushirul Hasan and Zoya Hasan in India, Professors Ahmed Sharif, Latifa Akanda, M. Sirajul Islam, Sufia Ahmed, Abdul Majeed Khan, B.M. Chowdhury, Mufakharul Islam, Muhammad Yunus (Grameen Bank), Ahmed Kamal, Sirajul Islam Chowdhury, B.K. Jahangir, Perween Hasan, Durgadas Bhattacharjee, Chowdhury Abrar, Tasneem Siddiqui and Ahmed Jamal in Bangladesh, and Drs Belal Baaquie, Habib Khondker, Gyanesh and Medha Kudaisya, Paul Kratoska, Andrew Major and Karen Snow in Singapore. I am thankful to all of them for their support and encouragement.

Dr Gowher Rizvi of the Ford Foundation deserves exclusive and special thanks for his support and encouragement throughout the project. I am also thankful to Luthfur Rahman Chowdhury, Ziaul Haque, Iqbal Sobhan Chowdhury (*Bangladesh Observer*), Enayetullah Khan (Editor, *Holiday*) for their support and encouragement. I am thankful to all the commentators of my conference and seminar papers which have been later incorporated in this book. I gratefully acknowledge the help of all of my interviewees including Taslima Nasreen herself, who gave a four-hour interview in late 1993, when things were turning from bad to worse for the controversial writer.

I am thankful to all the members of my extended family including my mother, sisters and scores of in-laws for their assistance. My wife, Neelufar, deserves very special thanks for all her help and encouragement. To me, she has been a living example of an over-worked loving woman from Bangladesh. She inspired me most. My daughters, Shakila and Sabrina, contributed to the completion of the work in various ways. While Shakila read and improved upon my manuscript, Sabrina has always been appreciative of my endeavour.

I would like to thank Mona Rahman and Saimum Wahab for their assistance in preparing the index, and Ms Rokeya of Narpokkho for providing the jacket illustration.

No 'thank you' is good enough to acknowledge the debt of Regina who painstakingly but cheerfully prepared the whole manuscript of this work. I am thankful to Macmillan and to St. Martin's Press for publishing this work.

I am solely responsible for the drawbacks and limitations of this work.

Taj I. Hashmi
Professor of History and Director,
School of Liberal Arts & Science
Independent University,
Bangladesh

1
Introduction

Sangsar sukher hoi ramanir gooney [The family becomes blissful only with the virtue of the woman].
                                                              Bengali saying

I never had any wish fulfilled at my father's home, neither did I have any better luck at my husband's.
                                      Jorimon, a poor village woman in Bangladesh

This study aims at understanding the dynamics of the predominantly Muslim and peasant society of Bangladesh *vis-à-vis* the overall position of women – their status, rights and opportunities – and examines whether the lack of opportunities for women and their persecutions at the hands of patriarchy have any positive correlation with Islam. As we know, Bangladesh is the third largest Muslim country in the world (after Indonesia and Pakistan). It is only natural to assume that, since about 90 per cent of the population are Muslims, Islam plays an important role in moulding its politics, socio-cultural norms and political culture of the bulk of the population. If mass poverty, illiteracy, backwardness and mass unemployment or underemployment have any positive correlation with Islamic resurgence and militancy, then potentially Bangladesh is one of the most fertile breeding grounds of the syndrome, often wrongly defined as Islamic 'fundamentalism'. Again, if Islamism or 'fundamentalism' has a negative correlation with feminism or any movement that tries to establish equal rights and opportunities for women in every sphere of society, then Bangladeshi women are likely to suffer more discriminatory treatment if the Islamists take over the country.

1

However, Bangladesh is not another Afghanistan, Iran, Saudi Arabia or even Pakistan. Although various 'Islamic' groups have gained more prominence and power, both socially and politically, in post-independence Bangladesh (since 1972) than ever before in the twentieth century, it would be facile to assume that 'Islamic' militants will be taking over the country in the foreseeable future. The rise of 'political Islam' in the country may be attributed to various historical, economic, socio-political and cultural factors.[1]

Without being engrossed in the debate as to whether total 'Islamization' of the polity – *à la* Afghanistan under the Taliban regime – is a possibility or not, it may be assumed that both secular as well as the *Sharia*-based Islamic personal law of Bangladesh are bad enough for the women in the country. We need to find out if the 'Islamic' personal law and other customs and traditions that go in the name of Islam are in accordance with the teachings of the religion and if women in the region can have a better deal in every sphere of life. In this book I investigate whether patriarchy and misogyny are mainly responsible for the misery of Bangladeshi women. Last but not least, I aim at discovering whether globalization and the advent of market economy are equally responsible for the exploitation of the poor rural and urban women, ironically in the name of the empowerment of women and the establishment of a civil society in the country.

Unlike the pre-independence period, in the post-independence Bangladesh the role and status of women in society have increasingly become important issues. Although the Bangladesh constitution has granted equal rights for men and women in every sphere of the state and public life,[2] there has been a substantial rise in the number of violent acts against women in the post-independence period.[3] The enactment of several laws and amendment of several pieces of legislation to protect Bangladeshi women's rights have not redressed their grievances.

While the Child Marriage Restraint Act of 1929, amended in 1984, has raised the minimum age of marriage from 16 to 18, in rural areas the average girl is married at the age of 15 or 16 and according to one report, girls as young as six or seven are being married to boys of nine or ten years by poor parents.[4] Although the Dowry Prohibition Act of 1980 (amended in 1982) makes the giving, taking or demanding of a dowry an offence punishable by fine, imprisonment of up to one year or both, it has failed to achieve its goal owing to lack of administrative support and also because it is contrary to the social norms and practices of the people.[5] The Cruelty to Women Act 1983 made the rape, sexual exploitation for gain, abduction, kidnapping or attempted murder of women offences subject to life imprisonment or death, yet there has been a substantial rise in the number of rape, abduction and murder of women throughout the country. The traffic in Bangladeshi women in the 'slave trade market', mainly to Pakistan and India, remains 'a major human rights concern'. As many as 5000 Bangladeshi women and children are smuggled out of the country every year.[6] By the first half of 1998, there had been several cases of brutal rape and murder of women, including children, throughout the country. Consequently the Government tabled the Suppression of Violence against Women and Children Bill 1998 in Parliament in April 1998. The Bill, enacted afterwards, was intended to protect women and children from the indiscriminate acts of violence, including the offences of using flammable substance and acid, trafficking of women and children, rape and abduction, and came in the wake of the sudden rise in the number of violent acts against women in 1997. During that year, as many as 420 women were killed and 487 raped. Of these, more than 100 were killed following disputes over dowry, 26 were victims of *fatwas* by rural *mullas* and about 200 girls reportedly received injuries from acid-throwing by local men. Out of the 487 rape victims, 192 were minor girls.[7]

Prior to the enactment of the Violence against Women and Children Act 1998, the Government enacted the Cruelty to Women Act in 1983, also known as the Deterrent Punishment Act. In 1992 the Government brought in the Anti-Terrorism Ordinance, which provides stiff penalties for the abduction or harassment of women, among other offences. It is noteworthy that the Government introduced direct election to the reserved seats for women members in the Union *Parishads*, the second tier in the local self-government. In the local government elections of 1997, 13 402 women were elected Union *Parishad* members, including those who won the elections to general seats by defeating male candidates. But female members of the Union *Parishads* blame 'male chauvinism' of their male counterparts as the main hindrance to female empowerment in rural Bangladesh. However, as this book reveals, the various laws enacted to protect women in Bangladesh did not ameliorate their condition. Another ineffective piece of legislation in this regard is the Muslim Family Law, derived from the Family Law Ordinance of President Ayub Khan (1961). Despite the restrictions on polygamy, as under the Family Law, by which husbands require the consent of the first wife before marrying another woman, Bangladeshi Muslim women are not in a position to oppose their husband's remarrying in a system where there is no alimony for divorced women and where women in general lack appropriate education to earn their own living.

Muslim women's rights to obtain divorce through the court, as under *Sharia* law and the Family Law, also remain unattained in most cases. Besides the stigma attached to a woman who seeks divorce, the lengthy and expensive litigation process also operates against the women. Victims of rape are reluctant to go to the police because of harassment and it is difficult for them to prove that they have been violated by men. The social stigma is so intense that thousands of Bangladeshi women, raped by Pakistani soldiers during the Liberation War in 1971, were not accepted by their own family members. Most Bangladeshi women have no protection against domestic violence. As the police generally view domestic violence as 'a non-criminal, marital and social problem and not as a law and order issue',[8] a large number of women commit suicide out of desperation.

Consequently what appears in this study is that although the Constitution and other laws establish equality between men and women in civil law, 'social norms and customs based primarily on religious laws discriminate against women in practice'.[9] The rehabilitation of Islam-oriented political parties, especially the 'fundamentalist' Jamaat-i-Islami, by the military government of Ziaur Rahman (1975–81) and the transformation of the State into an 'Islamic' one by making Islam the 'state religion', by another military ruler, General Ershad, in 1988, alarmed many human rights activists and women both within and outside Bangladesh. Various women's organizations in the country opposed the move to make Islam the state religion in the name of preserving the 'sovereignty of the country' and the 'spirit of the Freedom Struggle'.[10] The sudden growth in militancy among Islam-oriented groups and students, especially at the Chittagong and Rajshahi universities, the issuance of *fatwas* against feminist writer Taslima Nasreen and the large-scale persecution of rural women through *fatwas* in the first half of the 1990s, further alarmed human rights activists, liberal democrats and feminists in Bangladesh and abroad.

This book explores whether 'political Islam' is as pervasive in Bangladesh as perceived by many; and if under the influence of

Islamization of the polity women's rights and opportunities have been further circumscribed in this country. Contrary to the alarmist views of many Western and Bangladeshi observers, these conclusions are in line with the view that:

> While Islam is the dominant ideology governing relations between women and men in Bangladesh, . . . the country's geographic and historic isolation have made it resistant to the 'divine, theocratic, centralist and establishment – based' version of Islam, linked to Arabic learning and oriented to the Middle East, practised for instance in Pakistan.[11]

As it is evident from the overall socio-economic and political situation of the country, women have been lagging behind men in every sphere of life – from life expectancy to literacy, nourishment to power and status – while the 'divine' and 'theocratic' Islam has not taken the helm of government. It would be naïve to assume that with the assumption of political power by the armed forces, after the overthrow of a 'secular liberal democracy' under Sheikh Mujib in 1975, Islamic orthodoxy and the 'rural rich' came to the ascendancy to the detriment of Bangladeshi women.[12] There is no reason to believe that 'Islamic orthodoxy' and the 'rural rich' (whom Tazeen Murshid has identified as the real problem for gender equality in the country), had become politically irrelevant and socially less influential during the Sheikh Mujib era (1972–5). The origins of gender discrimination and patriarchy may be traced to the traditions and norms of the society rather than singling out the process of Islamization under Zia and Ershad as the main culprit in this regard; the reality is that Bangladeshi women have achieved more rights and privileges during the post-Mujib period.

It is not clear whether Tazeen Murshid has succeeded in establishing a positive correlation between the three to fourfold increase in the number of *madrasahs*, their teachers and students during 1977 and 1992 and the persecution of women and the rise of Jamaat-i-Islami in Bangladesh.[13] Contrary to Murshid's assertion, an empirical study reveals that while only about 18 per cent of Jamaat leaders were trained at *madrasahs*, more than 70 per cent of them have university diplomas. A large number of Jamaat followers come from schools, colleges and universities with a rural and petty bourgeois background.[14] Although the Jamaat gained 18 seats and more than 12 per cent of votes in the 1991 parliamentary elections, their abysmal performance in the 1996 elections is also quite significant. If their 1991 success is attributed to the rise in the number of *madrasahs*, some convincing argument is required to evaluate their failure in 1996. It is noteworthy that the Jamaat did not spearhead the anti-Taslima Nasreen movement in 1993, but rather jumped on the bandwagon afterwards. Consequently it is essential to examine some other socio-economic and cultural factors besides the 'Islamic factor' in order to arrive at a proper understanding of the backwardness and persecution of women in the country.

It may be asked why Bangladesh is one of the very few countries in the world where men outnumber women. There are about 1067 males to every 1000 females in the country. This is mainly due to the lower life expectancy of women, the corollary to malnutrition in young girls, who receive far less attention and medical care than their brothers.[15]

A recent study has revealed that 76 per cent of rural women fell under the category 'poor' in terms of income and resource endowments. Nearly 43 per cent of women are involved in agricultural activities, but 70 per cent of them work as unpaid family labour. There has been a rise in female-headed households in the countryside as women have been abandoned by their husbands. Despite government attempts to reserve 10 to 15 per cent of government jobs for women, no more than 7 per cent of government employees are women at the officer level and 9 per cent at other levels. This accords with the view that '[w]omen's socio-economic status differs from the legal status', and that this is 'due to the lack of enforcement' by the government and due to 'the lack of knowledge of women and men about internationally and nationally recognized women's rights'.[16]

It is interesting that many orthodox Muslim villagers in Bangladesh do not acknowledge the right of women to inherit land. They only acknowledge 'women's inheritable entitlement to maintenance', which only entitles them to maintenance at regular intervals. This is done by the institution of *nayor* or periodic home visits by married women to their parents' or brothers' homes. The custom is characterized as *'ashbi, jabi, khabi'* ('she'll come, go and eat). Similarly widowed mothers have the right to be maintained by their adult sons, but they cannot claim the produce of the land left to them by their husbands. They are simply entitled to *'pet-bhati'* (literally, 'an allowance for the stomach').[17]

There is no reason to assume that the gender hierarchy in Bangladesh is a by-product of Islamic law. An empirical study by Rahman and van Schendel has shattered this myth. Its findings reveal that the 'living law' is more powerful than the 'lawyers' law', especially with regard to marriage and inheritance by Muslim women. The village community's autonomy is reflected in the decisions taken at the grassroots level by village elders or *matbars/mondols* at the informal village court (*salish*), flouting the law of the land and the *Sharia*. Administering the Bengali rule of inheritance is simply a village affair. Thus, in accordance with the 'Bengali system', which reproduces a gender hierarchy quite different from the teachings of Islam, Muslim women may be disinherited. The subjection of women in the region is done in accordance with the Bengali concept of 'masculinity', there is nothing Islamic about it.[18]

Since this book aims at correlating the Islamization process with the problems of women's rights and status in Bangladesh, Chapter 2 highlights the teachings of Islam in relation to women's rights and status in the family and the society. What is being investigated in this chapter is not altogether a new subject of study. However, an attempt has been made to shed new light on the subject by differentiating the teachings of the Quran and the subsequent interpretations of the scripture, the *hadis* literature and opinions of Muslim jurists and scholars *vis-à-vis* women's rights and status in Islam.

1 Contrary to the general assumption of women in Islam and Muslim societies, that Muslim women are perpetually subservient to men and are forced to wear veil and live in seclusion as per 'Quranic instructions', the Quranic instructions are very liberal in relation to women's rights and position in the society.

2 Women in Muslim societies in general have been undergoing persecution in the name of Islam in almost every sphere of life since the eighth century. In fact, Muslim rulers and their subservient jurists and theologians justified polygamy, the institution of *harem*, male supremacy and other anti-women practices by subjective interpretations of Islamic law and by false traditions and sayings of the Prophet;

3 Islamic law and traditions are subject to change and modification as various Islamic thinkers and jurists have been suggesting measures to improve the status of downtrodden Muslim women throughout the world in accordance with the teachings of Islam. Local customs and traditions prevalent throughout history from the days of Plato to modern times of justifying the subjection of women are not typical to Islam or Muslim societies.

In short, what is being propounded here is that man-made law and pre-Islamic customs and traditions, not Islamic teachings, are responsible for the promotion of misogyny and subjection of women in Muslim societies. Bangladesh is no exception to this.

Chapter 3 aims at exploring the correlation between Islam and women in Bangladesh with special reference to the subjection and persecution of women both in the urban and rural areas at the hands of the self-proclaimed custodians of Islam. It is quite interesting that although Sunni Islam does not require a formal clergy as the intermediary between men and God, in the region of this study where Sunnism is the creed of more than 99 per cent of the Muslim population, the clergy is quite well-entrenched and very influential. In some sub-regions, especially in the rural areas, the *ulama* (both the well-versed religious scholars and the half-educated *maulvis* and *munshis*) are powerful enough to exert their influence in the 'dispensation of justice' in village-courts or *salish* undermining the authority of the government of Bangladesh. Quite often, poor rural women have been victims of these courts, run by rural *ulama* and village elders.

Unlike north-western India and Pakistan, the demarcating lines between the urban (and sophisticated) and the rural (and rustic) *ulama* in Bangladesh are very blurred and quite often, the two are inseparable. This is mainly due to the preponderance of rural and peasant culture in this predominantly rural society. Even big cities like Dhaka and Chittagong are not urban in the sense Bombay, Calcutta, Delhi and Karachi are, because of various historical factors.

This chapter aims at exploring the outcome of the reciprocity between popular Islam and popular culture at the grassroots level. While on the one hand, under the devouring influence of *mullas* the average Bangladeshi Muslim has been encouraged to accept the subjection of women as natural and efficacious, on the other, local traditions and culture, which also promote misogyny, have further influenced the misogynous *mullas*.

Chapter 4 argues against the prevalent (and trendy) view that NGOs and the Grameen Bank have been working towards the empowerment of rural women and alleviation of poverty in Bangladesh. On the contrary, it shows that most NGOs are no different from business establishments and have been mainly benefiting (as well as enriching and empowering) their organizers. NGOs' unaccountability to the people and government of Bangladesh and their exploitation of cheap labour of women and children, together with the transfer of the surplus from rural to urban areas, are reminiscent of the colonial mode of exploitation.

With regard to the Grameen Bank, I have argued that credit alone cannot eradicate poverty but only provide some subsistence to the poor, and that at the current pace, covering about two million people through its microcredit network in 20 years, the bank would take decades to reach the entire population of Bangladesh. Even if the entire poverty-stricken population of the country were covered by the bank, say in another 50 years (which is highly unlikely), they would barely attain some subsistence. In sum, the core of the main arguments is that any attempt to empower only the poor women by ignoring the poor men, would lead to 'gender-war' and the fragmentation of society.

Chapter 5 deals with the persecution of rural women at the hands of village *mullas* and headmen. The sudden rise in the declaration of *fatwas* by *mullas* in rural courts (*salish*) against women, which has even led to several deaths (by suicide and murder) of poor women in the countryside, further aggravated the situation. By 1995, hundreds of women had been tried in sham rural courts, run by village elders and their associates (*mullas*), for allegedly violating the *Sharia* law and Islamic codes of conduct. In some cases women 'offenders' were publicly caned, stoned and even forced to drink their own urine for the alleged commission of adultery and other crimes by these courts.

It is often believed that the emergence of the new female working class in the garment industries in urban areas (whose workers mostly come from rural areas) and among NGO-workers and beneficiaries in the villages is the main reason why *mullas* and village elders whose interests conflict with the garment industries and NGOs, because the latter have taken away their clients by providing credit and jobs, have been terrorizing women to dissuade them from working outside their villages. *Mullas* often allege that the NGOs are spreading Christianity and 'anti-Islamic' Western ideology. Hence the persecution of rural women!

The chapter explores the reasons why village elders and *mullas* are persecuting women and considers how far it is true that women working for NGOs and garment industries are the main victims of the *salish* courts in rural areas. There is reason to believe that most of the victims, on the contrary, have nothing to do with NGOs, but are non-working poor women without organization. The chapter attempts to show how Islamization at the state and grassroots levels, nourished by vested interest groups for political reasons and through ignorance, respectively, are responsible for the emergence of the megalomaniac 'mini Khomeinis' throughout Bangladesh and how and why *mullas* are losing ground in this transitional phase of socio-economic changes (and market-oriented reforms) in a politically stagnant and culturally backward Bangladesh which is semi-feudal and colonial to a great extent.

Chapter 6 examines militant feminism as represented by Taslima Nasreen in juxtaposition with Islam, society and politics in Bangladesh. While secular politicians and feminist groups were fighting the reactionary *mullas* and other obscurantist forces in the country in order to assert the rights of women and other fundamental freedoms, especially during the military regime of General Ershad (1982–90), a young, radical feminist writer (Taslima Nasreen, born 1962) emerged as a champion of Bangladeshi women in the late 1980s. She mainly wrote poems and columns in Bengali newspapers and periodicals depicting the plight of women at the hands of Bangladeshi men. Although she rightly criticized many 'secular' 'liberal democrats' and 'socialists' for not treating women with respect and dignity, she also criticized all religious texts, including the Islamic ones, for their male-oriented bias and prejudice against women.

Her writings soon earned her notoriety. Her advocacy of promiscuity and her criticism of Islam and Muslims in general angered different sections of the community: both Islamic and secular groups were alarmed by her writings and activities. Consequently conservative forces attacked feminism in general and Taslima Nasreen in particular as anti-Islamic and anti-Bangladesh. Although controversial, Nasreen has undoubtedly given a new dimension and meaning to the feminist movement, especially with regard to its relationship with Islam in modern Bangladesh.

What is evident is that Bangladeshi society is in a state of transition from backwardness to modernism and enlightenment. But the quest for modernization has again and again been retarded by illiteracy, poverty and the vested interest groups (both urban and rural) who benefit most from the country's perpetual backwardness.

Fortunately for the country, a large number of educated Bangladeshi men and women are coming forward to eradicate poverty along with illiteracy and obscurantism. Despite the opposition of *mullas* and other conservative/reactionary forces, women (both urban and rural) are joining the work-force and educational institutions with the belated realization that literacy and economic independence would eventually liberate women from the age-old customs of male supremacy. However, it is noteworthy that while *mullas* and other traditional elites have been gradually giving way to the rising new elites, who represent the 'liberal-secular' and 'NGO culture', Bangladeshi women have been going through the transition of facing new groups of superordinates and exploiters. Consequently while tradition-bound patriarchal exploitation and subjection of women has remained unabated, the newly emerging agents of exploitation of women are engaged in perpetrating the process and institutions of exploitation in the name of empowering and liberating women from obscurantism and 'fundamentalism' of the *mullas*.

2
Women in Islam: a Reappraisal

'And for women are rights over men similar to those of men over women'.

Al-Qur'an [2:228]

'The most perfect believers are the best in conduct. And the best of you are those who are best to their wives'.

Hadis

Introduction

'Women in Islam' is not a new subject of study. Some scholars have recently classified the subject as 'the mother of all battles'.[1] Scholars in both the East and the West have published scores of works on the status of women in Islam as well as in Muslim countries. Unfortunately, quite a substantial number of such works lack objectivity as they are either reflective of the age-old 'Orientalist' prejudice against Islam and Asian societies or of the subjectivity of Muslim apologists. There is another genre of writings which is reflective of the sheer ignorance of the authors about Islam, its history and the spirit of the religion. However, one should be aware of the difficulties of making an appraisal of the status of women in Islam and Muslim societies as scholars and laymen, 'Orientalists' and their opponents, Muslims and non-Muslims, liberal and orthodox Muslims, feminists and their opponents might raise various questions to any such appraisal. It seems that no objectivity is good enough to defend one's position on the problem.

Trying to defend the stand of some feminist writers who regard the Quran as a 'feminist bill of rights'[2] involves the risk of being branded as a Muslim apologist; but the danger of portraying Islam as a sexist religion, responsible for the promotion of male supremacy and the consequential subjugation of women through 'Islamic' institutions, practices, customs and laws, is not insignificant either. One may simply be branded as an 'enemy of Islam' both by traditional *ulama* and Muslim apologists for attacking the institutions of polygamy, seclusion of Muslim women and their inferior status *vis-à-vis* men in almost every sphere of life.

The very question about the 'status of women' is problematical, and one to which there are different answers when we apply it to women's lives. To many, the woman's ability to earn enhances her status. 'Is she working?' or 'Is she able to work?' are embedded in the question about her 'status', which is also determined by the level of her educational achievements. Women's legal rights, especially with regard to inheritance of property, voting and divorce, are also important determinants of their status. Besides gainful employment, educational achievements and legal rights, other quantitative indicators include women's longevity and the rate of infant mortality in a particular society under review. Often how much freedom women have in a particular society or whether they have the right to make their own choices are relevant questions with regard to their status in society. Sometimes researchers ask whether women are 'content with their lives.'[3] As has been stated by Diane D'souza, 'if legal rights alone were enough to determine how women were treated, Indian women and Indian society would be a shining example in today's world', and there is no way of quantifying the level of 'contentment' either.[4]

However aware of the 'Orientalist' and Western prejudice against Islam which have been reflected in Western discourses on the subject, we simply cannot blame the West for the negative image of Islam, especially in regard to the treatment of women. No one can be lynched for portraying Islam and its adherents as sexist and misogynous, because many ardent followers of the religion have no qualms about proclaiming unambiguously that since according to Islam women are inferior to men, they cannot have equal rights and status in any sphere of life. Some Muslim apologists, on the other hand, try to justify 'the inherent inequality of the sexes' as natural or 'desired by God' for the sake of maintaining social order and harmony, suggesting that order prevails only where men 'order' and women 'obey'. Under the rising pressure and criticism of Western liberalism and feminism, some Muslim apologists try to justify the

'Islamic injunctions', the seclusion of women, for example, as efficacious, natural and as part of God's desire to separate the domains and roles of the sexes for the sake of better cohesion and promotion of family values in the community.

However, of late many Muslim scholars and activists, both men and women, have challenged the traditional notions about 'women in Islam', nourished by both Muslim scholars/apologists and Western scholars/critics, as 'un-Islamic' and 'heretic'. Some Western and Afro-Asian non-Muslim scholars have also jumped on the band wagon of 'Islamic feminism', justifying a better deal for Muslim women in the name of 'Islamic justice' and the 'spirit of *Sharia* law'.

While both 'Islamic feminism' and 'Islamic modernism' are in the nascent stages, traditional Islam as practised and followed by Muslims and perceived by others represents the main stream of the religion. Consequently any discussion on women in Islam conjures up a situation where:

- Women are inferior to men, having lesser rights and privileges than men.
- Women have been created for the comfort and enjoyment of men. They are primarily sex-objects and must always remain subservient to men.
- They must observe seclusion and must not come out without wearing a veil.
- Men enjoy absolute freedom to keep more than one wife and concubines in special circumstances.
- Men may divorce their wives at will while women may only disengage themselves from their husbands by returning the dower to them with the permission of the court.
- The testimony of one man is equivalent to that of two women.
- Women are defective, not intelligent enough to run governments and lead nations.
- Since women are only supposed to keep their husbands in good humour and raise children, they do not need higher education.
- Islamic inheritance regulations imply that women should inherit half of what men inherit.[5]

However, before judging the status of women in Islam against this backdrop, it should be pointed out that what goes in the name of Islam is not always consistent with the tenets of the religion. Questions should also be raised about the particular circumstances, when and where a particular regulation about women ascribed to the Quran was introduced, whether the prevalent situation in the early days of Islam (in Madina after Muhammad's migration to the city in 622 for example) was unique and very different from other places and whether the period has striking dissimilarities with the modern age. Was the particular Quranic instruction only meant for a particular place in a particular time-frame or it has universal applicability? What is the relevance and validity of other sources of the *Sharia* law besides the Quran? The *hadis* or traditions of the Prophet of Islam and the various interpretations of the Quran and the *hadis* by Muslim jurists or *imams* are the mainstay of the *Sharia* law. We are not only confronted with diverse interpretations of the *Sharia* and contradictory *hadis* or sayings of the Prophet but also with a host of varied translations and interpretations of the Quran.

Jan Hjarpes has aptly evaluated the problems of understanding Islamic laws and regulations as emanating from the Quran:

> The problem is that of interpretation. What do these instructions mean? In what way are they norm-giving? How are they correctly applied?. . . . to determine the literal meaning of, for example, a Koran text is usually not difficult, but in what sense is it normative?[6]

Unlike the traditional *ulama*, some 'Islamic modernists' insist that since Islam signalled greater security, justice and economic liberty for women – from the abolition of female infanticide (prevalent in pre-Islamic Arabia) to the granting of the inheritance right to women – the Islamic law 'represents a radical improvement on earlier practice' when women inherited nothing. According to this mode of thinking, in the spirit of Islamic law, 'this means in our time' . . . men and women should have equal inheritance rights'.[7]

In view of the above, mere classification of the views of Muslim scholars *vis-à-vis* the status of women in Islam as 'traditional' and 'modernist' does not help us understand the intricacies of the problem. Firstly, because Muslim scholars do not represent a monolithic group as there are Sunni traditionalist scholars who hold different views in regard to the rights and status of Muslim women from the Shiite *ulama*, the latter also differ from their Sunni counterparts, especially those representing different countries, traditions or schools of thought. Again, what traditional *ulama* of the pre-modern era thought of women's rights and status in Islam is not always acceptable to their modern counterparts either. The same is the case with Islamic 'modernists': pre-modern 'modernists' often represented quite a different school of thought with regard to the rights and status of Muslim women from their modern counterparts. Consequently we will have to examine, accept or reject the diverse views of Muslim as well as non-Muslim scholars on the status of women in Islam for the sake of objectivity.

Women in Other Religions and Civilizations

It is noteworthy that besides the Islamic 'modernists', many non-Muslim scholars who have no prejudice against Islam have argued that far from being inferior to men, Muslim women from the Quranic point of view are actually entitled to even more rights than are non-Muslim women as laid down in their scriptures. It may be argued that both the Old and New Testament despise women in general and Eve in particular for committing the 'original sin', yet despite the fact that 'women's essential equality with man is more complete in Islam than it is in Judaism and Christianity',[8] Muslim women in general and those living in Afghanistan, Saudi Arabia, Iran and the Sudan in particular are worse off than their Jewish and Christian counterparts. One may in this regard cite the following Biblical and Quranic texts *vis-à-vis* the status of women:

> I will greatly multiply thy sorrow and thy conception; in sorrow thou shalt bring forth children; and thy desire shall be to thy husband, and he shall rule over thee.
> [Genesis 3:16, King James Version]

> Let the woman learn in silence with all subjection. But I suffer not a women to teach, nor to usurp authority over the man, but to be in silence. For Adam was first formed, then Eve. And Adam was not deceived but the woman being deceived was in the transgression. Notwithstanding, she shall be saved in childbearing, if she continues in faith and charity and holiness with sobriety.
> [Paul in the First Epistle to Timothy,
> Ch. 2, King James version]

In the Quran, on the other hand, one finds, Adam and his consort (Eve) jointly responsible for transgression:

Then they twain ate thereof, so that their shame became apparent unto them, and they began to hide by keeping on themselves some of the leaves of the Garden. And Adam disobeyed his Lord, so went astray. [20:121]

In general, the Christian tradition may be seen as androcentric, stipulating that Adam was created in God's image and that only men are 'creationally God-like' and women can achieve 'salvational Christ-likeness' by only 'becoming male'.[9] Christian traditions have justified women's subordination by their 'lack of a fully human God-like capability'.[10] Even many modern Western philosophers and theologians under the influence of Christian traditions regard Adam as a *sinner* in relation to God and a *victim* in relation to Eve. He represents 'the freedom and responsibility of the victim', and is 'partly innocent' as 'Eve's victim' and Eve is more guilty as she is 'the serpent's victim'.[11]

One finds misogynous exposition in Buddhist and Hindu texts as well. Buddhist 'birth-stories' or Jataka tales as well as the Hindu laws of Mannu portray women as demoniac, licentious, immoral and dangerous. According to the *Laws of Manu*, women irrespective of their age must not do anything independently and must be subject to their fathers in childhood, husbands in youth and sons when their 'lords' (husbands) are dead. 'A woman must never be independent', Manu stipulates.[12] According to Manu's laws: 'Though destitute of virtue, or seeking pleasure (elsewhere), or devoid of good qualities (yet) a husband must be constantly worshipped as a god by a faithful wife.'[13] These laws also lay down that widows should never remarry because: 'By violating her duty towards her husband, a wife is disgraced in this world, (after death) she enters the womb of a jackal, and is tormented by diseases, (the punishment of) her sin.' The obedient wife, on the other hand, is assured of exalted position in heaven.[14]

Manu also did not repose any trust in women. Men have been repeatedly urged to guard their women because, according to Manu: 'Women do not care for beauty, nor is their attention fixed on age; [thinking], "[It is enough that] he is a man", they give themselves to the handsome and to the ugly'.[15] Manu also regarded women as 'destitute of strength and destitute of [the knowledge of] Vedic texts' and '[are as impure as] falsehood'.[16] With regard to inheritance Manu is very definitive – only sons or the eldest 'may take the whole paternal estate' and daughters may receive one-fourth from their brothers, but this is an exception. Sons, according to Manu should be the sole inheritors, 'because a son delivers (*trayate*) his father from the hell called *Put*, he was therefore called *put-tra* (a deliverer from Put) by the Self-existent (*Svayambhu*) himself'.[17]

In *Mahabharata* one finds women being considered as much more dangerous and harmful than poison, snake, fire and *Yama* (the angel of death). In several other Buddhist and Hindu texts women are simply depicted as beings full of deceit and venom.[18]

Besides the religious texts, the popular culture of the Afro-Asian, European, Middle Eastern, Indian and the Mediterranean regions throughout history, as reflected in their literature, sayings and proverbs, also portrays the preponderance of male-oriented and misogynous predispositions of the people. While one hears that: 'The man who follows his wife's advice will never look on God's face' [Maltese proverb], and that: 'The fool praises his wife, the wise man praises his dog' [Turkish proverb], Arabic proverbs depict women as 'handful of trouble', 'devoid of God's mercy' and hold that: 'When a daughter is born the threshold weeps for forty days.' It is noteworthy that very similar to the Hindu notion of women, Arabs also despise women as unreliable, adulterous and deceitful. Consequently we hear that: 'What the devil accomplish in a year, an old woman may accomplish in an hour' (Moroccan proverb) and that: 'If it were not for shame, there would be no honest women' (Arabic proverb), so they should be perpetually kept inside the house and 'when the hen crows like a cock, it should be killed' (Arabic proverb).[19]

These adages are not the only specimens of misogyny in the region which was the first to witness the rise of Islam in the seventh century. Arabia and the adjoining countries were also influenced by ancient Greco-Roman and Judeo-Christian traditions. The Indian subcontinent, which had been an important centre of Islamic civilization for more than 700 years, up to the consolidation of the British Raj in the nineteenth century, also influenced and moulded the culture of the already Persianized Muslim conquerors. Indigenous converts, to a great extent, also retained Hindu-Buddhist and animist traditions, including those pertaining to the status of women. Consequently long before the advent of Islam, the would-be-converts in the Middle East, North Africa, India and elsewhere had been under the influence of misogyny. Islam could hardly transform the converts and their descendants into tolerant libertarians *vis-à-vis* the rights of women, non-Muslims and slaves. Although Islam brought about revolutionary changes with regard to the rights of women, minorities and slaves, its libertarian philosophy did not go beyond the notion of treating these groups 'kindly'. In other words, women, non-Muslim subjects or *zimmis* and slaves remained subservient to their (male) Muslim superordinates. The ascendancy of non-Arab Ottomans, Safavids, Mughals and some other dynasties, including those run by slaves or *mamlukes* of India and Egypt, had been the only departure from Arab supremacy (Arab and Islam being synonymous) after the fall of Baghdad in 1258.

As we know, despite its egalitarian, emancipatory programme, Islamic rule did not signal the ascendancy of the underdogs. Although women, slaves and other under-privileged groups of Makka had been the first among the early converts, not long after the demise of the Prophet of Islam and the end of the Early Caliphate in 661, Islam's egalitarianism and democratic principles were set aside by the Umayyad Caliphs. The Umayyads not only introduced monarchy (hitherto non-existent in Arabia) but also ushered in an era of Arab aristocratic rule and feudalism. Afterwards all the Muslim rulers from Spain to Indonesia for over 1200 years ruled as monarchs and despots adopting indigenous or foreign institutions, customs and traditions, often quite alien or contradictory to the precepts of Islam, albeit in the name of Islam. The Abbasids, Ottomans, Safavids, Mughals, Qajars or Saudis and other Muslim rulers profusely borrowed traditions, customs institutions and ideas from their non-Muslim neighbours. The subjugation of women in 'Islamic' empires and kingdoms and in the Muslim society in general by Muslim men, along with its justification by the *ulama* and ordinary Muslims, have been precipitated by their exposure to non-Muslim culture and traditions.

Against this background, it is unfair to blame Muslims and their religion for the subjection and persecution of women in every sphere of life. We know that long before the advent of Islam Aristotle prescribed the subjection of women as a 'social necessity' and 'natural'. To him, the rule of men over women was like the rule of the 'soul over the body, and of the mind and the rational element over the passionate'.[20] According to Aristotle, man's nature 'is the most rounded off and complete' while woman is 'more jealous, more querulous, more apt to scold and strike . . . more void of shame and self-respect, more false of speech, more deceptive'. He also saw female bodies as defective and women being 'as it were an impotent male, for it is through a certain incapacity that the female is female'.[21] Aristotle influenced not only Europeans but also Arab or Muslim philosophers and *ulama* including Imam Ghazzali (1058–1111), especially during the Abbasid and Ottoman periods.

It is noteworthy that Ghazzali and Abul Hasan al-Ashari (died 935), the most influential proponents of orthodoxy and scholasticism, brought back mysticism as the main guiding philosophy for the Sunni Muslims by discarding rationalism and free thinking developed under the early Abbasids in the ninth century. One may, in this regard, agree with Hitti that:

> The scholastic shell constructed by al-Ashari and al-Ghazzali has held Islam to the present day, but Christendom succeeded in breaking through its scholasticism, particularly at the time of the Protestant Revolt. *Since then the West and the East have parted company, the former progressing while the latter stood still* [emphasis added].[22]

The Muslim world's stagnation and backwardness, nourished by *sufism* and scholasticism, have also contributed to the subjection of Muslim women, because prior to the transformation of the Madina-based Islamic republic into monarchy in 661 under the Umayyads, Muslim women enjoyed more rights and freedom than their counterparts during the Umayyad and Abbasid periods.

A parallel may be drawn between Christianity and Islam in regard to their respective egalitarianism and failure to grant equal status to women. The spread of Christianity despite its lofty egalitarianism failed to get rid of Jewish patriarchal ideas about women. The Biblical account of Eve's creation from Adam's rib and Jewish customs allowing concubinage, men's unrestricted rights to divorce and women's lack of inheritance rights were accepted by Christians in Mesopotamia and Palestine. The (Christian) Byzantines were even more stringent with regard to the subjection of women. Respectable Byzantine women were not supposed to be seen or heard outside their home. With the exception of prostitutes, women had to wear the veil and those belonging to the ruling classes lived in segregated quarters (*harems*), guarded by eunuch slaves. Byzantine women were also excluded from religious activities, including study.[23] Church fathers such as Augustine, Origen and Tertullian considered women as 'inferior, secondary, . . . and useless to man – and, worse, as causing sexual temptation, corruption, and evil'. Augustine failed to understand why God had created woman as a man could be a better companion and helper of man. He concluded: 'I fail to see what use woman can be to a man, . . . if one excludes the function of bearing children.' Tertullian's misogyny was even more relentless. He wrote of woman:

> *You* are the Devil's gateway. *You* are the unsealer of the forbidden tree. *You* are the first deserter of the divine law. *You* are she who persuaded him [Adam] whom the Devil was not valiant enough to attack. *You* destroyed so easily God's image, man. On account of *your* desert, that is death, even the Son of God had to die.[24]

The situation of women under the Persian Sassanids (224–640) was not any better than under the Greek Byzantines. Like the Byzantines and other Christian kingdoms in the Middle East and Mediterranean regions during the ascendancy of Islam in the seventh century, the Sassanids also kept their women segregated and they were required to veil as well. The veil not only served to mark the upper class women but also differentiated 'respectable' women from those who were publicly available. Sassanid kings also maintained *harems* with thousands of concubines. It is noteworthy that neither the Sassanian law nor the Code Hammurabi (1752 BC) of Mesopotamia and the Assyrian law (1200 BC) granted equal status to women. Under these laws, men could easily divorce their wives, pull out their hair, mutilate their ears and could even kill them with 'good reason'. Under Zoroastrian regulations, women were 'somewhere between personhood and thingness' or properties owned by men. Under Zoroastrian laws reproduction was the primary function of women.[25] Arab, Persian and Turkish Muslims who inherited the Byzantine and Sassanid empires borrowed profusely from their culture.

While the Muslim empires from the seventh century onward underwent the process of adaptation of Judeo-Christian, Assyrio-Sasanid and Zoroastrian institutions from the vanquished empires, they simultaneously absorbed Aristotelian and Platonic ideas. Hence the preponderance of Platonic ideas of 'natural hierarchy in society' in the Muslim empires. This led to the marginalization of the lower classes, non-Muslims and women throughout the 'Islamic' empires while the egalitarian principles of Islam receded to the background or were only applicable to the dominant members of the royalty and aristocracy.

Pre-Islamic and non-Muslim practices and traditions are so well entrenched in Muslim societies throughout the world that both Muslim and non-Muslim scholars and laymen would hesitate to accept them as alien, let alone incompatible with the teachings of Islam. Consequently while there is no mention of Eve or *Hawwa* (one who is created from another being) in the Quran, Middle Eastern traditions and the so-called *hadises* reproduce the Biblical stories about how Eve was created from a rib of Adam and Muslims throughout the world believe in these stories, considering them as Islamic. It is noteworthy that non-Muslim institutions of the *harem*, concubinage, the veil and 'female circumcision', for example, are acknowledged as 'Islamic' institutions, both among their Muslim advocates and Muslim/non-Muslim critics.

The Muslim empires and kingdoms of the Indian subcontinent from the early thirteenth century to the modern times inherited feudal and tribal institutions form the Middle East, North Africa and Central Asia and absorbed many indigenous Brahmanic institutions and doctrines. These institutions helped them to maintain the *status quo* by legitimizing their rule. Consequently lower classes, slaves and women remained marginalized throughout the Muslim rule in India. As the caste system legitimized inequality with the concurrence of the upper and lower castes and classes, who considered the system as pre-ordained by God, the notion about women's perpetual inferiority *vis-à-vis* men was also accepted as part of the natural order both by men and women in India. We are not aware of any organized movement against subjugation and dehumanization of women in the Hindu society in the pre-modern period. Consequently even now, such derogative expression as *ramani* to denote women in Sanskrit-based languages is acceptable throughout the subcontinent to women as well as men. The term stands for an object of sex or *raman* from the male point of view.

Against this backdrop, one may assure that in both religious and secular matters, pre-Islamic and non-Muslim customs and traditions have overshadowed their Islamic counterparts to such an extent that the latter have managed to survive only in adumbration. The pre-Islamic and non-Muslim brutal practice of 'female circumcision' or genital mutilation, for example, still survives in many Muslim countries in Africa, the Middle East and South-East Asia as an 'Islamic' institution. The late Sheikh Gad al-Haq, an influential Egyptian cleric of the al-Azhar University, defended this institution as 'Islamic' despite the opposition of many Egyptian human rights activists along with those of the West.[26] Another Egyptian cleric, Sheikh Yousef El-Badry, in his defence of the institution asserts that: 'It prevents diseases like AIDS and bad smells. It makes the woman control her sexual urges'.[27]

It is noteworthy that the so-called 'female circumcision' is said to have begun with Hagar, the Egyptian concubine of Abraham, who incurred the jealousy of Sara (Abraham's wife) after she had conceived. In her jealousy, Sara (who was yet to give birth to Isaac) vowed to cut 'three limbs' of Hagar's and so, according to the tradition, Abraham ordered Hagar to pierce her ears and mutilate her genital. 'These customs', therefore, 'began with Hagar, and consequently the custom is mainly revalent in the Nile valley and adjoining regions'.[28]

Interestingly, from a report of the London-based Minority Rights Group ('Female Genital Mutilation: Proposals for Change'), the practice called 'female circumcision', one of the great 'unmentionable African horrors', is widely practised in West Sahara and eastern Africa as well as in Yaman and Oman by Muslims, Christians, Jews and animists. The report reveals that: 'Although often associated with Islam, it is not ordained in any Islamic text. The practice continues thanks to superstitious fears of female sexuality, habit and the mistaken belief that it is hygienic.' It is noteworthy that opponents of the practice of removal of the clitoris have been accused of racism. Jomu Kenyatta, the first president of Kenya [who was not a Muslim], made the defence of the practice part of his campaign for Kenya's independence.[29]

In view of the above, before lynching Islam as a sexist religion one must not ignore what has been going on both in the West and the Orient *vis-à-vis* women's rights and status in the modern times. Western women were gradually being enfranchized between the 1890s and 1970s. While women in New Zealand were the first to get the right to vote in the 1890s, those of Britain got it only during the 1920s, and in Switzerland, women were enfranchized as late as 1971. The Roman Catholic Church even today does not approve of divorce and female priests. Famous French philosopher and libertarian, Rousseau, is known to have favoured patriarchy and the subjection of women.[30] Women in Britain gained inheritance rights only in the 1870s. Prior to the Married Women's Property Act of 1870, amended in 1882 and 1887, 'all real property which a wife held at the time of a marriage became possession of her husband'.[31] As John Stuart Mill wrote in 1861, neither civilization nor

Christianity restored to the women her just rights. Mill also pointed out that under the common law of England, the wife was the 'actual bond-servant of her husband', she could not acquire any property and her position was 'worse than that of slaves'.[32]

In the Indian subcontinent, leading Hindu reformers like Ramakrishna Paramhansa (1836–86) and Vishnubawa Brahmachari (1825–71) for example, favoured patriarchy and subjugation of women. Ramakrishna, the guru of Swami Vivekananada (the 'patriot prophet' and 'patron saint' of Hindu revivalists, 1863–1902), despised women, likening them to human excreta and objects not worthy of love by men. He held modern educated Indian women responsible for turning their husbands into 'fools and worthless'.[33] The Brahmachari, on the other hand, was concerned with the decline of Vedic Hinduism, holding women responsible for 'distracting' men from the pursuit of Vedic knowledge. He believed that unless women lived as dependants of men, there would be disaster in every aspect of life.[34] It is interesting that not only *mullas* regard women as 'distractions' and thus justify segregation of the sexes, but Ramakrishna, and other Hindu ascetics and leaders also regarded them so. Hindu women were not only barred from inheritance but were also subject to *sati* or the ritual of widow burning at the funeral pyre of their husbands up to the 1830s. Hindu widows were not allowed to remarry either, up to the 1850s.

However, despite the fact that religious sanctions against non-Muslim women are much more stringent in their respective texts than those on Muslim women in the Quran, yet Muslim women living in Muslim countries are much worse off than their non-Muslim counterparts with regard to their rights and status both within and outside the perimeter of the family. One wonders why despite the restrictive religious rules and regulations affecting non-Muslim women, these women in general are freer than Muslim women living in Muslim countries! It is difficult to understand that despite the leniency shown to women by the Quran and early Muslims, why on earth Muslim women in Saudi Arabia are barred from driving cars on their own, are forced to live in segregated quarters for most of their life and are forced to cover their hair and entire body! There seems no reason either why women are simply treated as animals or objects in Afghanistan in the wake of the Taliban takeover in September 1996. They are not only forced to cover their entire body including face but also not allowed to attend schools and consult a male physician. Women in Iran and Sudan along with those of

most other Muslim countries are discriminated against and subject
to regulations which are tantamount to violation of human rights.
In Muslim countries, including Pakistan and Bangladesh, women
inherit less or nothing in comparison to men, they cannot move
freely, sometimes they are forced to wear *hijab* or head-cover, especially in some Arab countries and Iran. However, in some Muslim
countries women move freely, hold public offices, including that
of the prime minister, and do not have to wear *hijab* or observe
seclusion, albeit at the risk of a reprimand from the *ulama* and
other conservative Muslims. At times they are subject to physical
violence.

There is, however, nothing to indicate whether a Muslim country would maintain the status quo *vis-à-vis* the status and position
of women in society. Countries like Turkey, Iran and Afghanistan
were the first in the Muslim world to make laws granting more
freedom and rights to women in the first half of the twentieth
century. By 1979, with the Islamic Revolution, Iranian women came
across a totally new set of laws restricting their freedom and rights.
As mentioned earlier, women in Afghanistan have received an even
worse deal than their Iranian counterparts after the Taliban takeover of the country in 1996. Algerian women are very likely to
face a similar situation to that prevailing in 'Islamic' Iran and
Afghanistan if the Islamic Salvation Front (FIS) comes to power.

Consequently what is pertinent to our understanding of women
in Islam is not only an evaluation of Islamic laws and regulations
with regard to women, but also an understanding of the ebbs and
flows in Muslim societies which are by-products of their perpetual
struggle to cope with modernism and the forces of global capitalism, since the dawn of Western colonization of the Muslim world.
Side by side with attempts to understand Islamic laws and Muslim
societies one should understand that neither Islam nor Muslim
societies are monolithic. As Sunnis (about 85 per cent of all Muslims) are at variance with Shiites, Quranic instructions and regulations
are sometimes at variance with *hadises* or sayings of the Prophet of
Islam on various matters, including the position of women. Again,
Muslim countries are at variance with each other on many issues
due to cultural difference. Even the four Sunni schools of thought
do not see eye to eye with each other with regard to various socio-
political and economic matters.

So, in a nutshell, it appears that given the diversities of Islamic
societies, schools of thought, sectarian differences, interpretations

of the Quranic texts and contradictory *hadises*, it is not an easy task to understand the position of the religion with regard to the rights and status of women. For a proper comprehension of the problem, one should take into account all these diversities, contradictory practices and opinions of Muslim jurists and leaders along with an overview of the literature on the subject, including those reflecting Orientalist prejudice and Muslim obscurantism.

Women in the Quran

Women along with slaves and other under-privileged groups of Makka were among the first converts to Islam. In fact, Khadija, Muhammad's first and only wife till her death at 65, was the first convert to the new faith. She also wholeheartedly supported her husband in establishing the religion, which 'in a surprisingly contemporary manner' concerned itself with women's rights.[35] The rights accorded to women by Islam included the right to receive education, to earn and manage their income, to inherit property and rights in matters relating to marriage, divorce and maintenance. With the ascendancy of Islam to political power, with the Prophet's assumption of the new role as the head of the polity or *ummah*, composed of Muslims and mostly Jews and other non-Muslims in Madina in 622, gradually many pre-Islamic cruel practices, including (female) infanticide, were abolished. However, many other vices, such as slavery, prostitution, concubinage and temporary marriage (*muta*) were still in vogue both among Muslim and non-Muslim members of the *ummah* in Madina.

Since the ascendancy of Islam to political power did not signal the beginning of a social revolution, one may assume that the Prophet did not believe in taking revolutionary steps so that powerful elders were not alienated from the polity in the nascent state of Madina. Consequently many vices and immoral practices, including slavery, concubinage, prostitution and male supremacy remained unscathed. However, owing to the transformation of the polity (which was republican and egalitarian by nature) into a monarchy with all the paraphernalia of authoritarian, dynastic rule, with well-entrenched feudalism as the main mode of production, in the post-Madina period of the Khilafat from 661 onwards, the overall position of women further deteriorated. Henceforth, not only were the Quranic verses, according better rights and status to women, were interpreted in a way which justified patriarchy, but both the ruling elites and jurists also started relying more on *hadis*. Muslim jurists and philosophers during the Umayyad and Abbasid periods (661–1258), with their

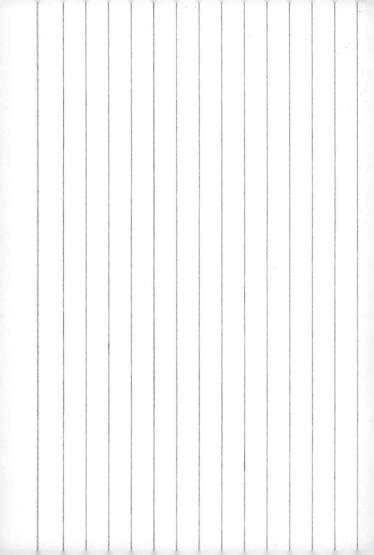

patriarchal interpretations of the Quran and reliance on scores of spurious *hadises*, struck the last nail into the coffin of women's rights. The collective efforts of the ruling classes, jurists and philosophers to deprive women from their due did not look odd during the medieval and early modern periods as women's rights and status in non-Muslim societies were not much different, if not worse, from the situation prevailing in the Muslim world.

An elucidation of the Quranic injunctions with regard to women's rights and status in juxtaposition to those of the *hadis* literature and Islamic jurisprudence is useful for a proper understanding of the inherent contradictions and dialectic in Islam *vis-à-vis* the position of women. Quranic verses affirm that there is absolutely no difference between men and women with regard to their relationship to God and that God has addressed both men and women assuring them similar rewards and punishment for good and bad conducts respectively. The following verses substantiate this:

> For Muslim men and women, for believing men and women, for devout men and women, for true men and women, for men and women who are patient and constant, for men and women who humble themselves, for men and women who fast, for men and women who guard their chastity, and for men and women who engage much in Allah's praise, for them has Allah prepared forgiveness and great reward. [33:35]

Emphasizing equal rights for men and women the Quran declares: 'And for women are rights over men similar to those of men over women' [2:228]. The Quran admonishes men who expropriate and oppress women:

> O you who believe! You are forbidden to inherit women against their will. Nor should you treat them with harshness, that you may take away part of the dowry you have given them, except when they have become guilty of open lewdness. [4:19]

The equality of the sexes is further highlighted in the following verses:

> O mankind! Revere your Guardian-Lord, who created you from a single soul. From that soul He created its mate, and through them He bestowed the earth with countless men and women. [4:1]

Some Muslim scholars point out that the term, 'the single soul' (*nafs* in Arabic) is a feminine noun and hence they believe it is man who was 'created from the rib of woman'. They denounce the well-known *hadis* which suggests that the first woman, Eve (Hawwa in Arabic), was created from the left rib of Adam as this view goes against the very text of the Quran.[36] It is interesting that while *nafs* or 'the single soul' is a feminine noun, the partner or spouse (*zawj*) created from the same soul is a masculine noun.

There are, however, Quranic verses which may be cited to justify male supremacy from the Islamic point of view. Both traditional *ulama* and ordinary Muslims cite these verses to justify the subjection of women. The ambiguity of some of these verses and their androgenic interpretations by Muslim scholars who are not enlightened enough to understand the Quranic text with regard to relationships between the sexes, have further made the issue very problematic.

The *Sharia*, which is the basis of all androgenic arguments, is again based on the Quran as well as on the *hadises* or traditions and sayings of the Prophet of Islam and the opinions of the *fuqaha* (jurists). Both the *hadis* literature and the major schools of thought in Islam developed during the early Abbasid period, in the ninth and tenth centuries. Although both the *hadis* literature and the various Sunni and Shiite schools of thought (*mazhabs*) lack universal acceptance among Muslim theologians: the bulk of the present-day *ulama* are not prepared to accept that medieval Muslim jurists – imams and mujtahids – were either influenced by 'different influences of their times' or they lacked the foresight and vision of modern scholars as their problems were different from those of their modern counterparts.[37] Their unwillingness to accept that the *Sharia* law also incorporated human opinion is a stumbling-block in the way of rational thinking.

One has to understand the context in which particular Quranic verses were revealed, particularly the pragmatism and exclusive applicability inherent in these verses. Ironically, however, both the dogmatic, close-minded *ulama*, who assiduously defend what they understand as Islam, and the critics of Islam, often cite the same Quranic verses and *hadises* in support of their mutually contradictory arguments on the subjection of women under the *Sharia* law. The following Quranic verses may be conveniently cited by both the defenders and critics of Islam:

Men are the maintainers of women, with what Allah has made
some of them to excel others and with what they spend out of
their wealth. So the good women are obedient, guarding the un-
seen as Allah has guarded. And as to those on whose part you
fear desertion, admonish them, and leave them alone in the beds
and chastise them. So if they obey you, seek not a way against
them. Surely Allah is ever exalted Great. (4:34)

It is noteworthy that different scholars, both Muslim and others,
have translated and interpreted the above verses in different ways.
To some scholars, men have been simply classified by the Quran as
'protectors', 'maintainers' of women, not as their masters or over-
lords.[38] Ahmed Ali's translation of the Quran, along with his
interpretations of some of the Quranic verses, are quite radical and
thoroughgoing. His translation of verse 4:34, from *Sura An-Nisa* (the
Women), gives us altogether a different meaning and substance of
the text. According to this version:

Men are the support of women as God gives some more means
than others, and because they spend of their wealth (to provide
for them). So women who are virtuous are obedient to God [Ac-
cording to Ahmed Ali "*Qawwam* . . . does not mean lord or master,
but provider of food and necessities of life, and through its form
qaim, to take care of; and *qanitat* only means devoted or obedient to God, as in 2:116, 16:120, 33:35 etc.] and guard the hidden
as God has guarded it. As for women you feel averse, talk to
them suasively; then leave them alone in bed (without molest-
ing them) and go to bed with them (when they are willing). If
they open out to you, do not seek an excuse for blaming them.
Surely God is sublime and great.[39]

The following Quranic verses may be cited to dispel the myth
about the male bias of Islam: 'If a woman fears aversion from her
husband, or ill-treatment, there is no harm if they make a peaceful
settlement; and peace is an excellent thing. *But men keep self-interest
uppermost*' (4:128; emphasis added).

However, some scholars accept the androgenic interpretation of
the Quran, holding that the verses which suggest male supremacy
should be taken as 'pragmatic in approach, not normative', and
that these verses should be examined in their proper context. Since

women were confined to their houses in the seventh century and men alone were their providers, these scholars argue, taking reality into account, the Quran accords men superiority over women without glorifying such a social structure and declaring it normative. One such scholar, Asghar Ali Engineer, further argues that Quranic verses, such as: 'And women have rights similar to those against men in a just manner', are the normative ones. According to Engineer, 'contradictions in the Quran are the reflection of the contradictions of a complex situation which provided the immediate context of its revelation'. He feels that while the normative verses are 'transcendent', the 'contextual pronouncements' are to be 'discarded with the change of context'. He is not prepared to accept all the views of earlier *fuqaha* (Muslim jurists) as transcendental and immutable under the changed circumstances and context.[40] Shah Waliullah (1702–62), the most influential Islamic reformist and scholar of his time in India, also felt that both the Quranic verses and *hadises* were subject to particular conditions and time. He agrees with classical legal theory that 'not all traditions are legally applicable' either. According to him particular rules of *Sharia* are 'in a sense specific to [a particular] people'.[41]

While some liberal scholars insist on 'liberal interpretations' of 'subtle' verses of the Quran, suggesting that the Quran has only allowed the husband to punish his wife 'only lightly, as a warning', or 'only after the guilt has been determined by a court of law',[42] scholars like Ahmed Ali, as cited earlier, do not accept that the Quran has ever empowered the husband to beat up his wife. Some scholars, on the other hand, argue that the economic superiority of men, not only in Arabia in the seventh century but everywhere in the world, even down to the present day, is the basis for male supremacy. Some Western scholars regard the Quranic verse which recommends sexual abstinence as a mode of punishment for an obstinate wife (*nashiza*), as 'proof of the importance attached to sexuality and sexual fulfillment for women as well as men in Islam'.[43]

In view of this, the position of women in Islam may be better explained by means of a discussion on Muslim women's rights with regard to marriage, divorce, inheritance and their overall position in the society, especially their socio-political and economic position and role. One may, in this context, take into account the differences between Quranic injunctions and pronouncements of *hadises* or sayings of the Prophet. The different Sunni and Shiite

sects also differ on matters relating to the rights and status of women
as regards marriage, divorce, seclusion, and so on.

Marriage in Islam

Marriage in Islam is contractual where both husband and wife are
bound by certain regulations and obligations. Contrary to the popular
notion in the West, a Muslim women cannot be legally forced into
marriage without her consent. She has every right to stipulate any
reasonable condition, including the delegated right to divorce (*talaq
tafwiz*) if she is displeased with any act of her husband, including
his taking another wife. There is no scope for arbitrary divorce by
the husband in Islam. There must be two witnesses for the consummation of a divorce.[44] As far as the Quranic injunctions are
concerned, a Muslim woman does not need a *wali* or a male marriage guardian. She is absolutely free to marry herself to anyone of
her liking on her terms.[45]

In accordance with the Quranic law, in a Muslim marriage the
wife is entitled to *mehr* (dower), which solely belongs to her and
the amount is to be fixed only with her consent. Although there is
no limit to fixing of the *mehr*, the Quran encourages men to give
as much as possible and advises the husbands: 'And if you have
given one of them a heap of gold, take nothing from it' (4:20). If
the husband fails to pay the portion of *mehr* which is immediate
(*mu'ajal*) to the wife, she can refuse to stay with him without losing her right to claim maintenance from him. The husband has
the sole responsibility of maintaining his wife and children while
the wife is free from this obligation even if she is rich and has her
own sources of income. The wife would lose her right to maintenance from her husband only if she elopes with another person.
The wife has the right to sue her husband if he fails to pay her
maintenance. It is significant that even after the husband divorces
his wife, he is under an obligation to pay for the maintenance of
the children so long they are in the custody of the mother. The
Quran is very specific about it: 'And mothers shall suckle their children
for two whole years. . . . And their maintenance and their clothing
must be borne by the father according to usage' (2:233).

Some other thorny issues with regard to women's rights in Islam
involve questions about polygyny, seclusion and veiling of women,
women's rights of testimony and their position as leaders in the
society.

Polygamy

It is almost universally believed both by Muslims and non-Muslims that Islam permits men to have more than one wife, up to the maximum of four at a time, in addition to concubines and slaves (either purchased or taken as prisoners of war). The most convenient way of justifying polygyny is either by citing the Quran or the personal life of the Prophet of Islam. The most frequently cited Quranic verse in this context is as follows:

> If you fear that you may not act with equity in regard to the orphans, marry such of the women as seem good to you, two, three or four – but if you fear that you may not be fair, then one only or what your right hands possess (captives of war); that is more likely to secure that you be not partial (4:3).

There is, however, a variant translation and interpretation of the verse by Ahmed Ali. His translation is as follows:

> If you fear you cannot be equitable to orphan girls (in your charge, or misuse their persons), then marry women who are lawful for you, two, three, or four; but if you fear you cannot treat so many with equity, marry only one, or a maid or captive. This is better than being iniquitous.

He also asserts that literally the expression, 'what your right hands possess' is used in the Quran 'for women one has married'. *'Aiman-u-kum*, your right hands', according to Ahmed Ali, 'has also been used for pledging in marriage, as in 4:33. The verse also virtually restricts the number of wives to one, for treating even two with absolute equality is well-nigh impossible'.[46] Another Quranic verse warns Muslims: 'Howsoever you may try you will never be able to treat your wives equally. But do not incline (to one) exclusively and leave (the other) suspended (as it were)' (4:129).

It may be pointed out that the Quranic verses deemed to have legitimized polygyny should not be taken as *inducements* to polygyny. Some of these verses just imply the pragmatic cognizance of the reality and status quo by nascent Islam, while others were solely meant for the Prophet. One may cite the following verse from the *Sura* (chapter) *Al-Ahzab* (the Clans), which was exclusively meant for the Prophet, not all Muslims:

We have made lawful for you, O Prophet, wives to whom you
have given their dower, and God-given maids and captives you
have married, and the daughters of your father's brothers and
daughters of your father's sisters, and daughters of your mother's
brothers and sister, who migrated with you [to Madina]; and a
believing women who offers herself to the Prophet if the Prophet
desires to marry her.

This is a privilege only for you and not the other believers.
We know what we have ordained for them about their wives
and maids they possess, so that you may be free of blame, for
God is forgiving and kind (33:50).

An elucidation of the verse (which was revealed in Madina) is pertinent
to our understanding of the complex issue of Muslim men's rights
and privileges with regard to marriage. Nothing could be more ex-
plicit than the way this verse spells out that while the Prophet had
certain privileges in regard to marriage, his followers had to follow
a different set of rules ordained by God. It is further evident from
the verse that the Prophet did not enjoy absolute power and authority
over his followers in Madina. He could only impose restrictions on
his followers with the authority of revelations from God, so that he
would remain 'free of blame'. However, most Quranic regulations
were not revolutionary in nature, they rather reflected a compromising
stand of Islam which did not want to alter the status quo overnight.

Many Muslim jurists and *ulama*, both in the medieval and modern
periods, despise polygamy, considering the Quranic verses concerning
polygamy as exhortations in favour of monogamy. Some of them
argue that what was necessary in the wake of the Battle of Uhud
(in 625), when the Quran permitted the Prophet's followers to marry
up to four women with a view to rehabilitating war-widows and
orphans (4:3), is not applicable in normal circumstances. As Wiebke
Walther suggests, the Quran recommended marriage to widows and
female orphans 'at a time when marriage represented the only way
for a woman to be provided for'.[47] It is noteworthy that although
the Prophet himself set example for his community by marrying
two Muslim war widows, he is said to have registered his contempt
when his son-in-law, Ali, contemplated marrying another woman.
He is said to have remarked that he would not allow Ali to marry
another woman as his daughter did not approve it. 'Fatima is part
of my body and I hate what she hates to see, and what hurts her,
hurts me,' he remarked.[48]

Some other examples from the annals of the early Islamic period show how polygamy was despised by society and how women enjoyed much more freedom and higher status than their counterparts did in the later Islamic period. It would be facile to assume that the Prophet adopted or legalized polygamy. He not only made it more difficult for polygamy to survive as an institution among Muslims but also prohibited conditional marriages and temporary marriages (*muta*) in the third year of the Hegira. Although a section of the Shiites still regards temporary marriages as lawful, there is no valid reason in support of the practice other than the desire and personal inclinations of the sovereigns who manipulated the *mujtahids* or jurists to justify the institution.[49]

Early Muslim scholars as well as rulers despised polygamy. The 'free-thinking' and 'rational' Mutazilite jurists as early as the third century of the Hegira considered the Quranic prescription on polygamy as a prohibition rather than an encouragement. A Mutazila marriage is essentially a monogamous marriage, a voluntary union for life of one man and one woman to the exclusion of all others. The Mutazilite doctrine was the official creed of the Abbasid empire until Caliph Mutawakkil, the 'mad bigot' (847–61), prevented the general diffusion of the school and persecuted its followers.[50] Henceforth polygamy and subjugation of women were institutionalized under the Abbasids and the successive Muslim empires throughout the Muslim world. The institutions of the veil, concubinage, harem – along with that of eunuch (castrated) slaves and guards already borrowed by the Umayyads of Damascus (661–750) from the Greeks and Persians, were institutionalized by the Abbasids and other Muslim rulers.

The Prophet's Marriages

It is noteworthy that both the defenders and critics of polygamy cite the Prophet's marriages as justification and criticism, respectively. One may point out that he was not a role model for his followers in every sphere of life. There are Quranic verses which were exclusively meant for him and his family. An elucidation of his conjugal life and circumstances leading to his numerous marriages (fourteen in total) is essential for our understanding of Muslim women's rights and status, especially with regard to polygamy and confinement of women.

Khadija was his first wife. The Prophet married this wealthy 40-year-old widow when he was 25. He led a monogamous life till her death at 65. Several months after Khadija's death, the 51-year-old Prophet married Sawda, the widow of a persecuted early convert who had fled to Abyssinia from Makka at the behest of the Prophet and who died in exile. By marrying this utterly destitute, elderly and not at all attractive widow of his faithful disciple who had been persecuted for embracing Islam, Muhammad simply showed his generosity and humanity.[51] His next wife, Ayesha, twelve-year-old daughter of Abu Bakr, his closest companion and friend, was married to him as the father of the bride had 'the desire of his life to cement the attachment which existed between himself and the Prophet'.[52] As Karen Armstrong observes, 'neither Sawdah nor Aisha were chosen for their sexual charms', and both the marriages had political dimensions. His marriage with Sawdah made Suhayl, a powerful Makkan, a relative by marriage. He also needed a closer tie with Abu Bakr. Although Muhammad was organizing an alternative kind of clan which was not based on kinship but on ideology, 'yet the blood-tie was still felt to be very important'.[53]

Muhammad's other wives included war-widows, destitutes and slaves, some of whom had connections with influential tribes and warriors. He married Hafsa, daughter of Umar (the second caliph), who had lost her husband at the Battle of Badr (the first decisive battle in the history of Islam). Her father failed to find a suitable husband for her because of her extremely fiery temper. The Prophet's marriage with Hafsa strengthened his ties with Umar, a very powerful and influential leader from Makka; 'And public opinion not only approved, but was jubilant over it'.[54] Three other wives of the Prophet, Hind Umm Salma, Umm Habiba and Zainab bint Khuzayma, were widows as well. Zainab and Hind lost their husbands in the Battle of Uhud. None among the Prophet's companions ever asked Zainab's hand. Umm Salma was neither young nor attractive. His marriage with Umm Habiba was very significant. She was a daughter of Abu Sufyan, the most prominent Makkan leader to oppose Muhammad until the conquest of Makka by the latter in 630. She embraced Islam against the wish of her father and other members of her family. After her husband died she had no one to look after her since by becoming Muslim she had already alienated her parents.[55]

His marriage with Juwairiya, daughter of a tribal chief of the Banu Mustalik, who fought against Islam, led to the conversion of the whole tribe to Islam. Safiya, a Jewish prisoner of war, was liberated and the Prophet married her at her request. Another wife, Maimuna, was a close relative of two arch-enemies of the Prophet, Ibn Abbas and Khalid bin Walid, who later proved to be able lieutenants of the Prophet. She was more than 50 years old at the time of her marriage with the Prophet.[56] He also married two slave girls. His marriage with Zainab bint Jahash, a former wife of his adopted son and freedman Zaid, raised eyebrows as it went against the prevalent custom. Zainab, a high-born lady, was related to the Prophet and she was never happy with her marriage to Zaid (a former slave) which was arranged by the Prophet. After she managed to divorce Zaid she wanted to marry the Prophet. Meanwhile, he had tried in vain to dissuade Zaid from divorcing her. It is possible to take the view that he married her considering himself responsible for arranging her marriage with Zaid. There is no reason to believe that the Prophet married her because he was enchanted by her beauty. She was already 39 years old, malnourished and exposed to the 'merciless sun of Arabia' at the time of her marriage with the Prophet. This marriage demonstrated the fact that a fostering or adoptive relationship (between the Prophet and Zaid) was not a tie of blood, creating a bar to marriage.[57] In view of the above Barbara Stowasser thinks that:

> Muhammad had as little use for mere sensual pleasures as he had for material luxuries. He was a man of seriousness and equanimity who could have lived like a king but chose to live like a pauper ... clearest proof of the Prophet's freedom from base instincts (especially lust), however, are the historical facts of his celibacy until his twenty-fifth year and his monogamous marriage with a women fifteen years his senior to whom he was completely devoted until she died and he was more than fifty years old.[58]

Since the Prophet's marriages, excepting with his first wife, were due to political and protective reasons, all attempts to buttress polygamy as an Islamic institution, citing his marriages as examples, do not hold ground.

Early Islamic Women

There are examples from the early Islamic days (during the lifetime of the Prophet and afterwards, up to the mid-ninth century) which highlight the fact that Muslim women had higher status and better rights than were enjoyed by their counterparts in the later periods. Two of the Prophet's great-grand-daughters Sakina (Sukaynah) and

Amina, for example, were independent enough to exercise their right to divorce and oppose polygamy. Amina was so opposed to polygamy that before marrying she set conditions that her husband would not touch another women; would not prevent her from spending his money and would not oppose any decision she might have made.[59]

Sukaynah (died 735), daughter of Husayn and grand-daughter of Ali, 'the proud and beautiful', was a resident of Madina. She is regarded as the most brilliant, most accomplished and most virtuous woman of her time. Like Sukaynah, other ladies from the Prophet's family 'were noted for their learning, their virtues and their strength of character'.[60] Sukaynah's rank and learning are said to have combined with her fondness for music, poetry, fashion and beauty. She was noted for her jests and hoaxes. Her hair-style, *à la Sukaynah* (*turrah Sukayniyah*), to paraphrase Hitti and Ibn-Khallikan, respectively, became popular among men until prohibited by the puritan Caliph Umar II (717–20). She is said to have married and divorced several men. She made 'complete freedom of action a condition precedent to marriage'.[61] She never pledged *taa* or obedience to any of her husbands and refused to acknowledge her husband's right to practise polygamy. She took one of her husbands to court for infidelity. She received visits from poets and used to attend meetings of the Quraysh tribal council. She never hesitated to express her contempt for the Umayyads who killed her father at Karbala in 680. She used to condemn them in the mosques of Madinah and insulted Umayyad governors and representatives of the dynasty 'every time she had an opportunity'.[62]

Sukaynah had a rival in the city of Taif. Aishah bint Talha, daughter of a distinguished companion of the Prophet and grand-daughter of Caliph Abu Bakr, was also known for her beauty and independent nature. Her appearance in public and her defiance of traditions and customs were even more striking than those of Sukaynah. She is said to have refused to veil herself on the grounds that since God had put upon her the stamp of beauty, 'the public should view that beauty and thereby recognize His grace unto them'.[63]

Like Sukaynah, she also negotiated her own marriages, three in total. Among other renowned Muslim women to have negotiated their marriages are Umm Kulthum, wife of the famous general, Amr ibn al-Aas, and Umm Salma, wife of al-Abbas, the founder of the Abbasid dynasty. The latter is said to have sent her slave to the young and handsome Abbas with her proposal of marriage.[64]

Three of the Prophet's wives, Asma bint al-Numan, Mulaika bint Kaab and Fatima bint al-Dahhak, repudiated their marriages with him. These repudiations are indicative of the state of independence and equal rights of early Muslim women. Fatima Mernissi seems to be correct in saying:

> The right to polygamy and repudiation granted exclusively to males seems to have been an innovation in seventh-century Arabia . . . the Prophet himself, despite his powerful attraction as a triumphant military leader and successful statesman, was himself faced with female sexual self-determination. He was solicited in marriage by many women and was rejected by many as well.[65]

Muslim Modernists on Women's Rights

Although polygamy has existed as an exclusive privilege for Muslim men since the seventh century, Muslim jurists and scholars from time to time have raised questions about the utility of the institution. Some nineteenth-century Muslim scholars in the Indian subcontinent, Sir Sayyid Ahmad Khan, Chiragh Ali and Maulana Mumtaz Ali, for example, believed that the Quran had virtually prohibited polygamy by demonstrating its underlying shortcomings.[66] Another Muslim historian, Syed Ameer Ali (1849–1928), of Calcutta, regarded polygamy as undesirable and unjustified. According to him:

> The task of abolishing polygamy . . . is not so difficult as is imagined. The blight that has fallen on the Moslem nations is due to the patristic doctrine which has prohibited the exercise of individual judgment [*Ijtihad*].[67]

Even some Western scholars believe that polygamy has not been sanctioned by Islam as

> nowhere does it say in the Koran that man should take women as they wish according to their own desires and whims, let alone shut them away in harems. Polygamy is allowed only on the condition that a man treats his wives equally – to which the Koran adds, 'This is impossible' (Sura 4, Verse 4).[68]

Sheikh Muhammad Abduh (1854–1905), the famous Egyptian Islamic thinker and disciple of Jamal al-Din Afghani, while opposing polygamy went to the extent of stressing that women's liberation from male oppression was 'an essential precondition for the building of a virtuous society'. He called for the immediate abolition of polygamy in Egypt.[69] Although a total ban on polygamy could not be enforced in any Muslim country, the institution has been substantially weakened in countries like Turkey, Tunisia and Algeria, mainly due to the concerted efforts of lawmakers and feminist pressure groups. The situation in Bangladesh in this respect has remained more or less unchanged. Despite certain legal restrictions on polygamy, introduced by President Ayub Khan's Family Law Ordinance in the early 1960s, Muslim men practise polygamy with total impunity, especially in rural areas.

The Veil and Inheritance Rights

We may now examine some other contentious issues such as the veil, rights and status of women *vis-à-vis* inheritance, testimony given in courts and the holding of high offices in the light of Islamic teachings. Before appraising women's rights in Islam, we must bear in mind that the Quran and *hadis* literature may quite often give contradictory views in this regard. Not only has what the Quran has given to women been taken away by the *Sharia* law and *hadis* literature, but also Muslim women up to the early eighth century enjoyed better rights and status than their later counterparts.

It is noteworthy that while women in Saudi Arabia are barred from driving automobiles on their own and Afghan women after the Taliban takeover can neither go to school nor consult a male physician, women in early Islam fought side by side with male soldiers. Ayesha, widow of the Prophet, rode a camel and actively took part in the Battle of the Camel against Ali, the last of the Pious Caliphs. Several female members of the Prophet's family took part in battles as well as in the decision-making process in the early days of Islam. Safiyah, an aunt of the Prophet, was the first Muslim woman to kill an enemy in battle. Asma bint Yazid killed nine enemy soldiers at the Battle of Yarmouk and Khawla bint al-Azwar charged the enemy riding beside the Prophet. Nusaybah bint Kaab is perhaps the most celebrated among the 'female warriors of Allah'. She was one of the ten brave fighters who held their ground at the Battle of Uhud (625), shielding the Prophet's body with their own when he was lying unconscious. In a later battle, she lost a hand. The Prophet honoured Nusaybah's contribution and often visited her house.[70]

There are scores of other examples from the early days of Islam to establish gender equality in Islam. It is evident from history that Umar, the second caliph of Islam, tilted the balance in favour of Muslim men, in accordance with the Makkan tradition, which, unlike the Madinian one, did not allow female independence and assertiveness. With the ascendancy of Umar as the caliph in 634 (he held the office till his death in 644), women in Madinah were confined to their houses and later were segregated from men at the mosques, having separate *imams* (prayer leaders) and prayer chambers in the mosques. It is noteworthy that while under the Prophet, one Umm Waraka, a woman acted, as *imam* for her entire household which included men, Umar appointed male *imams* for women, barring them from acting as *imams* any more. While after the Prophet's death, his widows, Ayesha and Umm Salama acted as *imams* for other women, Umar prohibited Prophet's widows even from going to *hajj*.[71]

Some contemporary sources reveal that Umar did not like the way women in Madina exerted their influence on their husbands and unlike their Makkan counterparts, did not accept their husbands' shouting with bowed heads. He did not like his wife shouting back at him either, like other women in Madina. He was even told by his wife that the wives of the Prophet often answered him back and that one of them even ran away from him until nightfall. Umar, who was rough and harsh with women, had every reason to be alarmed by the level of freedom enjoyed by women in Madina. He even reprimanded his daughter Hafsa, one of the wives of the Prophet (and through her other co-wives), for answering back to the Prophet.[72] In view of the above, there is no reason to be surprised that women enjoyed far lesser freedom in Madinah and elsewhere during his tenure as the caliph.

However, both Abu Bakr (the first caliph) and Umar entrusted their daughters (not their sons), Ayesha and Hafsa, respectively (both widows of the Prophet), with important responsibilities. While Abu Bakr before his death entrusted Ayesha with disposing of certain public funds and properties and his own properties among his successors, Umar passed on the first copy of the Quran to Hafsa's keeping before his death.[73] The Quran, as it exists today, is based on this preserved copy. The high position enjoyed by the Prophet's widows is further evident from the political role of Ayesha, who in the wake of the murder of Caliph Usman in 656 not only publicly proclaimed in a speech at the Mosque of Madina that his death would be avenged, but also opposed Ali's succession as the caliph and took part in a battle against Ali.

This, however, does not mean that Muslim women throughout history remained as assertive and independent as Ayesha, Sukaynah and some other prominent women of the early Islamic period. Even the Prophet's wives were subject to veiling during his lifetime and by the late seventh century the process of institutional subjection of women had been accelerated throughout the Islamic domain. Veiling and seclusion had been the two most significant aspects of the Islamic community to signal the lesser and inferior status of women both in the private and public domains. Both the critics and admirers of the institutions highlight the inferiority of Muslim women citing veiling and seclusion as points of reference in this regard.

An historical appraisal of veiling and seclusion of women reveals the pre-Islamic, mainly Persian (Sassanid) origins of the institutions. However, the institutions were so well-entrenched in Muslim society that Ibn Battuta (the famous fourteenth-century traveller) tells us that the only unveiled women he came across were the Berber women in North Africa. By the tenth century, as the Islamic empire had incorporated various non-Muslim, Greek, Egyptian and Persian institutions, the veil which was meant for the so-called free, upper-class Persian women, was also adopted by the Muslim ruling classes and elites.

The state of subjection and inferiority of Persian women throughout history down to modern times is well-reflected in Persian literature. While tenth-century poet Firdausi regarded women and dragons as 'impure creatures', his thirteenth-century counterpart, Sheikh Saadi, felt that: 'The eye of a woman should grow blind before a stranger, outside the home she should be as if in her grave.' The great medieval Persian historian Rashid al-Din apologizes to his readers for including an account of women in his history of the Mongols. He, however, used the terms *awrat* (genitals) and *zaifah* (the weak female) in reference to women.[74]

Against this backdrop, one may assume that since misogynous exposition and subjection of women (both through the veil and total seclusion) antedate the advent of Islam in the Middle East and North Africa, there is nothing Islamic about these institutions. Respectable women among the Sassanids and Arabs in Makka used the veil as a symbol of class distinctions.[75] However, the adherents of the veil who consider it an Islamic institution cite the Quran and more precisely, the *hadises*, traditions and customs of the Middle Eastern region. The following Quranic verses are frequently cited by Muslim adherents of the veil and total seclusion of women:

> O believers, do not enter the dwellings of the Prophet for a meal without waiting for the proper time, unless permission be granted to you. But if you are invited, enter, and when you have eaten, disperse. Linger not for conversation. Lo! that would cause annoyance to the Prophet, and he would be shy of asking you to go; but Allah is not shy of the truth. And when you ask of the wives of the Prophet anything then ask them from behind a *hijab* [curtain]. That is purer for your hearts and for their hearts. And it is not for you to cause annoyance to the messenger of Allah, nor that you should marry his wives after him. Truly this with God would be enormous.
>
> [33:53]

> O Prophet, tell your wives and daughters, and the women of the faithful to draw their wraps [*jalabib*] a little over them. They will thus be recognised and no harm will come to them. Allah is forgiving and kind.
>
> [33:59]

Interestingly, none of these verses imply that women are required to wear the veil, as neither *hijab* (curtain) nor *jilbab* (a cloak or garment to be worn in public) stand for the veil. Fatima Mermissi is right in her assertion that the *hijab* 'descended', not to put a barrier between a man and a woman, but between men, the Prophet and his male visitors, who lacked certain niceties such as not entering a dwelling without asking permission.[76] It is noteworthy that the verse on *hijab* was revealed in the fifth year of the Hejira (627) and is part of the *Sura*, *Al-Ahzab*, which narrates the turbulent situation that prevailed in Madina. The Prophet had to fight three defensive battles with his Makkan adversaries (the Badr, Uhud and Khandaq) during 624 and 627 and the law-and-order situation in the city was far from good as well. The Prophet and his small number of followers had external as well as internal enemies, especially the 'hypocrites' and Jews of Madina. One may agree with the view that the verse on *hijab* on the one hand touches on the rules of etiquette for the Prophet's Companions and on the other the last part of the verse forbids them from ever marrying his wives after him. The Prophet was threatened by men that they would marry his widows and this was symbolically dangerous. The verse on *hijab*, in short, 'came to give order to a very confused and complex situation . . . to be the solution to a whole web of conflicts and tensions'.[77] The verse was also meant to protect the Prophet's privacy as it was revealed on the wedding night of Zaynab bint Jahsh and the Prophet. *Hijab* provided 'an element of privilege' for the Prophet's family and was also a protective device in the turbulent days of Madina when many enemies of Islam, especially the hypocrites (*munafiqeen*), intended to harm the Prophet and his family. Umar (the second caliph) is said to have warned the Prophet to conceal and segregate the female members of his family as he felt that 'both the righteous and the wicked enter into your houses'.[78]

While *hijab* or seclusion was meant for protecting the Prophet's family in the turbulent days of Madina when the city state lacked regular armed forces and police, *jilbab* or cloak was meant for distinguishing free women from slaves so that they were not molested by hypocrites and those 'in whose hearts is a disease, and those who stir up sediton in the city' [33:60].

However, even after the restoration of order in Madina and elsewhere in Arabia in the wake of the conquest of Makka by the Prophet in 630, women had to walk the streets wrapped in their *jilbab*. Those who defied the *hijab* and went out *barza* or unveiled were looked down upon as loose women. Only the very brave and those belonging to influential families, Sukaynah (granddaughter of Ali) for example, could defy the *hijab* with impunity under the Umayyad and early Abbasid rulers. Quite often, the specificities of the Quranic regulations were ignored by Muslim jurists and rulers. The following verses may be cited in this context:

> Oh women of the Prophet, you are not like other women. If you fear God, do not be too obliging in your speech [or, be complaisant of speech], lest someone sick of heart should covet your person, so speak with conventional [or, befitting] speech.

They were also asked to stay at home and not to deck themselves with ostentation or *tabarruj* (revealing dress, ornaments and make up) as in the days of the *Jahiliyya* or paganism [33:32–3].

Historical evidence corroborates the view that veiling and seclusion were only observed by the Prophet's wives during his lifetime. According to Ibn Ishaq (died 767), the Prophet's Madina-born biographer, Ayesha, veiled her face while passing the grave of Abu Lahab, an uncle of the Prophet who had been an arch-enemy of Islam and tormentor of the Prophet.[79] Accordingly, we may assume that the 'Islamic' dress code for women, which had a positive correlation with disorder in the early days of Islam, was introduced by the Abbasid rulers in accordance with the prevalent custom of their empire, hitherto ruled by the Sassanids and Byzantines. There is no reason to believe that only Muslim women are required to be modest and chaste, Muslim men are also impelled by the Quran to lower their gaze and guard their private parts. Muslim women have an additional requirement – they need to 'draw their kerchiefs [*khumur*] over their bosoms' [24:30–1]. The Quran has not asked women to cover their face with *burqa* or *niqab*, contrary to the custom in South Asia, Afghanistan and elsewhere.

It is noteworthy that many Muslim women in different Muslim as well as Western countries have recently adopted the *hijab*. This is not necessarily due to their adherence to the traditional tenets of Islam. This rather reflects their dislike for the West which is held responsible for the plight of Arab and non-Arab Muslims. This voluntary adoption of the *hijab* and *niqab* or full face-veil by Muslim women often has deep political overtones. The re-emergence of the so-called Islamic dress (*al-ziyy al-Islami*) has a positive correlation with the resurgence of political Islam in the Muslim world after the 1967 Arab-Israeli war. It is interesting that Muslim women who face *mullas* and other conservative forces as their adversaries have been critical of the veil while those who confront the West (directly or indirectly) have simply adopted the *hijab* as a weapon to assert their identities and establish their rights.[80]

Against this backdrop, one needs to understand the symbolic, cultural, social and political overtones of the veil. Undoubtedly, as the Western and Muslim critics of the institution point out, the veil has been institutionalized with a view to subjugating women by creating a barrier between women and a means of livelihood and opportunities to become self-reliant. Although one cannot deny the moral and pragmatic reasons for its initial adaption in Madina, especially for the Prophet's wives, one may point out the excesses committed by both the critics and advocates of the institution. While the traditional conservative *ulama* such as Mawlana Mawdudi favour complete seclusion of Muslim women, including their covering the face, the 'liberal progressive' *ulama* such as the influential Sudanese leader Dr Hasan al-Turabi, believe that Muslim women do not have to cover their face as veiling was peculiar to the wives of the Prophet. Turabi also maintains that Muslim women have the right to participate in politics, including the right to stand for any public office (except the office of *khalifah*) and that they may mingle with men in places of worship, education, and in 'decent, innocent family gatherings'.[81]

It is not necessarily true that a woman in *hijab* represents servility, bondage and powerlessness. An empirical study of a Bangladeshi village shows how erroneous the typical Western feminist discourse is in equating *purdah* or seclusion with 'rape, domestic violence and forced prostitution', denying cultural and historical specificity.[82] The same study by Katy Gardner, a British anthropologist, reveals that one Kudderza Bibi, a pious, *purdah*-observing village woman in Sylhet district, is one of the most powerful women in the community. 'She owns a large amount of land, and runs her family with a will of iron. She, rather than her sons, is indisputably head of the household; there is no question that, ... she is passive and subordinate', observes Gardner.[83] She is critical of Western scholars who think that only the Western aid agencies would eventually 'liberate' these 'other' women, suffering under *purdah*. She has rightly pointed out that so long the women concerned have accepted *purdah* as their protector, having linked it to 'a wider cultural construction of femininity, sexuality and biology', it cannot be regarded as a means of controlling women by men.[84]

Leila Ahmed has pointed out that Islamic reformers such as Afghani and Abduh; the militant Islamists of today; Marxists such as Fannon, Samir Amin and El-Saadawi; and liberal intellectuals in the East are all awe-stricken by the West and 'whether they acknowledge it or not, they draw on Western thought and Western political and intellectual languages'.[85] Since 'the West is everywhere', in the 'discourses of collaboration and resistance', both pro- and anti-West scholars, reformers and activists in the Muslim world promote the notion of 'equality of the sexes' and are the 'foremost champions of unveiling'.[86] However, as mentioned earlier, many radical anti-Western Islamists, in Iran, Algeria and elsewhere in the Muslim world have been using the veil as a symbol of anti-colonial, anti-Western movements. As Frantz Fanon has pointed out, the anti-colonial struggle of the Algerians against the French was later turned into the 'battle of the veil', as the former affirmed the veil as part of their tradition and also because '*the occupier was bent on unveiling Algeria*'.[87]

In view of the above, there is no point in attacking or defending *hijab* so long as Muslim women regard it as a 'way of dressing' rather than a 'way of life', imposed by male superordinates on them. One may agree with the view that *hijab* is a veil rather than a 'fixed domestic screen/seclusion' in most Arab countries.[88] It is also 'a sign of propriety and a means of protection against the menacing eyes of male strangers', in the eyes of many Iranian women. The significance of the veil as a means of resistance to Western domination cannot be underestimated. It is true that the veil 'came to symbolize in the resistance narrative' rather than a symbol of 'the inferiority of the [Muslim] culture'.[89] Undoubtedly Muslim traditionalists who are apprehensive of the West, especially its secularism and free-mixing of the sexes, defend the *hijab* including the face-veil and gloves, as 'Quranic in spirit'.[90] It seems, until the Muslim world is able to sort out its problems with the West, Muslim women in general are not going to be salvaged by the writings of Qasim Amin (a nineteenth-century French-educated Egyptian writer) and others who hold *hijab* responsible for the 'ignorance, superstition, obesity, anemia, and premature aging of the Muslim women'.[91]

In regard to other contentious issues such as Muslim women's rights to inherit property, testify in the courts of justice, hold high positions such as rulers, judges and administrators, one finds the *Sharia* law and *hadises* rather than the Quran as the main impediments to such rights and opportunities for women. Although the *Sharia* laws (codified during the ninth and tenth centuries) are theoretically based on the Quran, in practise they rely on the *hadis* literature and collective and individual judgments (*ijma* and *qias,* respectively) of medieval Muslim jurists, *imams* and *mujtahids.* Needless to say, local customs and traditions promoting misogyny and male supremacy played the most vital role in perpetuating the status quo with regard to the deprivation of women, albeit in the name of Islam.

Although the Quran is very clear about the right to inheritance, allowing women to inherit half the share given to a man, one must consider the specificity of the regulation. Islam allowed women a share in the property when women in general did not enjoy such right as they were deemed to be 'properties' from the male point of view. Muslim scholars such as Afghani, Abduh, Ali Shariati and Mahmud Taha believed in the evolutionary development of Islam, stressing that Islamic dogma had to be regarded as determined by space and time. While only the Makkan verses had universal validity, those revealed in Madina were subject to modifications as they were determined by the age and the place. The Madinese verses again reflected the period when the Prophet was simultaneously a politician. Consequently Makkan verses gave more rights and equal status to women than the Madinese ones. As Fazlur Rahman has pointed out that although the Quran is the 'eternal Word of God', it nevertheless addressed 'a given society with a specific social structure'.[92]

One may argue that in view of this specificity, Muslim women's inheritance rights, as stipulated in the Quran, may be re-evaluated in accordance with the changed circumstances of the modern era. It may be pointed out that the *Sharia* law has gone through radical changes since the nineteenth century under the influence of Western civilization in most Muslim countries. Consequently the criminal and general civil law of the *Sharia* have been abandoned in most Muslim countries as well. Only certain civil matters – marriage, divorce and inheritance – are still regulated by the *Sharia* in most of these countries. However, there are broad discrepancies in the interpretations and application of *Sharia* laws in regard to civil matters, including inheritance. The *Sharia*, for example, allows male agnate relatives or *asabah*, (who are more than one degree removed from the deceased through male links) to have shares in the property of the deceased. In accordance with the Shiite law of inheritance, both male and female agnate relatives have shares in the property and like the Sunnis, a male relative normally takes double the share of the corresponding female relative.[93]

Some Muslim scholars consider the system which allows the half-share for women a generous one, as according to Islamic law only men have the obligations to maintain their family members, having no right to disinherit the wives. Some scholars justify the system as all those who have shares in the property of the deceased, as members of the extended family, are duty-bound to look after and protect the female relatives of the deceased 'financially, morally, socially and otherwise', as these female successors 'are the flesh of their flesh and the bones of their bones'.[94]

In view of the above, one may assume that there are scopes for modifications in the *Sharia* law of inheritance, especially when women are no longer dependent on their husbands and other male relatives for maintenance and protection under the modern urban setting. Female members of nuclear families again do not get the financial, moral and social support of any relatives other than those of their fathers and brothers. Consequently one may argue that since extended families have ceased to exist in urban areas, the *Sharia* law of inheritance is simply obsolete and contrary to the best interests of female members of nuclear families. One modern Islamic scholar suggests that 'the proportion for the female of one-half the proportion for the male is not the sole mode of property division [in accordance with the Quran, 4:11–12], but *one* of several proportional arrangements possible'. She further argues that 'if in a family of a son and two daughters, a widowed mother is cared for and supported by one of her daughters, why should the son receive a larger share?' It is a persuasive view that: 'All distribution of the inheritance . . . must be equitable', such equity in distribution must take the actual *naf'a* (benefit) of the bereft into consideration and that 'the Quran does not elaborate all possibilities'.[95]

It is noteworthy that a noted modern commentator of the Quran from Pakistan holds that the inheritors can inherit only what the deceased has left behind (*ma taraka* or, 'what one leaves behind', verse 4:11); and that the Quran does not take away the right of a person to make his own will. One can give away one's entire property to someone and thus nothing is left for the 'inheritors' to inherit. It is not the Quran but Muslim jurists who have barred Muslims from giving away their entire properties to someone to deprive their relatives.[96] However, as Engineer has observed, the law of inheritance in Islam is governed more by sociological than theological realities. As far as Muslim women are concerned, there have been more breaches than observance of the law, especially in agrarian societies, where women even do not get their due shares as specified in the Quran.[97]

In Muslim countries such as Bangladesh, where almost every aspect of life is regulated by Western or secular laws, Muslim men are very particular about implementing the *Sharia* law with regard to inheritance, with a view to depriving their female relatives from getting equal shares. In many cases, Bangladeshi women, both in the rural and urban areas, have to give up their shares (half the share of the corresponding male relatives) in accordance with the non-Islamic indigenous custom. Women who assert their right to their due shares, are generally looked down upon by their male siblings and other relatives throughout Bangladesh and among other South Asian Muslims. Elsewhere in the Muslim world, in Jordan for example, custom and pressure have been depriving women from property rights granted by Islam. In some rural areas in the region fathers often distribute their land among their male heirs before their deaths, thus totally depriving women of any shares. The Muslim Brotherhood is also supportive of local customs and strongly opposed to giving equal shares to women.[98]

Leadership and Testimony by Women

Other contentious issues, such as Muslim women's position as leaders and their rights of testimony in the courts of justice, may be examined in the light of the Quran and *Sharia* law. In general it is believed by both Muslims and non-Muslims that Islam does not favour women's authority over men as men have been given a degree or *darajah* above women in the Quran. However, a closer look into the verse distinguishing a *darajah* between men and women reveals the specificity of the verse, refuting the view that men have this edge in every sphere of life. The verse allows men an advantage over women as the former are individually able to pronounce divorce without any arbitration. Muslim women may divorce their husbands only through the arbitration of a court.

> Women who are divorced shall wait, keeping themselves apart, three (monthly) courses. And it is not lawful for them that they conceal that which Allah has created in their wombs if they believe in Allah and the Last Day. And their husbands would do better to take them back in that case if they desire reconciliation. And [the rights due to the women are similar to (the rights) against them, (or responsibilities they owe) with regard to] the *ma'ruf* [conventionally accepted kind treatment of women], and men have a degree [*darajah*] above them [women]. Allah is mighty, wise. [2:228]

It would be a mistake to assume that the Quran has given men a higher status than women and hence women are disqualified to be leaders in the society. In fact, there is nothing in the Quran which disqualifies women as rulers. On the contrary, Sura 27, *al-Naml* (The Ants) glorifies Queen Sheba (Bilqees) of Yamen as a competent and powerful ruler. She is the only ruler other than the prophets to get a positive mention in the Quran.

It is noteworthy that the remark, 'a people who entrust their command to a woman will not thrive', ascribed to the Prophet, is based on faulty chains of authentication or *isnad*. Although this tradition is part of Bukhari's *Sahih* or 'authentic' *hadises*, since the first transmitter of the *hadis*, Abu Bakra (a freedman of the Prophet), was once punished for giving false testimony, this tradition cannot be accepted as authentic. Again, the transmitter narrated the so-called tradition to disqualify Ayesha (widow of the Prophet) as a leader, who took up arms against Ali. Abu Bakra, the transmitter, is said to have had pro-Ali sympathies.[99]

The contentious issue of women's testimony in Islam is another by-product of ignorance, prejudice and misogyny on the part of Muslim jurists and laymen. Although there is only one verse out of the nine on testimony in the Quran which stipulates that the testimony of one man is equal to that of two women, Muslim jurists throughout history have been supportive of this inequitable arrangement. Since jurists regard the testimony of women as defective, it is theoretically possible that in a case of murder witnessed by 50 women in which there are no male witnesses, their testimony would not be accepted by a *Sharia* court of criminal justice.[100] As one Muslim scholar has pointed out:

> And because of this same defect a woman can be neither a judge, nor an officer in the government, nor the guardian of her own children or of her ownself. And she cannot marry herself, her son can give her in marriage.[101]

Now the problematic verse which 'suggests' that one man is equal to two women may be clarified in the light of common sense and reason. The verse concerned deals with a commercial agreement or a debt. It stipulates that when an agreement is contracted it should be recorded in writing witnessed by two men and 'if two men be not at hand then a man and two women, of such as you approve as witnesses, so that if the one errs [*tudilla*] the other can remind her'. [2:282] It is interesting that both the women are not considered as witnesses, one is supposed to 'remind' the other.

Although there are scholars (mostly Muslim apologists), who argue in favour of this two-to-one ratio, stressing that women have 'short-term memory loss', attributed to premenstrual syndrome and other physical and psychological disorders solely affecting women,[102] there may be more convincing explanations than those given by the apologists, such as the explanation that two female witnesses are required in a society where women could be coerced and forced to disclaim their testimony by men. 'When there are two women, they can support each other – especially in view of the term chosen: if she (*tudilla*) "goes astray", the other can (*tudhakkira*) "remind her", or "recall her attention" to the terms of agreement', so goes the counter-argument, which also stipulates that the verse is significant to a particular circumstance which has become obsolete in our time.[103] Muslim scholars in the early days of Islam, al-Tabari and al-Qurtubi for example, regarded the rule in this problematic verse as a 'recommendation, not an obligation', that is, the rule was based on social conditions where women do not take part in business and are unable to understand the transaction. Consequently the verse is not only applicable to a specific situation, having no basis of a universal law of evidence for women, it is also absurd to assume that a woman cannot be a judge or hold high positions as 'she cannot be a full witness'.[104] It is not insignificant that in accordance with the Quran a woman's oath, by which she defends herself against the accusation of adultery by her husband, outweighs the allegation and saves her from punishment.

> As for those who accuse their wives but have no witnesses except themselves; let the testimony of one of them be four testimonies [required to prove adultery], ... And it shall avert the punishment from her if she bears witness before Allah four times that the things he [the husband] says is indeed false. [24:6–9]

There is an example of the Prophet punishing a rapist on the basis of the testimony of the female victim. There was no other witness to corroborate her assertion.[105] It is said that the fourth caliph Ali would have tried the murderers of Usman, the third caliph, on the basis of the testimony of the sole witness, Naila, widow of the victim, but on grounds of political expediency (to avoid a civil war) Ali refrained from trying the murderers.[106] In view of the above, there is no reason to believe that Islam does not regard the testimony of women as equal to that of men.

Hadis and Fiqh

As pointed out earlier, while the Quranic injunctions in regard to women's rights and status are liberal and often libertarian, the *hadis* literature and the *Sharia* law, codified by both the Sunni and Shiite *faqihs* (jurists) by the late ninth century, are full of inflexible, prejudiced, biased, intolerant and reactionary injunctions *vis-à-vis* the rights of women. Consequently it is often said that, 'what the Quran has given to women has been taken away by the *Sharia* law'. However, a close look at the *hadises* or 'sayings of the Prophet', collected more than two hundred years after his death in 632, reveals that not only do they contain diverse views but some are also contradictory and often go against the teachings of the Quran. This is true of the so-called *sahih* or authentic *hadises* compiled by al-Bukhari (817–70) and others as well. One is not sure how to react to the following contradictory *hadises*:

> I (the Prophet) have left behind no temptation more harmful to my community than that which women represent for men.
>
> or
>
> The whole world is delightful, but the most delightful thing in it is a virtuous woman.[107]

There are scores of 'authentic' *hadises* like the following ones, full of misogynous exposition, even in the compilation of al-Bukhari:

> The Prophet said that the dog, the ass, and woman interrupt prayer if they pass in front of the believer.
>
> [Bukhari, *Sahih*, Vol. I, p. 99]

> Three things bring bad luck: house, woman, and horse.[108]
>
> [Bukhari, *Sahih*, Vol. III, p. 243]

Some scholars have challenged the authenticity of many *hadises*. It is noteworthy that even at the very early stage of *hadis*-compilation, some leading companions of the Prophet, Caliph Umar and Ayesha (widow of the Prophet) for example, questioned Abu Hurayra, one of the leading narrators of *hadises*, about the authenticity of his narratives. It is interesting that Abu Hurayra, who only spent three years in the company of the Prophet, narrated 5300 *hadises*. Al-Bukhari cited him as the source of 800 *hadises*. Umar is said to have remarked about his narration of *hadises*: 'We have many things to say, but we are afraid to say them, and that man [Abu Hurayra] there has no restraint.'[109] Ayesha rejected Abu Hurayra's narration of the *hadis* where women have been compared with asses and dogs. She rejected the so-called *hadis* by asserting that: 'In the name of God, I have seen the Prophet saying his prayers while I was there, lying on the bed between him and the *qibla* [the holy *Kaaba* in Makka].'[110] With regard to the comparison of a woman with a horse and a house as things that bring bad luck, attributed to the Prophet by Abu Hurayra, Ayesha responded:

> Abu Hurayra learned his lessons very badly. He came into our house when the Prophet was in the middle of a sentence. He only heard the end of it. What the Prophet said was: 'May Allah refute the Jews; they say three things bring bad luck: house, woman and horse'.[111]

It is interesting that although Imam Bukhari and other compilers of the *sahih hadises* had been meticulously strict in selecting *hadises* (Bukhari selected only about 7000 *hadises* as authentic from over 600 000 memorized items), contradictory *hadises*, including those contradicting some Quranic teachings, with regard to Islamic eschatology for instance, abound in their compilations. The following *sahih hadis* from Bukhari are examples:

> Abdullah Ibn Umar said: The Prophet said: 'I took a look at paradise, and I noted that the majority of the people were poor people. I took a look at hell, and I noted that there women were the majority!'[112]

One wonders, how could this be accepted as authentic by Bukhari since according to Islamic eschatology men and women are supposed to go to heaven or hell only after the Day of Judgment?

Consequently before passing judgement on the status of women in Islam solely based on the *hadis* literature, it should be realized that:

1 *Hadis* is neither infallible nor is faith in it essential to remain a Muslim (unlike the Quran).
2 *Hadis* lacks universal acceptance among Muslims – Shias and Sunnis rely on different sets of *hadises*.
3 Many early narrators of *hadises* invented traditions to propagate their own ideas.
4 Many narrators or *rawis* were non-believers and *munafiqeen* or hypocrites, who wanted to harm Islam.
5 *Hadises* were compiled in the eighth and ninth centuries when rulers and politicians concocted them to legitimize their regimes.

Falsehood, hypocrisy and the spread of heretical doctrines were so pervasive in the Muslim world in the eighth and ninth centuries, the heyday of *hadis* collection, that a pious Muslim such as Yahya bin Said (died 760) is reported to have said: 'I have not seen more falsehood in anyone than in those who have a reputation for goodness.' Another pious Muslim made a similar statement: 'I have not seen the good man lying about anything more than about *Hadith*.'[113] Al-Tabari (died 923), who wrote a commentary on the Quran, was sceptical about the authenticity of many *hadises*. He cited many *hadises* in his work, frequently indicating his reservations with the phrase *wa-llahu a'lam* (God knows best). The *hadises* on the creation of Eve or Hawwa from a rib of Adam have been attributed to 'the people of the Torah' or Biblical tradition by Tabari.[114] Sir Sayyid Ahmad Khan, a renowned Islamic 'modernist' of the nineteenth century, pointed out that it is difficult to judge the character of living people, let alone those long dead. So he raised the question about the authenticity of *hadises* narrated by people who had been long dead when their narrations were collected. Even many defenders of the *hadis* literature agree with this view considering that the collectors of *hadises* 'were simply too distant in time from the Prophet to be able to rescue authentic *hadith*'.[115]

Notwithstanding this mental reservation about the authenticity of *hadises* by Tabari and some other pre-modern Muslim scholars, Muslims in general blindly follow the consensus (*ijma*) of Muslim jurists (*faqihs*) and *imams* of the Sunni and Shiite schools, who mainly depended on the *hadises*. The *hadis* materials on women's inferiority, including their 'lack of full personhood and moral responsibility', were generally accepted by the bulk of *ulama* until eighteenth-century reformists began to question the authoritative status of the *ijma*. Since the nineteenth century, Islamic modernists have virtually denied the authenticity of medieval interpretations of the Quran and the *Sharia* law, including those pertaining to women.[116]

Leading Islamic scholars such as Fazlur Rahman and Asghar Ali Engineer have also challenged the authority of medieval Muslim jurists and their followers for closing the doors of *ijtihad* or 'original thinking' in Islam. Modern Muslim scholars believe that there is nothing sacerdotal about the authority of the *ulama* or *mujtahids* who exercised their individual or collective reasoning, *qiyas* and *ijma* respectively and that *ijma* is the *'method and principle'* to interpret the scripture, its contents may be regarded as 'authoritative, not infallible'. According to Fazlur Rahman:

Like an organism it [*ijma*] both functions and grows; at any given moment it has supreme functional validity and power and in that sense is 'final' but at the same moment it creates, assimilates, modifies and rejects. . . . It [*ijma*] was more akin to an enlightened public opinion.[117]

However, our experience tells us that despite their mutual differences of opinion, the conservative *ulama* or the lawyer – theologians throughout history have interpreted Islam basing on the authority of *ijma* or community consensus which is again the core of the *Sharia*. The *ijma* again, does not necessarily always represent the 'great tradition' of Islam but was largely moulded by local or 'little traditions', symbols, perceptions and customs. It is noteworthy that most *ulama* cite a very small number of Quranic verses to justify segregation, and inferiority and subordination of women. What they cite most are *hadises* and *fiqh* (books of Muslim jurisprudence). Many of them also love to issue *fatwas* depending on their own judgments, mostly reflective of their prejudice, ignorance and mysogynous bent of mind. Fazlur Rahman may be cited to highlight the close-mindedness of most *ulama*, trained in *madrasahs*:

For the *madrasahs* have, almost from the beginning of their organized existence, aimed at merely imparting a system of ideas, not at creating newer systems; and therefore they have not been interested in inculcating the spirit of enquiry and independent thought. . . . Otherwise, their *raison d'etre* would be gone.[118]

The reason the bulk of the *madrasah*-trained *ulama* resist changes in certain *Sharia* edicts concerning women

is not because they are based on the Quran and *sunnah* (slavery was also based on the Quran and *sunnah* and yet it was abolished when the time came for it) but because societies are still male-dominated and it hurts the pride of men to accept change.[119]

One may assume that the *ulama*, devoid of liberal education and receptive mind, will be eventually more accommodating to women's liberation as they no longer protest against photography, cinema and television. Since Islamic scholars like Imam Ibn Taymiyya of the fourteenth and Shah *Waliullah* of the eighteenth centuries believed that Islamic edicts change with time and circumstances, there is no reason to accommodate the immoderate views of the *ulama* concerning women's rights and status in Islam. Since the *ulama*, who have no legal or religious authority and status in the Muslim community or *ummah*, as Islam does not recognize any priestly class, liberal Muslims may formulate their own views in accordance with the teachings of the Quran and common sense.

One may lynch the early *fuqaha* (jurists) who arbitrarily closed the doors of *ijtihad* (creative interpretation) in the eighth century for formulating the *Sharia* depending more on *hadises*, local traditions and practices than on the Quran. As the Quran can cancel the *sunnah* and not the vice versa, 'there is much in it [the *Sharia*] which is contextual and hence needs to be re-assessed in the changed context'.[120] Before we accept the so-called *sahih hadises* transmitted by Bukhari, Ibn Hanbal and other compilers, especially with regard to women, we should recognize that Bukhari believed that '[W]omen are naturally, morally and religiously defective', and Ibn Hanbal did not have a high opinion of women either.[121]

It is generally believed that unlike the average conservative *mulla*, sufis have been much more tolerant and liberal with regard to women's rights and status in the society. Several powerful female *sufis*, such as Rabiah Basri (717–801), sold as a slave and freed by her master, Fatima of Nishapur (died 849) and Nafisa (born 762), a great-granddaughter of Hasan (grandson of the Prophet) were revered by both men and women. Other *sufis* are said to have accorded equal status to women throughout history. However, one should be careful before stereotyping all *sufis* as tolerant and liberal with regard to women. Although *sufis* promoted mysticism and esoteric doctrines, in general, they were adherents of the *Sharia* and Islamic schools of jurisprudence (*mazhabs*). With the ascendancy of Abul Hasan al-Ashari (died 935), Imam Ghazzali and other orthodox ideologues in the Muslim world, the so-called liberal *sufis* and rationalist Mutazilites simply disappeared from the mainstream of Islamic thought and socio-political life.

Ghazzali's influence is pervasive in the Sunni world. He is often glorified for 'saving' Islam from the clutches of heterodoxy and the influence of Sufism. He believed that the most ordinary men should surpass the most gifted women. He considered women as a dangerous distraction for men, as the main source of *fitna* or chaos, and advised Muslim men to use them for the specific purpose of procreation and sexual enjoyment. He regarded the woman as the hunter and the man as the passive victim. He even interpreted the Quranic verse 3 of sura 113 (*al-Falaq*) to denigrate women. According to him, during coitus, the male is embracing a woman, 'symbol of unreason and disorder' and 'disciple of the devil', and men seek refuge in the Lord of daybreak, 'from the evil which He created and from the evil of darkness when it is insane' [3:113]. Ghazzali reminds the man that during coitus he is not in Allah's territory. Hence the necessity to invoke his presence to save him from 'the evil of darkness'.[122] It is noteworthy that Ghazzali's sentiments about women are more in conformity with ancient Greek philosophy of Tertullian or Augustine than with the Quran.[123]

Conclusions

In sum, any discussion of women's rights and status in Islam is very problematic. Firstly, neither Muslim nor non-Muslim scholars are unanimous about the stand of Islam on the subject. Secondly, there has traditionally been an unbridged gap between the faith of Islam and the practices of its adherents. Last but not least, neither Islam nor its followers hold monolithic views. There are differences between the teachings of the Quran and those of the *hadis* literature as there have been different opinions on the subject among the adherents of different sects, schools of thought and among Muslims living in different countries. Local cultures and traditions, and modes and relations of production prevalent in different Muslim communities in the past and in our times determine to a great extent the status of Muslim women. In a nutshell, one may conclude that despite the concerted opposition of the conservative *ulama* and agents of patriarchy, Muslim women have recently attained greater rights in most Muslim countries. However, there have been exceptions to this. Iran, Afghanistan, Pakistan and Algeria for example, have moved in the opposite direction after improving women's rights and establish a kind of gender equality in the first half of the twentieth century. There is, however, no reason to blame only the so-called Islamic fundamentalists for retarding and reversing the process of giving equal opportunities and rights to Muslim women. Secular leaders such as Habib Bourgiba of Tunisia and Ben Bella of Algeria also sent women to the kitchen. Women workers of the Sudan Communist Party, which was quite influential in the 1950s and 1960s, did not have an independent voice in the Party and similarly, the PLO has not given autonomy to the General Union of Palestinian Women, part of the Palestinian movement.[124] It is equally significant that while Ayatollah Khomeini praised Iranian women for their role in the Islamic Revolution of 1979 ('Any nation that has women like the Iranian women will surely be victorious'), the so-called enlightened and liberal Muhammad Reza Shah considered that: '[W]omen are important in a man's life only if they're beautiful and charming and keep their feminity'.[125]

As Islam is not a monolithic religion and Muslims throughout history have not been the only people to subjugate women, there is no reason to be pessimistic about the future of Muslim women, at least in the relatively progressive Muslim countries, including Bangladesh. Since Islam does not sanction any priestly class and God has never addressed the *ulama* as a special category in the Quran (although many *ulama* preach the *hadis* that 'the *ulama* are the lieutenants [or *naibs*] of the Prophet'), Islamic modernists have insisted on relying on individual interpretations of the scriptures (*ijtihad*) by de-emphasizing the *Sharia* and collective interpretations of the scriptures (*ijma*).[126] However, since the conservative *ulama* are critical of individual *ijtihad*, Islamic modernists are bound to face the concerted opposition of the conservative forces in Islam. Yet this sort of confrontation between the conservative *ulama* and radical Islamic modernists has not taken place everywhere in the Muslim world. Turkey under Kamal Ataturk and Iran under Reza Shah are the only Muslim countries who have gone through the process and even here without similar results. One cannot, however, rule out the possibility of such a confrontation, especially in certain Muslim countries in the Middle East and North Africa, with a tradition of growing Islamic modernist and feminist movements.

What began with the writings of Islamic modernists such as Sheikh Abduh and Qasim Amin in Egypt and Sir Syed Ahmad Khan and Mumtaz Ali in north India in the nineteenth century later led to the foundation of a feminist movement among Muslim women in the Middle East and South Asia. Qasim Amin's *The Women in the East* (1894) and *Tahrir al-Mar'ah* (The Liberation of Women), which came out in 1899, influenced many Egyptian Muslim men and women. His call for an end to female seclusion and the abuses of divorce and polygamy had great symbolic significance. He demonstrated that female seclusion, veiling and polygamy had nothing to do with Islam. Soon he published *al-Mar'ah al-Jadidah* (The New Women) in 1900, applying secular and nationalist arguments for the liberation of Egyptian women. Amin's writings may be associated with the feminist movement in Egypt led by such women as Aishah al-Taymariyah (died 1902), Zaynab Fawwaz (died 1914), Huda Sha'rawi (1879–1947), Nabawiah Musa, and others. By the early twentieth century feminism had become a part of anti-colonial movements in countries like Egypt, Syria and India.[127]

By the Nasser period, Egyptian women had gained equal opportunity in education and in work and started playing an important role in society. However, feminists like Nawal Saadawi, author of *The Hidden Face of Eve* (1980), and Hoda Lutfi started a movement for not only rights but power. In 1979 amendments to the Family Law were made in Egypt by a presidential decree with the support of Sadat's wife, Jihan.[128] Women in Tunisia and Morocco by the 1970s had also achieved greater rights than before. In Tunisia, polygamy was prohibited, men could no longer divorce a wife by simple public repudiation but had to follow a civil procedure, women gained the right to initiate divorce and to choose to work and gained more inheritance rights. The lot of women has been improving in Morocco as well.[129] In general, women's rights have been recognized more widely throughout the Middle Eastern and North African countries, with a few exceptions such as Saudi Arabia and Sudan.[130]

Muslim women in South Asia and Southeast Asia have attained more rights despite the opposition of the conservative forces. Ayub Khan's Family Law Ordinance restricted polygamy and accorded more rights to Muslim women in the early 1960s. Since the turn of the twentieth century, Begum Rokeya (1880–1931), with her bold writings and actions, has made a breakthrough by, challenging patriarchy and the subjection of women in the name of Islam in Bangladesh. However, through the spasmodic and not so well-organized feminist movement, Bangladeshi Muslim women have attained many rights, including the right to hold public offices (two successive prime ministers since 1991 have been women). Despite these achievements, women in countries like Bangladesh and Pakistan have remained subservient to men. In Pakistan, this may be attributed to the predominance of feudal culture and 'political' Islam, in Bangladesh the gender-based oppression is more a Third World syndrome than an Islamic one. This is true of many backward and poor Muslim societies – the competition for scarce resources has polarized men and women into opposite camps. Both the Islamic and secular forces blame each other with a view to making inroads in the women's domain mainly for politico-economic reasons. Before rejecting the achievements of Muslim societies in regard to the liberation and empowerment of women, we should remember the words of Fatima Mernissi who rightly observes that:

> The traditional enthronement of women . . . has forced the Muslims in a few decades to face up to what Westerners took centuries to digest (and which they still have difficulty doing): democracy and the equality of the sexes.[131]

To conclude, it is a fair assumption that what the West has achieved with regard to establishing equal rights for women has been possible only in the post-Reformation, post-Renaissance period, and the Muslim world has not yet gone through these processes. We should not expect radical changes in the Muslim world with regard to gender equality. Most Muslim countries are still in the pre-capitalist, semi-feudal and pre-modern stage. Last but not least, not only are Muslim men divided over the issue of granting equal rights and opportunities to Muslim women, but Muslim women are sharply divided over the issue as well. This cleavage was reflected at the NGO Forum in Beijing in September 1995. While hundreds of women from half-a-dozen Muslim countries chanted slogans demanding equal rights for women and condemned 'the barbaric stoning' in Iran, scores of Iranian women demonstrated in favour of *Sharia* law, all dressed in black cloaks and headdresses. Their banner read 'Islam is our law'.[132]

3
Mullas, Popular Islam and Misogyny in Bangladesh

If you wish to praise women, rather praise dogs, for a dog is better than a hundred virtuous women! How shrewd was the King of the World Kay-Qobad who said: Let the good women be cursed!
Firdausi (tenth-century Persian poet)

God sends these fruits to us in 'packets' to save them from flies and insects, that is why they taste so good. All good things in life are shrouded with covers and mystery. That is why woman should be covered from head to toe.
Delwar Hossain Saidi, a Jamaat-
i-Islami leader, Bangladesh

Introduction

In this chapter I want to explore the correlation between Islam and women in Bangladesh with special regard to the subjection and persecution of women both in the urban and rural areas at the hands of the self-proclaimed custodians of Islam. It is quite interesting that although Sunni Islam does not require a formal clergy as the intermediary between man and God, in the region of this study where Sunnism is the creed of more than 99 per cent of the Muslim population, the clergy is quite well-entrenched and very influential. In some sub-regions, especially in rural areas, the *ulama* (both the well-versed religious scholars and the half-educated *maulvis* and *munshis*) are powerful enough to exert their influence in the dispension of justice in village-courts or *salish*, thus undermining the authority of the Government of Bangladesh. Quite often, poor rural women have been the victims of these courts, run by rural *ulama* and village elders.

Here I attempt to differentiate between the well-versed *ulama* and the half-educated rural *maulvis*, which respectively represent the 'great' and 'little' traditions of Islam in Bangladesh. The lines of demarcation between the two categories of *ulama* are in general not different from those drawn between the urban and rural ways of life – norms, behaviour and *modus operandi*. However, unlike in north-western India, the demarcation lines between the urban and rural *ulama* in Bangladesh are very blurred and quite often, the two are inseparable, mainly due to the preponderance of rural and peasant culture in the predominantly rural society.

This is important for our understanding as to how and why the rural *mullas'* versions of the *Sharia* law and interpretations of the Quran and sayings (both real and fictitious) of Prophet Muhammad have preponderated over those of the well-versed *ulama*, Islamic modernists and liberal reformists such as Jamal al-Din Afghani, Sheikh Muhammad Abduh and Syed Ahmad Khan. It is equally important to know how, under the overpowering influence of the rural *mullas* and popular Islam, the average Bangladeshi Muslim has been programmed to accept the subjection of women in every sphere of life as natural, efficacious and 'desired by God which is beyond the comprehension of human beings'. In short, we are considering here the development of misogyny as interpreted and understood by the average *mullas* of Bangladesh, rather than the way in which their gracelessness has led to the subjection (recently turned into tyranny) of women in the region.

Muslims in general and the *ulama* in particular are known to have sanctioned the seclusion of women and their subjection to men. Thus misogyny (the hatred of women by men) is associated with Islam and with the custodians of the faith, mainly because of the way women are subjugated in 'Islamic' countries such as Afghanistan, Iran and Saudi Arabia in particular. However, the dogma which glorifies the subjection of women in the name of Islam has no universal acceptance among the adherents of the faith. Not only are there Shia-Sunni differences in this regard, but also those between different ages and countries so far as the status of Muslim women is concerned. In this chapter I try to explore the correlation between the subjection of women and the teachings of the *mullas* in Bangladesh from a historical perspective, and to understand how and why the differences between the qualified *ulama* and the not-so-qualified ones (respectively representing the 'great' and 'little' traditions), have been blurred, especially with regard to the status and perceptions of women. In general, popular Islam portrays women as satanic, demonic, deceitful, difficult to control, insatiable, unfaithful, quarrelsome and in short, as the root of all evil. The bulk of the *ulama* and average Bangladeshi Muslims often say and do things which not only are derogatory but also harmful to women, who are the first to lose their properties, dignity and basic human rights in violation of both the basic tenets of Islam and the UN Charter of Human Rights. This is especially true of poor women.

The persecution of hundreds of poor rural women by village *mullas* and their patrons (powerful village elders) in the name of 'Islamic justice' through village courts (*salish*) in the recent past (1990–5), further aggravates the situation as several victims were killed and many committed suicide in disgrace. These acts of flagrant violation of human rights have not gone unchallenged. Scores of local and international organizations, intellectuals, feminists and others have been challenging the authority of the *fatwa*-dispensing *mullas* and the legal validity of the *salish* courts. The controversial writings of Bangladeshi feminist writer, Taslima Nasreen, in the recent past, which also highlighted the plight of women in Bangladesh in the name of Islam, and the issuance of another *fatwa* against her by some obscure *mullas*, condemning her to death, brought the issue of subjugation of women in 'Islamic' Bangladesh into the limelight.[1]

However, an in-depth study of the culture of misogyny, nourished by both secular and religious, rich and poor, urban and rural, literate and illiterate sections of the population, is essential for our understanding of why Bangladeshi women in general enjoy very low status, suffering in every spheres of life, for there is a positive correlation between popular culture and the 'great tradition' of Islam. It is noteworthy that the process leading to the growth of misogyny did not start with the Islamization of the region. Eight centuries of interaction between the indigenous peasant/tribal culture and the Middle-Eastern Islamic one led to the growth of a syncretic Bengali culture.[2] It is essential to understand this mishmash in order to evaluate the culture of misogyny and the role of the *mulla* in its promotion.

Mullas in the 'great' and 'little' traditions

Mulla is a generic term, primarily denoting Muslim theologians but actually connoting all sections of the people associated with the

Sharia law, its interpretation and application and those associated with *marifah* or Islamic mysticism. These categories include the *ulama*; *pirs*; *sufis*; *shaikhs* (*shaykhs*); *muftis* and *imams*. However, the term 'mulla' (often misspelled as 'mullah') is the Persian form of the Arabic 'maulawi' (*maulvi*) or a learned man. It also stands for a scholar 'filled' with knowledge (from *mala* to 'fill'). However in the local context, *mullas* are considered inferior in education and status to the well-qualified *maulanas* and *maulvis*.[3]

In medieval Bengal, the *mullas* enjoyed a highly respectable position and exerted great influence because they in society possessed religious knowledge. Muslim rulers and *qadis* (judges) held them in high esteem. In short, the *mulla* was 'a dignified person. . . . a religious scholar, teacher, preceptor and *imam* to the Muslims of his locality'.[4] Some conducted marriage ceremonies and performed the ritual slaughter of animals and were rewarded by Muslim villages.[5] The half-educated *mullas* were also known as *kathmullas* ('ignorant and bigoted ones') in the region.[6] Among the different species of *mulla* or *ulama*, *pirs* or mystic guides and *sufis* are the most important, having tremendous influence on both the ordinary people and the dominant class of Bengali Muslims.

Etymologically, the Persian word *pir* stands for old, but in the Indian subcontinent it denotes a mystic guide or *sufi*, who initiates *murids* or disciples in mystic *tariqas* or orders. In Bengali, the term 'is exclusively used in this mystic sense and has no other meaning than "the mystic guide" . . . . equivalent to the mystic terms "*Shaykhs*" and "*Ustadh*" used in different parts of the Muslim world'.[7]

Pirs in Bengal have generally enjoyed a much higher status than *sufis* elsewhere in the world. According to Asim Roy, 'the Bengali Muslim folk developed almost a cult and pantheon of *pirs*, to whom they resorted in the trials and tribulations of their hard everyday life'.[8] It is evident from different sources that *pirs*, also known as *shaykhs* (*shaikhs*), *murshids* and *gurus* in Bengal, were the most influential elements in the popular Islam of the country, some resembling Tantric *gurus* and many under the influence of the Vaishnava, Yogic or other Hindu-Buddhist-Baul cults. Many of them were even worshipped by their followers, as superhuman powers were ascribed to them such as being able to help the poor, cure the incurable and foretell the future.[9]

A recent empirical study of rural Bangladesh reveals that *pirs'* holy power and supposed ability to heal and bring wealth to their followers may be the basis of their legitimacy. It also tells us that 'women, far more than men, visit local *pir* in times of particular need', and that 'this is partly because women of whatever class are partly excluded from more formal means of gaining religious capital (they are less likely to perform Haj, for example, and are barred from the mosque and household *milad*)'.[10] Like landless men without power, women 'are more likely to desire the miraculous escapes from their circumstances which *pir* appears to offer'.[11]

Broadly speaking, the *pirs* in Bangladesh may be classified into the categories of *ba-shara* (those conforming to the *Sharia* law and morality) and *be-shara* (those who do not).[12] The former, representing the 'great tradition', are well-established and acceptable to the Sunni *ulama*, including those representing the Deoband *madrasah* in north India, who have a profound influence on the bulk of the Bangladeshi *ulama*.[13] The *be-shara* pirs, on the other hand, represent the so-called syncretic culture of Bengal, a blend of *sufism*, *yogism* and different animist and Hindu cults, such as the *Satya Pir*, *Panch Pir, Panch Pandit, Nath* and *Sahajiya*.[14] Under the pervasive influence of some of these cults, especially the *tantric* cult and Vaishnavism of Shree Chaitanya (1486–1533), free and extra-marital love has been glorified by some *be-shara pirs*.[15]

Despite the puritanical Islamic movements of the nineteenth century, such as the Tariqa-i-Muhammadiya, Faraizi and Tayuni,[16] many local and syncretic traditions and practices have remained dormant as well as active among Bengali Muslims. These traditions often undermine the status of women by turning them into sex objects for men. According to a recent study: 'pure Islam exists only as an aspiration' and is mostly confined to the well-to-do sections of the community. Poor masses, the study reveals, associate themselves with *be-shara pirs* and 'cults which reject the Quran and use *tantric* means to reach God', many revere Hindu deities and follow *be-shara pirs* who play music for prayer, smoke *ganja* (marijuana) and indulge in *tantric* practices believing that 'enlightened devotees may achieve salvation through the very acts which cause ordinary people to burn in Hell'.[17]

It may be mentioned here that even the puritanic Jaunpuri *pirs* (descendants of Maulana Karamat Ali of Jaunpur), who frequent the region, both from north India and from their local bases in Dhaka, Noakhali, Khulna and elsewhere, have not succeeded in preventing their *muridan* (disciples) from touching their feet in reverence and eating/drinking their left-over food, drinks and even chewed betel leaves (*paan*) as *taburruk* (spiritual blessings of saints).

Some *be-shara pirs* even encourage their followers (both male and female) to suck their toes and swallow their saliva and even semen as *taburruk*.

Side by side with the *be-shara pirs*, exists the puritanical *Tabligh* movement[18] to revive Islamic orthodoxy, which also implies the strict imposition of *purdah* or seclusion and servility of women. The influence of the growing number of *hajjis* and Bengali expatriate workers in Saudi Arabia and other Middle Eastern countries, has also been contributing to the reassertion of Islamic puritanism in Bangladesh.[19]

In addition to the *pirs*, *hajjis* and *Tablighi Jamaatis*, local *muftis* and *imams* are also very important with regard to the spread of orthodoxy in the country. *Muftis* and *imams* are often very difficult to distinguish from each other and from *pirs*. *Muftis* may be associated with both *madrasahs* and mosques or both, who issue *fatwas* or religious dictums sometimes on their own authority or at the behest of ruling classes, village elders, masses or individuals, with a view to establishing 'Islamic points of view' on important matters in the light of the *Sharia*. However, *muftis* may be manipulated and bribed by those who seek their *fatwas* to justify something. Traditionally, the influential Deoband *ulama* keep the functions of both *pir* and *mufti* 'united in a single person'.[20]

Imams, on the other hand, lead congregational prayers and simultaneously may perform the functions of *pirs* and *muftis* as well. However, *imams* are not priests, as there is no priesthood in Islam. According to Mohammad Arkoun:

> The *imam*, who prays before rows of the faithful in collective prayer, has no sacerdotal function; he stands apart from the rest of the believers by staying in a recess called *mihrab* to symbolize the unity of the praying community.[21]

Imams in Bangladesh are not regarded as authorities on Islam by the bulk of the population. They simply repeat and transmit the contents of the Quranic message, and their activities are 'strongly supervised and controlled' both in urban and rural areas by their employers who control the mosque management committees. Only in urban areas do *imams* enjoy slightly higher social status, in contrast to village *imams* who do not. While an urban *imam*'s average monthly salary is around 1200 *taka* ($30) his rural counterpart earns a paltry 200 *taka*. Consequently the village *imams* have to eke out a living by working as grocers, booksellers, tailors or teachers. In short, village *imams* are part of the village community and enjoy only the status of poor villagers without any power or prestige. They often live on charity and are dependent on village elders. The village *imam* is often referred to as *munshi* or 'employee of religion', while his urban counterpart is called *imam sahib*, which is clearly respectful.[22]

Because of their low social status and precarious living conditions, *imams'* jobs are not the most sought after by *madrasah* graduates, only about 10 per cent of whom aspire to become *imams* in Bangladesh.[23] However, many village *imams* nourish a tremendous sense of deprivation and social envy, and work for the establishment of an Islamic polity. This is not very dissimilar from what many Egyptian clerics have done by joining the radical Muslim Brotherhood to change the socio-political order.[24] Most of the itinerant *mullas* who travel around Bangladesh addressing religious meetings (*dharmio sabhas* or *waz mahfils*), testifying to 'the truth of Islam in the context of a popular religion where the fear of hell is more present than the discovery of truth', formerly worked as *imams*.[25] These demagogues also represent the hard-core anti-modern misogynist section of the *mulla*. Bernard Hours has most appropriately compared these meetings with un-Islamic animist discourse:

> One may wonder if this type of meeting is not the prolongation and the extension of the animist meetings organized around a medium, as is practised in the Indian subcontinent or in South-East Asia, whatever the dominant religion (Hinduism, Islam, Buddhism).[26]

In view of the above, the advent of the *ulama* (both indigenous and north-western Indian) in the socio-political arena of Bengal in different phases since the early nineteenth century, which culminated in the transformation of eastern Bengal into East Pakistan in 1947 with overwhelming Bengali support,[27] also led to the proliferation of Islamic *anjumans* or societies and an enormous rise in the number of *pirs*, *maulanas* and *maulvis* in the region. One designated as a *pir*, *maulana* or *mufti*, with or without any authentic *sufi* genealogy, was automatically elevated to the *ashraf* (elite) category despite his *ajlaf* or plebeian background. The success of Maulana Karamat Ali of Jaunpur (1800–73), north India, and his successors in championing the cause of Islamic orthodoxy and *sufism* in

Bangladesh,[28] also led to the proliferation of *pirs* in the region. As Rafiuddin Ahmed has aptly suggested, with the Islamic reform movements of the nineteenth century began the process of mass 'Islamization' and intense competition among semi-literate Bengali *mullas* vying with one another 'to establish the "correctness" of their interpretation of Islam', while lower-class Muslims 'continued their "idolatrous" practices long after the reformist purge'.[29]

Mullas and Muslim elites in the region, who proclaim to be the defenders of *Sharia* or the 'great tradition' of Islam, have never been totally immune to the indigenous culture, including superstitions, like their counterparts throughout the Muslim world. Arab Muslims, for example, indigenized Persian and Greek institutions, the veil and *harem* for women, respectively, in the early days of Islam. Asim Roy corroborates this.

> A culture is no less a determinant in recasting and reformulating a religion than is a religion in modifying a culture .... Islam in Bengal, therefore provided an uncommon paradigm of one religion's containing two great traditions juxtaposed to each other, one exogenous and classical, and the other endogenous and syncretistic.[30]

Consequently under the dual influence of the Middle-Eastern and indigenous cultures of misogyny, *mullas* in Bangladesh have been preaching their versions of the Islamic code of conduct with regard to the status and lifestyle of women in the society. As the bulk of the *mullas* come from humble peasant families from rural areas, they lack the refinement of urban *ulama* from northwestern India and parts of Pakistan.

In explaining the inherent peasant and misogynous culture of *mullas*, we need to shed light on the indigenous 'great traditions' of the region as depicted in the *Mahabharata*, *Ramayana*, *Puranas* and *Manusanghita vis-à-vis* women and their status in Hinduism, besides the 'little traditions' or Tantric and Baul cults. The traditional Bengali culture, as developed during the pre-Islamic period, was profoundly influenced by Hinduism and Buddhism. The inferior status of women is not only reflected in the cruel institutions of *sati*, female infanticide and denial of inheritance to women, as sanctioned by Hindu texts, but also in the Bengali expression, *raman* for 'woman', derived from Sanskrit, which literally means an object of sexual intercourse or *raman*. Hundreds of misogynous verses from the *Mahabharata*, *Ramayana*, *Arthashastra* of Kautilya and the stories of *Jataka* and *Panchatantra* may be cited as corroborative of the above assertion. Both Hindu and Buddhist religions as well as secular texts are full of cautionary advice with regard to the malevolent nature of women. They are portrayed as 'sexually promiscuous and insatiable', 'untrustworthy', 'vicious', 'conspiring', 'evil', 'demonic' and 'poisonous'.[31]

Similar misogynous expositions appear in the sayings of the famous nineteenth-century Hindu Bengali ascetic, Ramakrishna Paramahansa (1836–86), written in the *Kathamrita*, a diary-based record of his conversations between 1882 and 1886. This 'near illiterate', 'rustic brahman', who inspired the famous nineteenth-century Hindu revivalist, Swami Vivekananda, and hundreds of educated Bengali men and women, stressed that 'the insubordinate, unchaste woman was a principal source of evil' while *bhakti* or devotion 'had a feminine face, being personified by the pure dutiful wife or mother'.[32] Similarly, to Bengali *mullas* women are tolerated and even glorified only as obedient wives and indulging mothers. Although there is no evidence to suggest that *be-shara pirs* and other *mullas* were influenced by Ramakrishna's abhorrence of heterosexual sex and the female body, yet his espousing different obscure *tantric* cults, such as the *Baul*, *Sahajiya*, *Shakta*, *Kartabhaja* and *Sahabdhani*, drawing many devotees among Bengali men and women, might have affected Muslim villagers as well. The influence of *tantric* cults on rural *mullas* may perhaps be ascribed to the patronage of these cults by Ramakrishna and his disciples as well.

Mullas' background, gender bias and *weltanschauung*:

Any discussion on the backwardness of *mullas* and their promotion of misogyny needs to shed light on their socio-economic background, academic qualifications and place in the production relations of the polity. As discussed earlier, *mullas* enjoyed high social status as teachers and preachers and as members of the ruling elite in their function as judges and interpreters of the law in the pre-British as well as the colonial periods. Their privileged position declined gradually with several drastic measures taken by the British authorities curtailing the power and privileges of the *mullas* and other members of the Muslim aristocracy. These measures include the 'Resumption Proceedings' of the 1820s–1850s, which mainly expropriated Muslim elites (including the *ulama*) enjoying revenue-free estates under the

Mughals. The abolition of Persian as the official language in 1837 also hit the Muslim elites in Bengal hard.[33] The anti-British Wahhabi and Faraizi movements and the Mutiny of 1857 were mainly led by *ulama* and the Muslim aristocracy. Eventually their uncompromising, selfless and pioneering anti-British struggle led to the further emasculation of these people at the hands of the British *raj*, hence the decline and degeneration of the *ulama* in Bengal, who had their 'glorious past' during Muslim rule.[34]

Nevertheless, an even-handed study of the roles of the *ulama* in the liberation of the subcontinent places them in high relief. With their steep decline, both socio-politically and economically, after losing government patronage, the *ulama* in Bengal were fast turning into unemployed or under-employed members of the awe-stricken and backward Muslim community, nourishing a tremendous inferiority complex *vis-à-vis* the British *raj*. Many of them later found it convenient to collaborate with the British – not very dissimilar from the behaviour of many Al-Azhar *shaykhs* of Egypt who collaborated with Napoleon. The bulk of the *mullas* in Bangladesh either belong to this vacillating and pro-establishment group or to the poverty-stricken, backward and fatalist underdogs, nourishing a tremendous inferiority complex and anger towards modernization, capitalist growth and development.

Realizing the importance of the *ulama* for the interpretation of Muslim law for the Government, the British authorities established the Calcutta Madrasah in 1781 which followed the traditional curriculum in Arabic and Persian. The result was quite disastrous for the Muslims of Bengal, as the graduates of the *madrasah* had been

> good in their peculiar narrow way, but not in the least fitted to take their place in the competition of official or general life; and who were in consequence, as a class, bigoted, self-sufficient, disappointed, and soured, if not disloyal.[35]

We hear more about the fanatical and lewd behaviour of some of the *madrasah* students from a nineteenth-century account. Many of them were said to have brought prostitutes into their rooms and fought over the 'right way' of saying their prayers among themselves. Whether one should join their heels or keep them unclosed during prayers, for example, could be a very big issue among *madrasah* students.[36] The curriculum of the *madrasah* chiefly consisted of the *hadis* and 'law books of the fanatical medieval stamp – a sort of learning which fills the youthful brain with windy self-importance, and give rise to bitter schisms on the most trivial points within the College walls', as British civilian William Hunter observes.[37]

There is no reason to single out the Calcutta Madrasah as the centre of *obscurum per obscurius* as the other *madrasahs* in the region, including those of Deoband, Firingi Mahal and Nadwa in north India, for example, were equally, if not more, obscurantist and backward-looking. The Deoband Madrasah, which was established in 1867, adopted the age-old *Dars-i-Nizamiyah* curriculum. The learning of *hadis* is one of the main aspects of the curriculum. Deoband produced 1672 Bengali graduates (second highest after UP's 1896) between 1867 and 1967.[38] Since the *hadis* literature is full of controversial, misogynous expositions, one mastering the *hadis*, called *muhaddis*, would naturally convey a message which is supportive of misogyny to ordinary Muslims, in the name of Islam.

Besides the study of *hadis*, both Deoband and Calcutta Madrasah prototypes in Bangladesh, following the *Dars-i-Nizamiyah* and 'modern' curricula, respectively, also include the study of basic Arabic language and literature, *fiqh* or Muslim jurisprudence, logic and philosophy (pre-modern), the *Quran* and its interpretations, elementary mathematics, Urdu, Bengali and some English. However, the study of *hadis* remains the core of the curricula in every *madrasah* in the region.

It is, however, interesting that although all the *madrasahs* in the subcontinent stress the importance of *hadis* and regard *purdah* and the subordination of women to men as essential, the bulk of the north Indian *ulama* have been much more sophisticated, liberal and tolerant towards women than their counterparts in Bangladesh. Liberal north Indian *ulama* like (Sir) Sayyid Ahmad Khan (1817–98), Chiragh Ali and Maulana Mumtaz Ali (1860–1935) existed alongside the conservative Maulana Karamat Ali Jaunpuri (1800–73) and Maulana Ashraf Ali Thanawi (1864–1943). Although the conservative *ulama* did not favour equality of the sexes, they hardly portrayed women as perpetually inferior or defective in comparison to men. The liberal *ulama*, on the other hand, questioned the validity of those *ahadis* (plural of *hadis*) which contradicted common sense or the teachings of the *Quran*. They also favoured liberation and equality for women.

Both Sayyid Ahmad Khan and his 'more radical associate' in the Aligarh Movement, Chiragh Ali, opposed polygyny as well. Their interpretation of the Quranic verse making polygyny 'permissible' for Muslim men was quite liberal and modernist. They argued that 'justice in a man-woman relationship can only be synonymous with love; and since a man is emotionally incapable of loving more than one woman equally at any given time, in fact polygamy has been prohibited by demonstrating its underlying shortcoming'.[39] Maulana Mumtaz Ali, a Deoband-trained theologian, in the light of his liberal interpretations of the *Quran*, had similar views on polygyny. According to him, in Islam, there is no discrimination between the sexes.[40]

Although both Karamat Ali Jaunpuri and Ashraf Ali Thanawi wrote volumes on Islamic orthodoxy stressing puritanism, seclusion of women and their inferiority *vis-à-vis* men 'as destined by God', none of them used vulgar and humiliating expressions to undermine women. Thanawi's *hadis*-oriented knowledge did not turn him into a misogynist although he regarded women as inferior to men. Instead he favoured education for both the sexes. To him, 'women and men are essentially the same, endowed with the same faculties and equally responsible for their conduct'.[41] Although he believed women were 'more likely than men to be troubled by *nafs* [lower or "animal" faculty of human being]', he found this situation 'culturally, not genetically, determined'. He did not regard women as morally inferior to men either.[42] The essence of Thanawi's *Bihishti Zewar*, his book on 'perfecting women' (to paraphrase Metcalf) in Urdu, written in the early 1900s, is as follows.

1 Women are as good as men but 'are meant to be socially subordinate to men'.
2 Women are different but should be educated.
3 Women have suppressed *aql* (intelligence or sense on which a good life depends).
4 Women are entitled to rights 'obscured by custom'.[43]

However, Thanawi also believed that some literate women might, 'breaking through seclusion', indulge in illicit correspondence with men and read 'heaven-knows-what in novels'. He also advised 'perfect women' not to allow their husbands work for them or regard them as their equal.[44] Karamat Ali Jaunpuri, on the other hand, urged Muslims to educate women so that they would learn the basic teachings of Islam, cleanliness and hygiene. None of his books, including *Meftah ul-Jannat*, written in 1828 especially for women, contains any rustic or misogynous exposition.[45]

In contrast to the writings of the north-Indian *ulama*, already mentioned, who dealt with the problem of the position of women in Islam, Bangladesh produced ultra-conservative, obscurantist, and misogynous *mullas* like Maulana Gholam Rahman, Maulvi Shamsul Huda, Maulana Fazlur Rahman Anwari, Maulana Delwar Hossain Saidi and host of other qualified and semi-literate *mullas*. There is hardly any parallel with the relatively sophisticated north-Indian *ulama* like Maulana Karamat Ali Jaunpuri or Maulana Ashraf Ali Thanawi, let alone Maulana Sayyid Mumtaz Ali who opposed polygny and servility of women, considering them un-Islamic, in the Bangladesh region. The reason is not far to seek. As discussed earlier, the differences between the north Indian and East Bengali Muslim cultures are conditioned by the inherent differences between urban and rural cultures. The preponderance of rural culture is also visible in Bangladeshi cities, including Dhaka and Chittagong, as against the relative urban culture one finds in Delhi, Agra, Aligarh, Lucknow, Bombay or Calcutta.

Some other striking dissimilarities between north Indian and Bangladeshi *ulama* are:

1 While the former are respectable across the board, the latter are often ridiculed by different sections of the community.
2 Most north-Indian *ulama* are well-versed in their mother tongue, mainly Urdu, the bulk of the Bangladeshi *ulama* have no competence in any language. While their command of Bengali is very poor (with a few exceptions) their knowledge of Arabic is also grossly inadequate. Some of them can communicate in Urdu as it used to be the medium of instruction in most *madrasahs* in the recent past, but the rest have no recourse to other than pidgin Bengali or Urdu to communicate with the people.
3 While north Indian *ulama* in general avoid vulgar and offensive expressions, many Bangladeshi *ulama* frequently resort to such expressions both in their writings and public speeches.

In short, many Deoband, Jaunpur, Firangi Mahal, Nadwa and other north-Indian *ulama* despise the bulk of Bangladeshi *ulama* (*pirs*, *imams*, *madrasah teachers* and others) for their vulgarity, crudity, eating habit, manners and moral degeneration. In Bangladesh, *mullas* are traditionally ridiculed by the average people for their manners, opportunism, greed and lust. *Mullas'* proclivity for child abuse and homosexuality (taboo in Islam and Bangladesh), is widely known and discussed throughout the country. Rural *mullas'* unpolished manners and immoral code of conduct were even discussed in the Bengali folk-literature in the nineteenth century, as reflected in the following extract:

The *kathmullahs* [crude *mullas*] are a class of people in this world, who wear an enormous *pugree* [turban]. They prescribe amulets, and by means of incantations exorcise the *jinns*. If some one is ill he is brought before the *mullah*. He suggests that this must be the work of an evil eye .... Then the *mullah* asks for some remuneration; say, that he need a black hen and suggests that amulet will cure this illness.[46]

One may cite scores of examples to highlight the lack of knowledge, ethics and refinement of *mullas* from their writings, speeches and behaviour and from those of their Western-educated followers (also devoid of refinement), including doctors and engineers in the region. There follow a few examples of such writings which are in contravention of morality, common sense, truth and scientific knowledge.

Mullas' rusticity and misogyny: some reflections

We may begin with some of the writings of Maulvi Muhammad Shamsul Huda (BA, BL, and a retired magistrate of the Government of East Pakistan) to elucidate our point. His *Neamul Qur'an* (in Bengali), first published in 1940, a bestseller found in almost every conservative Bengali Muslim household, is full of unscientific and unrefined explanations for almost every natural phenomenon. According to the author, the main sources of his work are the traditions of the Prophet and some of the writings of Muslim saint Abdul Qadir Jilani and Maulana Ashraf Ali Thanawi of north India. One section stipulates 'the five situations when one can lie'. According to the author, 'for the sake of winning over the heart of one of the wives the husband is allowed to lie to her, telling her that she is the most beloved among all his wives', and 'with a view to encouraging children to study, parents may give them false assurance of rewards'.[47] It seems that the author has no qualms about adopting the wrong means to justify an end. The same author tells us: 'While every advanced country in the modern world is progressing because of its adherence to the basic Quranic principles, the Bengali Muslims have been doomed by drifting away from the *Qur'an*'.[48]

Neamul Qur'an also tells its readers how to use the different Quranic verses to heal disease, acquire power, position and honour by subjugating *jinn*, cure infertility of women (not men), subdue enemies, win litigations, bring and stop rains, cure male impotency and prosper in life. In short, this offers a magic formula for every malady of the poverty-stricken, backward peasant community in Bangladesh. One of the most interesting aspects of the work is the author's attempt to justify every Islamic ritual, Quranic verse and saying of the Prophet, with 'scientific' explanations. Quite often, the arguments are buttressed with some out-of-context quotations from some European or American scientists or philosophers. Some of the observations made in the work are simply unsubstantiated, such as 'ritualistic ablution and prayer enhance virility of men'.[49]

It is equally interesting that, although the author had college degrees in arts and law, he could not overcome his misogynous disposition, typical of many Bengali *mullas*. While describing the usefulness of washing one's hands, face, fingers and mouth, as required before praying, he thinks water soothes our nervous system after we [men] 'kiss with our tongue and enjoy the pleasure of touching soft and smooth female body with our fingers'.[50]

His defence of *purdah* or total seclusion of women is equally ludicrous and unscientific, despite his assertion that seclusion protects the 'acidic' female body from male 'alkali' and thus helps the world from getting depopulated, as he claims free mixing of the sexes would destroy fertility of women. He claims, even the shadow of a man, who is not related to the unveiled woman, is bad for her health, beauty and the foetus if she is pregnant. To him, *purdah* is essential for the prevention of adultery and rape. He also cites the German philosopher Nietzsche in support of *purdah* and to save the world from getting depopulated.[51] He even misquotes Quranic verses to support his theory of total seclusion of women. According to him in Verse 59 of *Surah Ahzab*, God prescribes *burqa*, which completely covers women from head to toe, including the face, 'whenever they go out'.[52] He also thinks *purdah* is essential for the preservation of feminine beauty.[53]

At times, the author resorts to narrating unhistorical 'fairy tales' to substantiate his arguments. We are told 'how' and 'why' Siraj ud-Dawla, ruler of Bengal, lost the battle of Plassey in 1757 to Robert Clive of the East India Company of Britain. From his account of the battle, one might be led to believe that the Indians were aware of the significance of it in 1757 and that it was decisive in determining the fate of Indians *vis-à-vis* the British domination. The author tells us that Hazrat Shah Zubayr, a renowned saint of a place called Palta (in Bengal), blessed Robert Clive before the battle, because of the saint's vision of Khwaz Khijr (the invisible living holy spirit or saint of the Muslims) who was marching ahead of the British troops, favouring their victory. The moral of the story is that the British conquest of India was essential for the survival of Islam and Muslims in the subcontinent, otherwise the Marathas and Sikhs would have become the masters of Indian Muslims.[54]

Maulvi Shamsul Huda's notion of race and 'purity of blood' smacks of his prejudice as well. He thinks inter-racial marriages among Muslims have destroyed their unity, cohesion and sense of belonging to the Muslim community. According to him, marrying outside one's *Kufu* (class and race) is a violation of the Prophet's instruction because it leads to the loss of the 'purity of the Muslim blood'. He also imputes Muslims' committing grave sins like killing and looting to their inter-racial marriages.[55] It is interesting that *mullas* in general get away with whatever they say in the name of the holy scripture. The bulk of the population, either semi-literate or illiterate, are too gullible to challenge the *mulla*. In general, the literate section is either ignorant of Islamic texts and their interpretations or is as gullible as the illiterate masses.

Some *mullas*, as discussed earlier, resort to 'science' to establish their assertions or to justify some vices or defects of their followers. Maulvi Shamsul Huda is quite defensive of Muslims (men), who according to him, 'are violent, impatient, dishonest and imbalanced, because almost all the Muslim countries are tropical where the hot blazing sun develops the body of the inhabitants before their brains are fully developed'.[56] One is not sure if by this explanation he is trying to justify wife-beating and other violent acts committed by many Muslims in the region.

While a college-educated '*mulla*' such as Shamsul Huda believed in 'the purity of blood' as well as in the Biblical theory that the advent of the first man on earth took place about 7000 years ago,[57] *madrasah*-educated *mullas* are no exceptions in this regard. From the onset of the British *raj*, for various reasons, *mullas* were opposed to British culture, dress and civilization. Many of them opposed the learning of English language. Some of them even discarded the radio when it first arrived in the region, 'for emitting the voice of Satan'. Many *mullas*, even today, oppose blood transfusion as un-Islamic[58] and some object to taking photos of human beings and other living objects. One village *mulla* even refused to say funeral prayers for the mother of a villager who took a snapshot of his dead mother.[59]

We could prepare a very long list of things *mullas* practise and ask their followers to do (in the name of following 'the right path' as virtuous Muslims), to highlight their lack of information and of any sense of history, geography, ethics or common sense. The following rhetoric and practices of *mullas* and those who blindly follow them are examples:

- *Mullas* throughout the region exhort their followers to use *kulukh* (dry stones or clods of clay), in addition to water, to clean themselves after defecation. They stress it as obligatory even when water is available. Their ways of stressing the utility of *kulukh*, including its usage, are simply revolting.[60]
- *Mullas* and others in the *Tabligh Jamaat*, including highly educated people, often eat cooked rice and curry with their fingers, two or three of them at a time from the same plate, to promote 'Muslim brotherhood'.
- *Mullas* often oppose birth control as un-Islamic in densely populated Bangladesh. Some of them even regard it as a Western conspiracy to depopulate Muslim countries, arguing that while in the West even children born of unmarried mothers get state support, 'the enemies of Islam' are distributing contraceptives in Bangladesh so that lawfully married couples cannot give birth to 'Muslim' children.[61]
- They often express their (negative) views about non-practising Muslims, and contrary to the teachings of Islam, condemn them to death. Urging their followers to kill those who do not say their prayer, 'because this is in accordance with the teaching of the *hadis*', they also tell them not to treat an ailing non-practising Muslim and never to attend their funerals, because by doing so they would be duly rewarded by God.[62] This extreme encouragement to ostracize non-practising Muslims smacks of the Faraizi influence (nineteenth-century reform movement in Bengal) on the *mulla*. The Faraizis forbade their followers from performing funeral rites for non-practising Muslims.[63]

From their treatment of rivals and victims of circumstances – whether men or women, Muslim or non-Muslim, rich or poor – Bengali *mullas* may be portrayed as heterogeneous groups combining their members' perpetual sense of inferiority, megalomania and incompatibility. They hardly tolerate fellow *mullas* holding views slightly deviant from their own. In a recent Bengali book, edited by a *mufti*, to 'expose' the 'new Islam' of Maulana Mawdudi, the founder of the Jamaat-i-Islami in the sub-continent, the author describes Mawdudi as 'evil', 'insane' and 'the creator of a new religion' because of his reservations about *hadis* and *fiqh* (Muslim jurisprudence) and, among other things, his granting of the right to divorce to women. Throughout the book, Mawdudi is referred to as 'Mr' not 'Maulana', to deny him the status of an Islamic scholar, a discourtesy which Mawdudi's secular opponents have not yet done to him. More than two hundred Bangladeshi *maulanas* have put their signatures to a document approving the text of the book.[64] In view of the above, we might class the misogyny, nourished by the different sections of the *mulla* in Bangladesh, as a by-product of their inherent crudity and intolerance which are also part and parcel of any peasant society.

Under the dual influence of the Middle Eastern and the indigenous Hindu-Buddhist-peasant cultures, which also undermine women, misogyny received a tremendous fillip, and acquired legitimacy as 'Islamic' throughout the Bengali region. This is reflected in the writings, speeches and behaviour of different sections of the *mullas* and their ardent followers.

With the rapid Islamization of the region, and owing to the overwhelming influence of Islamic puritanism from the 1820s, Bengali Muslims' culture, as reflected in their language, attire, food habit and ceremonies, was significantly transformed into what we might call the 'Muslim-Bengali' culture. The prevalent misogyny in the region retained almost all its features and adopted certain characteristics of that brought by the Turko-Afghan ruling elites, *sufis* and other categories of the *mulla*.

The following 'Muslim-Bengali' verses, written in the nineteenth century, reflect this synthesis:

> The Lord has given man the higher status; women must follow the orders of their husbands. A woman has no rest so long as she is alive. She has to serve her husband and thus worship Allah .... There are some cantankerous women who quarrel if their husbands take more wives. The holy books say such women are scoundrels.[65]

Hundreds of *puthis* (literature created by semi-literate Muslims in a mixture of Bengali, Arabic, Persian and Urdu) and other Bengali writings of the nineteenth and twentieth centuries are full of such sexist, misogynous expositions.

Modern *mullas* in Bangladesh are not much different from their rural predecessors either. Shamsul Huda tries to establish male supremacy, with what he thinks is a 'scientific' approach. He thinks that since men are physically stronger than women, having brains which are heavier than those of women (427 grams against 380, on the average), 'women in general are more stable and steady while men are restless and dynamic and *that is why women in general are monogamous while men are polygamous by nature*' [emphasis added].[66] After defending the polygamous nature of men with his 'scientific' analysis, he claims that 'while male intelligence has a qualitative growth, female intelligence is devoid of such quality.... In short, women lack creativity.... Our Prophet also said that "women's intelligence and energy are not on par with men's. Therefore, women cannot be equal to men".' According to him, one Austrian scientist, Dr Oswald Swartz, believed that 'while men excel outdoor in their offices and factories, women perform better at home'.[67] Since women by nature are immodest, unlike men, and lacking personalities or distinctive character, they fail to think about themselves and blindly follow the dictates of men.[68]

By glorifying the institution of *purdah* or strict seclusion of women he asserts that the mere reflections of male bodies on women, especially in the tropics, are harmful to women. He also advises Muslim women to love their husbands as '*there is no better tonic for women than serving their husbands* [emphasis added] and giving them constant company as these acts would enhance their beauty and keep them healthy'.[69] It is noteworthy that here, for women, 'love' stands for 'serving their husbands'. He believes that husbands often do not realize how wives enjoy serving their husbands.[70] Husbands are advised to follow the instructions of Sheikh Saadi (a medieval Persian poet), who is reported to have said: 'Never trust a woman', and 'never tell your secrets to women, enemies and fools'.[71] He also advises men never to be dependent on wives' income. Citing the example of the nomadic, matriarchal Bedey community of Bangladesh, he asserts 'not a single talented and spirited person has ever been born in their community'.[72]

According to the same *mulla*, the ideal wife is one, 'who does not have any interest in higher education'. He thinks women without any craving for knowledge would be loving and 'aspire to nothing but marriage and children', while the highly educated ones 'are by nature quarrelsome'. He thinks 'since women's brains are smaller than those of men, they cannot absorb college education'. All scientists have accepted 'this truth', he claims.[73] Here we find him not much different from the traditional *mullas* who also oppose higher education for women.[74] The only kind words one finds in his writings are to the effect that civilized men should not neglect their wives and deprive them of medical care. He thinks, since women are dependent, their prayers are quickly responded to by God. He also advises Muslim men to make their wives sexually contented and asserts, 'one who is charitable to his wife, lives longer and remains healthy and youthful'.[75]

Shamsul Huda's advocacy of male supremacy as a natural phenomenon and as sanctioned by God and Prophet Muhammad, is finally epitomized in his citation of a *hadis*, often quoted by most *mullas* in the region: 'Had I asked anyone to worship anybody other than God, I would have asked wives to prostrate before their husbands'. Citing this passage, said to have been uttered by the Prophet, the author argues, 'one need not argue any more about the rights of husbands over their wives'.[76] In another version of the same *hadis*, we find that Prophet Muhammad said this after some of his followers wanted to prostrate themselves before him, seeing some camels and deer prostrating before the Prophet.[77]

In short, both in their writings and speeches, *mullas* in general suggest that for women the best way to attain virtue is by serving their husbands, by always keeping them happy and contended as, for Muslim women, their husbands are only next to God.[78] One may illustrate this by citing examples from a selective writings and speeches of some leading *mullas* in Bangladesh, who often portray men as demigods and disobedient women as the off-spring of Satan.

Maksudul Momeneen: the Epitome of Misogyny

We may begin with the most controversial and very popular Bengali work, *Maksudul Momeneen* by Maulana Gholam Rahman, which first appeared in 1935 and had 45 editions by 1994. This work is the parallel of north Indian Maulana Ashraf Ali Thanawi's Urdu work, *Bihishti Zewar* (mentioned earlier), also written mainly for Muslim women. *Maksudul Momeneen*, however, is not another *Bihishti Zewar* or *Meftah ul-Jannat* by Maulana Karamat Ali, because of its inherent vulgarity and offensive, misogynous style. For many Bengali feminist and progressive writers and social reformers this work is nothing short of an enigma, while many others quote this book (sometimes without acknowledging it), in order to portray Islam as a promoter of male supremacy and misogyny. Most of Taslima Nasreen's vituperations against Islam are based on this work.[79] We may also cite *Maksudul Momin* by Maulana Fazlur Rahman Anwari, which is equally misogynous and seems to have been written following the 'grand success' of Gholam Rahman's work.

Both the above-mentioned books justify husbands' beating and punishing their wives (it seems by taking the Quranic injunction literally) under the following circumstances:

1 If the husband demands sex and the wife refuses to comply, whilst having no valid excuses.
2 If the wife does not dress up and go to her husband if asked to do so.
3 If the wife does not take a bath and clean herself for saying her prayers.
4 If the wife visits someone's house without her husband's permission.
5 If the wife does not perform Islamic rituals and fails to observe seclusion.
6 If the wife gives away things to others without her husband's permission or runs away after taking the dower.[80]

However, by citing a *hadis*, Gholam Rahman urges his readers not to beat their wives like slave girls. He, also cites Imam Shafi (the founder of the Shafi School of Jurisprudence) who is said to have regarded beating one's wife as *mobah* (neither an act of sin nor virtue), but not doing so as 'desirable'.[81] Both the authors of *Maksudul Momeneen* and *Maksudul Momin* have some kind words for women. Gholam Rahman insists that: 'since men want beautiful wives, women also aspire to handsome men. . . . Therefore, those who arrange marriages of their wards should be aware of this lest they mismatch partners'. He is also opposed to child-marriage.[82] The author of *Maksudul Momin* urges his readers, husbands and wives, to treat their partners kindly. He cites the following Quranic verse in this regard: 'As you deserve good treatment from your wives so are your wives entitled to similar treatment from you'.[83] In the rest of the writings dealing with men-women relationships, both the authors have tried their best to establish women, especially wives, as nothing short of slaves of their husbands. One is reminded of some of the 'sayings of the Prophet' in this context: 'The woman who dies leaving behind a contented husband, is assured of the paradise'.[84] One of the most repulsive examples which expound the worthlessness of women and the virtue of men is the citation of a 'saying of the Prophet', as it appears in both the works of the *maulanas*: 'If the wife of a leper cleans her husband's wound with her tongue, this act is not good enough to repay her debt to her husband'.[85]

Glorifying the submissiveness of wives, Gholam Rahman supports the view that:

1 'Disobedient wives are cursed by God, their prayers being never answered by Him.'
2 'The wife who spends one hour with her husband keeping him in good mood, earns the virtue one can get by saying prayers in a year.'
3 'The Prophet affirmed that whenever the husband calls his wife she should rush to him even if she is engaged in cooking or boiling milk.'

He also cites some stories from Arabic and Persian books high-lighting the virtues of obedient wives and how their parents are rewarded by God for the obedience of their daughters to their husbands. He also narrates the story of a disobedient wife, who suffered in hell-fire because of her defiance of her husband when she was alive. After narrating the story of the disobedient wife, the author addresses his female readers: 'Look what may happen to wives if their husbands are unhappy with them!'[86]

Maulana Gholam Rahman's *awrat-i-hasina* or 'ideal woman' is not only pious but one who also 'totally surrenders herself to the will of her husband'.[87] He has also classified two types of women – one, who should be preferred to others as wives and the other, who should never be selected as brides – not on the basis of their qualities of being God-fearing or obedient but on the basis of physical beauty and the lack of it. The first category of women consists of 'the beautiful ones with long hair, shapely eyebrows, beautiful teeth, thin waistline, big eyes and chastity'. The other category of women (who should never be considered for marriage) consists of the ones 'with squint (one who looks obliquely) or with restless, wandering eyes and women with dimples on their cheeks as well because they are most likely to be sterile'.[88]

One may point out that there is no similar classification of men as 'desirable' and 'most undesirable' from a woman's point of view in this book. The author has glorified the hard domestic chores done by women, as well as condemned their resentment against their husbands by citing a *hadis*:

> For women, grinding wheat is as good as going to a *jihad* (holy war). The moment a wife tells her husband that she is not happy with any of his activities, she is assured of losing all the virtues one can earn in seventy years.[89]

The epitome of the theory of male supremacy and the conse-quent subjugation of women, along with their 'justifications', is found in the 'Thirty five Commandments' of Maulana Gholam Rahman and the 'Duties of Wives' by him and Maulana Anwari, as they appear in their writings.

'The Thirty five Commandments to Women'

1 Follow the teachings of Islam and observe the rituals as pre-scribed in this book [*Maksudul Momeneen*].
2 Obey your husband, but his command cannot supersede that of God.
3 Never lie to your husband or to others.
4 Never speak against someone behind his back. Always observe *purdah* and protect yourself from sin. Because this is obligatory.
5 Observe the instruction with regard to menstruation.
6 A husband is a precious wealth. Always keep him in good humour because those who are on good terms with their husbands are the happiest in this world. Therefore, if you desire happiness in this world and the hereafter, love your husband.
7 Never let your husband be displeased with you. Follow his in-structions so long he does not ask you to violate the commands of God. If your husband asks you to stand erect, folding your hands whole night by his side, obey him as it would please God and his Prophet.
8 Never hurt your husband's feeling by rude utterances. This sort of rude behaviour might permanently antagonise your husband towards you.
9 If your husband asks you to go to him promptly follow his order and try to fulfil his wish if there is no physical difficulty such as menstruation or illness.
10 While your husband is around, never perform any non-obligatory prayer or fasting without his prior permission. Never eat ahead of your husband. It is more virtuous to obey one's husband than performing non-obligatory prayers and fasting.
11 Never give anything away without your husband's permission. Never visit your neighbours and relatives without your husband's permission.
12 Never expose your husband's limitations to others. Always share his happiness and sorrow.
13 Even if your husband is wealthy, never ask him to bring any-thing for you. Be patient and accept whatever he gives you to

eat and wear. Your forbearance would be rewarded by God.

14 Always keep yourself clean and tidy, otherwise your husband might be unhappy with you.

15 Even if it is against your will, never ever argue with your husband. Although you are innocent, never contest your husband's opinions about you and try to convince him of your innocence with an obliging tone. Consequently your husband would understand your viewpoint and he would be more loving and understanding.

16 Never ever speak ill of your husband's behaviour with you to others. Always be patient with your husband and happy with whatever he brings for you. Never undermine his gifts.

17 Never ever be ungracious and express your unhappiness in front of your husband telling him that you have never been happy with him and that your parents have committed a grave mistake by arranging your marriage with him. The Prophet told us that he had seen women outnumbering men in hell and this was because of their ingratitude to their husbands.

18 Always try to comprehend your husband's frame of mind. While he is in a jovial mood be smiling in showing your happiness but if he is not in good mood, never ever giggle in front of him. It might be too irritating for him and he might hit you back.

19 If finding fault with you your husband reprimands or beats you up, you should not be in a withdrawing, melancholic state of mind, you should rather be apologising to him, seeking his forgiveness, by grabbing his feet.

20 Be tactful and sly in leading your conjugal life. If sometimes out of love and affection your husband tries to massage your arms and feet, never ever allow him to do it. As you would never allow your parents to touch your feet, let alone your husband because his status is even higher than that of your parents.

21 If your husband is back from abroad (after a short or long stay) rush to his service by providing him with something to sit on, touch his feet to pay obeisance and fan him if it is a warm day and arrange for food if he is hungry. Never ever ask him if he has brought anything for you as it might make him annoyed or angry with you.

22 If your husband gives you money, accept it in good grace and if he gives his money only to his parents, be happy and remain contented with this as well. It is even better for you to ask your husband not to give you any money but to his parents

only. This gesture would enhance your position to your parents-in-law and other members of the family.

23 So long as your parents-in-law are alive serve them and never argue with them.

24 Always perform your household duties (domestic chores) to the best of your ability. Never ever tell anything bad about your husband's family to your parents.

25 Never ever tell anything bad about your parents' family to your husband's family.

26 Always keep your home and clothes neat and clean. God forbid, if there is any disagreement with your husband, never disclose it to others, because if your husband learns about it he would be very upset and angry. This would eventually be disastrous for you.

27 Never leave your husband's company for any duration without his permission. According to a saying of the Prophet if a wife stays away from her husband for a night without his permission, 70 000 angels curse that woman for the whole night. One who stops a wife from staying with her husband, is equally cursed by angels.

28 Never ever think of outwitting your husband in any matter, because it is extremely difficult to do so. If you really want to outmanoeuvre him, start crying by holding his feet and saying all the pleasing and flattering things to win him over.

29 Follow your husband's instructions and do whatever he wants you to do. Never express your dissatisfaction at your husband's lifestyle because you would not be held responsible for his sins, but try to dissuade him from sinful acts by mild persuasion.

30 Your husband is the greatest asset for you in this world. So long as he is alive, serve him to the best of your ability because your salvation in the hereafter lies in your selfless service and dedication to him.

31 If your husband asks you to give up your claim on the *mehr* or dower, do so immediately because nothing is more precious in this life than your husband's contentment. Ayesha and other wives of the Prophet also gave up their claims on the dower. Actually, the real virtuous women are those who gracefully give up their dower.

32 Do not be like those women who do not dress up or wear ornaments for the pleasure of their husbands but for the pleasure of others, because by doing so you would be assured of nothing but hell-fire.

33 The wives of the *ulama* should be considered as the most fortunate among all women, because the *ulama* are the most gifted and exalted among all men. The wives of the *ulama* earn a million times more virtue than other women by serving their husbands. One married to an *alim* should consider herself very lucky and should always try to make her husband happy.

34 You should be thankful to God even if your husband happens to be insane, stupid and illiterate. You should regard your husband as precious as the moon and spend your life at his feet so that you get eternal bliss in paradise.

35 Whether your husband is rich or poor, educated or illiterate, blind or crippled, good-looking or ugly always serve him as your master and be loving and caring. According to the Prophet, an immoral woman is worse than one thousand immoral men combined together and one virtuous woman is better than seventy saints combined together.

Ten Duties of a Wife to her Husband

1 To let her husband have sex with her.
2 Not to give away or lend anything to others without her husband's permission.
3 Not to fast (non-obligatory ones) without his permission.
4 Not to be critical of her husband.
5 Not to go anywhere without his permission.
6 Not to ask for anything from him more than the basic necessities.
7 To be happy with his happiness and sorry with his sorrow.
8 Not to rebuke him.
9 To remain well-groomed in his presence.
10 Not to rebuke their children.[90]

Among the dos and don'ts for the ideal wife, according to Gholam Rahman, the following are important with regard to her duties towards her husband:

1 She is not supposed to take her meal ahead of her husband and even if her husband advises her to eat ahead of him if she is hungry, it is better for her to wait for him.
2 She should be punctual in performing her various duties, especially with regard to the preparation of meals – breakfast, lunch and dinner.
3 She should be always grateful to her husband and should never be rude to him.
4 She should respect and serve her parents-in-law.
5 She should not squander her husband's wealth.

6 She should wash her husband's and parents-in-law's clothes.

7 She should always obey her husband.

8 She should not be jealous of other wives of the husband.[91]

Now to turn to the advice to men with regard to their treatment of women, one finds the *mulla* telling them either to be condescending to women or to keep them under strict surveillance and control. Since to the *mullas*, inferiority of women is an established fact, one finds them urging Muslim men to follow the following 'advice of the Prophet of Islam':

1 Always give good counsel to your wives. Most certainly women are created from a curved rib-bone of Adam. If you try to straighten it, you would simply break it into pieces. . . . Therefore, you should be happy with whatever is attained by advising your wives.

2 Women possess half of men's *iman* (faith) and *aqal* (intelligence). As women are devoid of intelligence, so do not pick on them, rather be forgiving.[92]

Mullas advise men to give their wives 'some basic education' and always to keep them under seclusion. Men are also told to divorce their wives in three circumstances:

1 If they pose threats to their husbands' lives.

2 If they are 'always engaged in adultery'.

3 If they are disobedient.

Husbands are also advised to reprimand their wives for wrongdoing, but they should not hit them on the face. However, they are also told not to undermine the gifts their wives bring for them from their parents. Husbands are also advised not to stay away from their wives longer than four months at a time.[93]

Misogyny and the ideal woman of the Village Mulla

If the above expositions are misogynous, one does not know how one would classify the speeches of itinerant 'mad *mullas*', delivered at *waz mahfils* (religious gatherings), mostly in small towns and villages in Bangladesh. Contrary to our expectation, with the passage of time and the transformation of 'Islamic' East Pakistan into 'secular' Bangladesh in 1971, there has been a tremendous growth in the number of such *mullas*, *pirs*, *muftis*, *shaykh ul-hadis* and 'internationally renowned Islamic thinkers' – throughout the country. Maulana Delwar Hossain Saidi, a member of the Central Committee (*Majlis-i-Shura*) of the Jamaat-i-Islami of Bangladesh and a member of the Parliament (elected in June 1996), basically an itinerant *mulla*, came to the limelight as a *bakta* (public speaker) in the 1980s. His speeches are available in audio and video tapes, not only in Bangladesh but also in the USA, UK and Middle-Eastern countries, especially in shops run by Bangladeshi Muslims. He is both despised and admired by tens of thousands of Bangladeshis. Many liberal secular groups and individuals demanded his arrest and proscription of his cassettes in the 1980s throughout Bangladesh, but owing to the changed socio-political situation, leading to the 'Islamization' of the polity in 1988,[94] he remained unscathed and continued spreading his message – in the name of Islam. From his numerous recorded speeches on audio and video tapes with catchy and misleading titles like 'Liberation of Women', '*Purdah* and Women's Rights in Islam', 'Rights of Husbands and Wives', 'Women and Non-Muslims in Islam', proceed vulgar and misogynous expositions, which not only undermine modern civilization but also degrade women to the level of animals, objects, fruits or eatables.

Women's liberation, to him, is the harbinger of the doomsday. He is firmly opposed to women working in the office with men. 'When a well-groomed, young and beautiful woman with dark and inviting eyes, coloured lips and low-cut, revealing dress sits on the other side of the desk, do you think office-work is going on there?' Saidi retorts.[95] He is also against women working in the police department. He attributes road accidents involving lorry drivers on the streets of Dhaka to the distractions provided by the tight-fitting uniform of policewomen. He ridicules policewomen in the following manner: 'How can police women protect national wealth when they need police force to protect their "wealth"'?[96] Like many other *mullas*, Saidi also thinks that employing women for office work is a 'national loss' because 'woman workers would spend their salary on lipsticks and clothes whereas men working in similar positions would maintain their families with their salary'.[97]

Sometimes the demagogy of Saidi can be so misleading as to be mistaken for a 'progressive' social reformer, especially in the light of his condemnation of those taking dowry from brides' parents or guardians. His true nature is revealed, however, when he exhorts, shouts, screams and sarcastically tells his audiences (both those who attend his *waz mahfils* and those who listen to his taped speeches) that Bengali Muslim men have lost all interest in 'half-naked' and 'easily available' women, hence the demand for dowries – cash, television sets, fridges and even cars. He thinks that *purdah* would save women from being raped or molested, and most importantly, that they would remain attractive to men. He even compares secluded women with the beautiful spotted deer from the Sundarbans, and the *'be-purdah* whores' – or unveiled women – with the stinking goat, since the former is very attractive because it lives in *'purdah'*, in the forest, and the latter is not attractive because, it is 'available' everywhere. He even compares *purdah*-observing women with fruits like bananas, mangoes and pineapples. He argues, 'God sends these fruits to us in "packets" to save them from flies and insects, that is why they taste so good. All good things in life are shrouded with covers and mystery. That is why women should be covered from head to toe'.[98]

In the name of defending 'Islam as the liberator of women', Saidi argues that those who oppose polygyny are agents of the West or enemies of Islam, because polygyny is better than having illicit sex with mistresses or prostitutes. He thinks that since the Prophet of Islam gave mothers much higher status than that of fathers, women in Islam are the most privileged in the world.[99] He is also opposed to female leadership in any sphere of life. According to him, in Islam man has a higher status than but equal rights with women.[100]

Muslim orators or *baktas* like Saidi are a prevalent part of popular Islam in Bangladesh. They are specially invited to address one- or two- nights-long *waz mahfils* and *urus* (commemorations of death anniversaries of local or renowned *pirs* and saints in the dry season during November to February). The *baktas* cast a magical spell on their audiences, mostly arousing a fear of hell, in conformity with the popular culture which glorifies death and the hereafter. The gifted *baktas* such as Saidi are in great demand in both urban and rural areas. Not only the gullible and illiterate or semi literate with their incomplete access to the Islamic texts but also the educated, whose knowledge is greater, listen to them and give the *baktas* a patient hearing.

The enchanting and convincing style of talking of the rural *mulla*, reflective of his lack of knowledge and patriarchal prejudice, if not misogyny, has been exquisitely reproduced by Hartmann and Boyce in their empirical study of a village in Bangladesh.[101] Mofis, the village *madrasah* teacher, who believes that 'a woman's heaven lies under her husband's feet', describes the virtues of the ideal women to the authors:

The Prophet's daughter Fatima was almost an ideal woman, but even she had her faults. One day her father told her she didn't observe purdah strictly enough. She quarrelled with him, saying, 'Why, I am the most discreet and proper girl in the world.' He laughed and told her to visit the wives of the woodcutter who lived in the forest. Then she would understand what he meant.

So Fatima went to the woodcutters' village. She called their wives, but they refused to come out of their houses. Discouraged, she finally left. When the woodcutters returned and heard of her visit, they scolded their wives. 'What, you didn't go out? Why, that was Fatima, the Prophet's daughter! If she comes again, you should greet her.'

Fatima told her father what had happened and he urged her to return. This time she brought her two small sons, Hassan and Husain. She called the women, but from their houses they could see the boys. They shouted, 'If you come back alone, we'll see you.'

That night, their husbands were angry. 'Those boys are only her sons,' they told their wives. 'They are religious people. You should not turn them away.'

On the third day, Fatima returned alone. (Mofis paused for emphasis, with a twinkle in his eye.) This time the women greeted her and took her into their houses. In one courtyard, Fatima saw a club and a rope laid carefully against the wall, and asked, 'What are those for?'

The woman of the house explained, 'I put them there for my husband. When he wishes to beat me he can use the club, and with the rope he can tie my hands.

Fatima was impressed, and that night she told her father, 'You're right, the woodcutters' wives are far better than I.'[102]

According to the study, Mofis *mulla* 'evidently took this story very seriously' as in his day-to-day relations with his two wives, he expects them to 'submit willingly to his blows', and beats them up quite often. 'My husband beat me with a bamboo staff because the children stole a few grains of rice', his first wife told Hartmann, lying on the bed and crying immediately after his latest beating.[103] The authors make the point that wife beating in rural Bangladesh, which is quite common among poor villagers, is 'an outlet for men's sense of powerlessness and frustration in the face of grinding poverty'.[104] This also implies, with regard to the persecution of women in Bangladesh, that there is a reciprocity between the misogynous teachings of the *mulla* and the prevalence of endemic poverty among the bulk of the population.

Conclusions

However, despite a section of liberal/secular male and female groups' and individuals' criticism of the misogyny of *mullas* in Bangladesh, the indigenous misogyny which undermines women and things associated with feminity has remained active throughout the region. So far as the legal status and position of Muslim women in the region are concerned, the advent of Islam brought about certain improvements with regard to their rights relating to inheritance, marriage and divorce, but in reality, these rights have been more illusory than real. In fact, whatever rights the Quran bestowed on Muslim women have been partially taken away by the *Sharia* law and by both Middle-Eastern and local customs ('little traditions'), glorifying male supremacy and the subjugation of women.

Although male supremacy does not necessarily connote misogyny, the proponents of the theory need misogyny for its justification. In a way, misogynous expositions by *mullas* as well as non-*mulla* sections of Bangladesh society provide the ideological framework to legitimize male supremacy. Both of them find religion a very useful tool in this respect. They often alter Islamic codes of conduct with regard to male-female relationships and the position of women in Islam. The acceptable *hadis*, 'heaven is at the feet of the mother', for example, in popular parlance glorifies 'husband' instead of 'mother'. In some rituals, the *qurbani* (sacrifice), for example, contrary to Islamic rule, married Bengali Muslim women performing the ritual are identified as 'wives' not as 'daughters'. In official documents, including passports, every married Bangladeshi woman is identified as so-and-so's wife. This is in accordance with the tenets of Bengali or South Asian culture where a woman is either someone's daughter, wife or mother. Her father's name is irrelevant both for religious or secular purposes. Muslim women in general are also barred from mosques in the region, which is not the case in the Middle East and Southeast Asia. There is nothing Islamic about these practices; they are integral parts of indigenous customs. *Mullas* simply follow these customs both out of ignorance of the Islamic texts and as a result of their subservient position in the society.

It is interesting that, even those Bangladeshis who are aware of the *mullas'* incomplete knowledge of Islamic texts and history condone their activities, as they could be useful in safeguarding their vested interests. This is why the least religious or even agnostic and atheist Bangladeshi men insist on *Sharia* law, especially with regard to the distribution of property (already questioned by some Muslim jurists and intellectuals) to deprive their sisters or other female relatives of equal shares in property throughout the region. These people also need the *mulla* to support them when they want to divorce their wives as well as to deprive them of the *mehr* or obligatory dower, due to the Muslim wives from their husbands. In rural Bangladesh, village elders often use the *mulla* to gratify their sexual desire by annulling or arranging marriages to their advantage and convenience.

As we have seen, the endemic crudity of the *mulla* in Bangladesh was not just created in the recent past. The age-old curricula (*Dars-i-Nizamiyah*) in which the *mullas* are trained and the *madrasahs* and the *mullas'* lack of initiative to overcome this lack of knowledge are some of the main reasons for their intellectual backwardness. Their social and economic backwardness may be imputed to their socio-economic background – the bulk of them come from the lower peasantry and other petty bourgeois sections of the society. Their parasitic and dependent youth, their harsh treatment and punishment from early childhood as *madrasah* students and, above all, their upbringing in an environment which is totally devoid of entertainment such as music, cinema, games and sports, are responsible for their unsocial and anti-social bent of mind. From early childhood they learn two things, punishment and discipline. They are also not aware of their limitations, and always regard themselves as the epitome of perfection. A poverty-stricken, illiterate and fatalist peasant society like that of Bangladesh is the perfect breeding ground for such *mullas*, who work as intermediaries between God and the people, nourishing and glorifying the culture of death and fatalism. They also work as agents of local power-brokers to maintain the status quo and inequality as 'pre-ordained' by God.

It is pointless to argue whether the prevalent misogyny is moulding the *mullas'* thought process with regard to women or the *mullas'* crudity is responsible for the promotion and glorification of misogyny in Bangladesh. There is truth in both the arguments, since the *mullas'* inherent peasant nature and their acquired misogynous values (which they come across in the *madrasah*), are complementary. The various institutions which perpetuate subjection of women in Bangladesh, including the marriage and inheritance laws, are also complementary to the prevalent backwardness and the indigenous culture of misogyny. The existing gap between the 'great' and 'little' traditions of Islam has been filled by the ignorance of *mullas*.

Consequently the modes of persecution of women in the region of this study reflect the indigenous misogyny and prejudice of *madrasah*-educated peasants-turned-*mullas*. This sheds light on the process of victimization of women, mostly in the rural areas of Bangladesh. Otherwise we have no explanations for the erratic behaviour of rural *mullas* which led to several deaths of women, persecuted in the name of 'Islamic justice' in village courts or *salish* in the region in the first half of the 1990s. Only the existence of barbarism explains why Razia Khatun, a 22-year-old housewife, was forced to drink her own urine for her alleged commission of adultery in a village in Kishoreganj district in June 1994.[105] Islam most definitely does not sanction this type of punishment for adultery. According to Islamic law, an adulterer and an adulteress may only be punished by a legally constituted court of justice after considering the testimonies of *four adult eyewitnesses*. The offenders are liable to receive 100 lashes each for their crime. Private individuals and *mullas* cannot constitute *Sharia* courts by defying the authority of the state, as Islam does not allow such defiance by anybody.

In sum, the misogyny of *mullas*, their urban and rural patrons and followers, is not necessarily synonymous with peasant culture. Their intolerant attitude towards women, especially towards those who are independent and assertive, is a by-product of ignorance. And ignorance breeds prejudice. Here the ignorance of the peasantry, combined with that of the *mulla*, has compounded the situation to the disadvantage of those professing equality of the sexes. It is, however, pertinent to our understanding of the problem of discrimination against and persecution of women at the hands of male supremists in the region that both the persecuted women and their persecutors are victims of ignorance, backwardness, poverty and social inequality.

A section of the male perpetrators of the outrageous crimes against women, as well as their victims, lack power and opportunity for upward mobility. The former victimize the latter to give vent to their own indignation towards their superordinates in society. Misogyny as a means to perpetuate male supremacy is also a hegemonic ideology promoted by the elites with the help of religion, customs, culture, norms and values. In short, it is another dimension of the cultural hegemony of the elites or male superordinates to subjugate women, not always by force but sometimes by mutual consent.

Mullas' plebeian background and perpetual dependence on the well-to-do sections of society turn them into either a frustrated group, angry with the whole socio-political set-up, or one nourishing a tremendous inferiority complex *vis-à-vis* their urban and rural superordinates. Their *madrasah*-education, which is not adequate to make them competitive in the shrinking job market, is also responsible for their parasitic position with regard to the production system and production relations in the region. They are not only socially inferior to the elites but also isolated from the mainstream as society does not approve of their participation in various secular and entertaining activities such as games and music. *Mullas* know quite well that their only utility to society lies in their performance as prayer-leaders or *imams*, as priests to marry people or to perform the funeral rituals. Their position as leaders is simply exceptional not normative.

It is interesting that while on the one hand, *mullas* are looked down upon by the well-to-do people, on the other, they are also respected for their piety and social utility. *Pirs*, *sufis* and *muftis* representing the 'great tradition' are respectable both in rural and urban areas. However, Bengali Muslim women, in general, either despise *mullas* for imposing so many restrictions on their activities or distance themselves from them with a mixed feeling of fear and respect, if not condescension. They are the least desirable as husbands among educated women throughout Bangladesh. This might be a factor in the way *mullas* in their turn despise modern educated women by portraying them as unchaste, evil and inferior to men as well as to the secluded, illiterate or semi-literate and 'submissive' women. It is noteworthy that some 'radical' Hindu reformers of nineteenth-century Bengal, Keshabchandra Sen for example, had prejudice against university education for women which, he feared, 'would unsex them'.[106]

The *mullas'* misogynous frame of mind is not only due to their peasant and plebeian background but also to their lack of liberal education. Some Bangladeshi technocrats, also lacking liberal education, are not much different from the *mullas* in this respect. Last but not least, both *mullas* and peasants also have common enemies in the liberalization and modernization of society. Modernization in technology or the means of production and the transformation of production relations, which also aims at altering the social structure to the disadvantage of the traditional rural elites (rich peasants and village elders), are not well received by *mullas* and others who have vested interests in the status quo. Village moneylenders, for example, are not at all happy with non-local, government or non-governmental organization (NGO)-backed credit schemes in the village because they drive away their potential clients from them. NGO-sponsored schools and medical centres are again *bêtes noires* to some *mullas* for taking away students from their *maktabs* (Islamic schools) and patients who would normally go to the *mulla* for amulets and 'holy water' as cure. Since women's liberation, self-sufficiency and literacy are synonymous with modernization, their weakness and lack of organization compared with men has caused them to be the main victims of the vindictive *mullas* and village elders. *Mullas* are but junior partners of those who have vested interests in keeping women away from power, authority and property. Islam is being used by both the *mulla* and non-*mulla* sections of society in Bangladesh in order to perpetuate the servility of women. Nothing could be more efficacious than the portrayal of women as inferior, subhuman, demonic and satanic for the nourishment of the culture of male supremacy, and nothing could be more effective in this regard than religion for legitimizing their actions in a peasant society like Bangladesh. In short, the understanding of the growth and development of misogyny in Bangladeshi society requires an understanding of why and how the persecution mania of a section of *mullas* and village elders fits in with that of other sections of the male population in the region as regards the persecution of women.

4
Women as Victims of the Salish: Fatwas, Mullas and the Village Community

Purush manusher ki dosh? [How can you blame a man] This bitch [18-year-old Beauty Khatun, a rape victim] is solely responsible for the 'illicit relationship'. She should be lashed 101 times for her crime.

A salish (village-court) verdict (1994)

Since Razia is no longer 'legally married' to her husband, she must marry someone else and only after getting a divorce from her 'second husband' she will be allowed to re-marry her 'first husband'. Both Razia and her 'adulterer' husband should receive 51 lashes for their crime.

A salish verdict

Introduction

While gender discrimination is a global phenomenon and treating women as inferior in every sphere of life is a norm in under-developed countries, the position of women in Muslim countries – such as Bangladesh – is generally assumed to be even worse than that of women in 'non-Muslim' countries. Undoubtedly, Bangladeshi women in general, the rural poor in particular, are on the lowest rung of life's ladder. Their persecution and degradation at the hands of patriarchy, strengthened and justified with the expulsion of Taslima Nasreen from the country in 1994 and the sudden rise in the dispension of *fatwas* by *mullas* in rural courts *(salish)* against women, which even led to several deaths (suicide and murder) of poor women

96

in the countryside further aggravated the situation. By 1995, hundreds of women had been tried in sham rural courts, run by village elders and their associates *(mullas)*, for allegedly violating the *Sharia* law and Islamic codes of conduct.

It is often believed that the emergence of the new female working class in the garment industries in urban areas (workers mostly come from rural areas) and NGO-workers and beneficiaries in the villages is the main reason why *mullas* and village elders having conflicting interests with the garment industries and NGOs for taking away their clients by providing credit and jobs have been terrorizing women to dissuade them from working outside. *Mullas* often allege that the NGOs are spreading Christianity and 'anti-Islamic' Western ideology. Hence the persecution of rural women!

This chapter explores the reasons for this persecution and the extent to which it is true that women working for NGOs and garment industries are the main victims of the *Salish* courts in rural areas. There is reason to believe that most of the victims, on the contrary, have nothing to do with NGOs, they are simply poor women. We also attempt to show how Islamization at the state and grassroots levels, nourished by vested interest groups for political reasons and out of ignorance, respectively, is responsible for the emergence of these megalomaniac 'mini-Khomeinis' throughout Bangladesh, and how and why *mullas* are losing ground in this transitional phase of socio-economic change in politically stagnant Bangladesh.

Persecution of women by men – male relatives, neighbours, strangers, employers and even members of the law-enforcing agencies – is quite common throughout the country. Various reports indicate that while about 3000 women are victimized annually in different parts of Bangladesh only a handful of them manage to obtain shelter and legal aid from the various government and non-government organizations. During 1991 and 1995, most of the victims (more than 10 000) of murder, rape, abduction, arbitrary divorce, polygamy and torture by husbands and other relatives were poor rural women. They failed to get any redress owing to poverty, ignorance and the prevalent social order which promotes male supremacy. Consequently in 1993 alone about 6000 persecuted women committed suicide in different parts of the country. The emergence of the *fatwa*-dispensing 'mad-*mullas*', who have been victimizing hundreds of poor village women almost with impunity, in the name of preserving the tenets of the *Sharia* or Islamic law, is yet another impediment to the attainment of equal rights and opportunities for Bangladeshi women.[1]

Since the victimization of these women has been going on using the excuse of preserving the *Sharia*, it may be assumed that the *ulama* in general and their rural counterparts, the semi-literate *mullas*, in particular, have been dispensing judgements in accordance with the *Sharia* and with a view to preserving the faith of Islam. At the outset, we should dispel the myth of a link between the judgements dispensed by the rural *mullas*, the self-employed custodians of Islam, and the *Sharia* law. As we have seen (Chapter 3), even non-practising and non-believing Muslim men in the region insist on the implementation of the so-called *Sharia* law in order to deprive their female relatives, mainly sisters, from getting equal shares in inherited properties. Hence, it would be hackneyed to single out the *Sharia* law (as practised in the region) and its custodians, *mullas*, as responsible for the persecution of rural women in Bangladesh. We may place 'the belligerent *mullas*' in subsumption of the village community which is primarily run by non-*mulla* superordinates. The *mulla* is just an accessory and collaborator of the powerful village elders, broadly known as *matabbars* or *matbars* (village headmen) and elected office-bearers of the local-government bodies, Union Parishads, known as 'Members'. So the *mulla* is the junior partner in the *member-matbar-mulla* triumvirate in the village community. However, as the interpreter-*cum*-custodian of the *Sharia*, he exerts great influence over the masses.

The *salish* court and the impoverished village community

Although the *salish* or village arbitration council is a traditional institution of conflict resolution through mediation, it is not part of the judicial system inherited by the state from the colonial or Pakistani period. As a council of elders, the institution passes informal judgements seeking compromise solutions in village-level disputes over property, family, marriage, divorce or inheritance matters. A *salish* is apparently established 'as and when the need for arbitration arises', and is quite effective in conflict resolution, allowing poor villagers to obtain quick and inexpensive or free justice. However, women activists and human rights groups are concerned that it is constituted by conservative village elders who are opposed to any changes in the existing social structures.[2]

In accordance with tradition, the *salish* may punish men and women for violating the moral or religious code and honour of the village community. In most cases, offenders are either beaten up with shoes or asked to hold their ears in public in the *salish*. In extreme cases, the offenders are ostracized by the villagers in accordance with the judgements of the *salish*. The judgements mostly reflect the wishes of the influential village elders, local *mullas* and occasionally, the local or itinerant *pir-sahibs*, who sit in the *salish*. Women in general are excluded from sitting in the *salish* and women plaintiffs must be represented by their male relatives. The *salish* as the custodian of *naye* (justice) against *annaye* (injustice) and *najjo* (approved behaviour) against *anajjo* (deviant behaviour), does not consider women as equal to men in any sphere of life. Not only women excluded from participation as *salishkars* or arbiters in the *salish*, but village elders may also intervene directly in the internal affairs of village households 'in issues related to women and their social status'. Women are often treated as 'symbolic objects' and their position and honour *(izzat)* may mark deeper conflicts about social, political and economic issues between male leaderships of the *shamaj* [village community] concerned. In short, women are often objects of disagreement between faction and individuals in the *shamaj*, and there is nothing to be surprised about it, because anything and everything could be a contentious issue in this faction-ridden, poverty-stricken village community. Things have not changed much since the days of Carstairs (a British civil servant), who at the beginning of the twentieth century observed that harmony was 'the exception rather than the rule' in the countryside of Bengal.[3]

Comprehension of the origin and nature of the *salish* requires an understanding of the village community in Bangladesh, along with the power brokers and hierarchies in the village and their mutual relationships. Villages in this region are quite different from their counterparts elsewhere in South Asia, where a close collection of houses belonging to the cultivators is situated over an area of two or three miles with a number of shops and a common meeting-place frequented by the villagers. In Bangladesh, on the contrary, the whole countryside, except what is actually required for residential purposes, is under cultivation and the villagers have no common meeting place other than the weekly market places or *hats*, the congregational mosques, school playgrounds or fields after harvest during the dry season. Homesteads are very closely packed together, especially in densely populated districts. The homesteads are built normally on high ground, surrounded by trees, with courtyards in the front and ponds or pools in the backyard surrounded by bamboo or banana hedges. In small villages while shops are practically non-existent, *hats* are in close proximity, where villagers sell and buy goods on market days. Nowadays, due to improvements in communication in the form of roads and bridges, most villages are in close proximity to towns and business centres with electricity and newspapers. Many villagers have access to radio and television as well.

Other links with urban areas are established through government officials, politicians and their clients, mainly the *members* and *matbars*, in the village. Traditional rural elites belonging to the *member-matbar-mulla* triumvirate not only link the masses with sub-regional or national leaders – politicians and members of parliament – but they are also 'makers of public opinion' in the village. The village-elders or *matbars*, mostly representing well-to-do peasant families, represent their factions based on kinship (*gushti*) and lineage (*bangsho*). Their dominance as land-holding, powerful and influential classes traditionally leads to factional frictions and rivalries (*doladoli*) among villagers.

With the intensification of competition for meagre resources among the bulk of the villagers (more than 50 per cent living below the poverty line), the traditional patron-client relationship and semi-tribal factionalism in the village community have become more conspicuous than ever before.

It is, therefore, pertinent to our understanding of why poor rural women are vulnerable to victimization by the *salish*, that we perceive how the intense competition for meagre resources among poor villagers and conflicts of interests between the traditional and newly emerging elites in the countryside for control over these resources, including land and labour, has become even greater since the advent of NGOs and Grameen Bank in the countryside. While the traditional elite belonging to the *member-matbar-mulla* triumvirate does not want to lose control over its clientele (mainly poor villagers), the NGO-Grameen lobby and its local beneficiaries are also desperate to dislodge the triumvirate in order to establish their hegemony in the countryside. The NGO-Grameen lobby is doing this in the name of empowering the poor, especially women. This intense competition for the control over meagre resources, labour and services of the poor villagers, on the one hand, has widened the cleavage between the traditional and modern elites, and on the other, has weakened the traditional patron-client relationship with the *member-matbar-mulla* triumvirate as the benefactor of the masses.

Despite some positive response from many poor villagers, both men and women, *mullas* and others are opposed to the NGO-Grameen lobby because of their aversion to new ideas, reforms and education introduced by outsiders, as these might loosen their hold on their unwitting victims. Their attitude towards NGOs is not altogether different from that of the *kulaks* (rich peasants) of Russia in the nineteenth century, who also found the break-up of patriarchy distressing, considering peasant woman as 'the primary culprit', vulnerable to evil influences and temptations as the 'rural Eve'. Like their Russian counterparts, it seems Bangladeshi *kulaks* and their associates firstly regard women as symbols of purity and fertility, to be placed exclusively in the private domain of the family; and secondly, as 'slyer than the devil', and 'less humane, more heartless'.[4]

One cannot, however, totally escape from the religious aspect in this anti-NGO sentiment of the village elders and their associates. The break-up of patriarchy and the institution of *purdah* have negative correlations with the tenets of Islamic 'orthodoxy' as perceived in the Muslim world. Rural as well as urban *ulama's* persistent opposition to NGOs is not very dissimilar to their counterparts' similar attitude towards English education, colonial rule and reforms throughout the subcontinent during the British *raj*. Like their predecessors in the nineteenth century, *mullas* and other conservative people in modern Bangladesh also invent the bogeyman and the spectre, said to have been 'spreading Christianity and alien, un-Islamic ideology' among the unwary masses through Westernization and modernization. What could be more 'Western' than NGOs and Grameen Bank as they are mainly funded by Western (and Christian) donors? However, it would be trite to assume that *mullas'* wrath against pro-Western NGOs is the only factor leading to the persecution of rural women. Several socio-political, demographic and economic factors may be ascribed to the victimization of women, mainly through the institution of *salish*.

As Shapan Adnan has suggested, changes in the position of women in Bangladesh in recent years have 'been impelled by a number of critical "parametric" shifts at the *macro-level*, involving economic, demographic and socio-demographic factors'. There is some truth in his view that 'uneven capitalist development' in which market forces by 'profit-oriented logic' have been making use of the available (cheap) female labour in the country. Consequently Adnan argues,

structures of family and kinship, social institutions and production relationships have been subjected to specific kinds of economic
compulsions (eg., ensuring subsistence or making normal profit),
requiring these to either adapt to the changed circumstances or
disintegrate.[5]

With the massive growth of population – 63 per cent in the twenty
years 1961–81 – by 1981 Bangladesh had nearly 90 million people,
a figure which by the mid-1990s had reached nearly 120 million;
and the process of tremendous differentiation and polarization has
taken place not only on class-lines but on gender-lines as well.
Along with the increase in the number of landless or semi-landless
categories of people, there has been an enormous rise in the number of nuclear/sub-nuclear families, especially among the landless
or semi-landless people. Consequently wives in these households
on the one hand have become free from the hierarchical authority
of mothers-in-law and other members of extended families, but on
the other, have also been exposed to 'greater risks of destitution in
the event of divorce or widowhood'. Demographic pressure and the
consequential intensification of poverty among the bulk of the rural population in the last three decades also led to a growth in the
number of 'female-headed households', relatively free from patriarchy and the institution of *purdah*, destitute women with no option
but to fend for themselves and their children.[6] These 'financially
independent' women either work for subsistence for richer households in the village or are available as the pool of cheap labour
and as clients of NGOs and the Grameen Bank. Some of them also
work as factory-workers, day labourers and maids, mainly in urban
areas.

The large-scale destitution of rural women, after the emergence
of Bangladesh, especially during the famine of 1974, coincided with
the emergence of hundreds of NGOs, mainly funded by foreign
donor agencies. The advent of NGOs and the Grameen Bank in
rural areas, on the one hand, led to the large-scale transfer of poor
women in the landless or semi-landless categories from their traditional patrons-cum-employers to these extraneous organizations for
patronage; on the other hand, they were held responsible for breaking
the traditional ethos and values by members of the traditional and
orthodox rural elites. The traditional elites, the *member-matbar-mulla*
triumvirate, have politico-economic and socio-religious reasons to
be aggrieved. Firstly, as we have seen, NGOs and other external

organizations are perceived as the triumvirate's competitors, taking away their clients (poor men and women) by providing jobs, microcredit, schools and clinics; and secondly, these organizations are blamed for accelerating the process of breaking up the moral codes of conduct or norms of 'approved behaviour' of rural men, especially women. Although the institution of *purdah* had become a 'luxury' for poor women, even before the advent of NGOs, since abject poverty had forced them to fend for themselves and work side by side with men, the way female clients of some NGOs and the Grameen Bank have been defying patriarchy and village-elders in particular, has alarmed the rural triumvirate. The incidents of persecution of women through the *salish* are, therefore, mainly parts of the defensive mechanism of the existing pre-capitalist village community. An appraisal of a few case studies involving persecuted poor women and their tormentors may help us comprehend both the nature of the so-called Islamic resurgence/fanaticism at the grassroots level and peasants' bewilderment as well as rational behaviour *vis-à-vis* the process of 'modernization', 'development' and 'exploitation in the name of development'.

However, before we consider the situation leading to the persecution of women through the *salish* and its short- and long-term consequences with regard to women, the peasant economy and Islam in Bangladesh, further light needs to be shed on the institution of *salish* and the immediate, remote, local, national and international factors responsible for the controversial judgements against women.

Although the *salish* court is a traditional institution, the Bangladesh government regulated its jurisdictions and activities in the 1970s. The Village Courts Ordinance of 1976 and the Council of Dispute (Municipal Areas) Ordinance of 1979 formally established village courts and conciliation boards (in urban areas) clearly defining their procedures, composition and jurisdiction. Their jurisdiction is strictly limited to minor civil matters and petty criminal offences. In criminal cases these courts may not pass any sentence of fine or imprisonment but may order the guilty person to pay the aggrieved person compensation of an amount not exceeding 5000 taka. The establishment and jurisdiction of all other courts are governed by the Constitution of the country and by the Code of Criminal Procedure of 1898 or specific acts passed by Parliament. In view of this, all *salish* proceedings in the recent past which convicted and sentenced people, mostly women, in criminal matters in accordance with the so-called *Sharia* law, had no legal sanction or the authority of government. These acts of arbitrary violation of the law were not only carried out in remote areas but also in villages near to Dhaka, the capital city.[7]

Since offences committed against the moral code of conduct of the villagers or the *Sharia* law as understood by them are also taken care of by the *salish*, the verdicts mainly derive from *fatwas* or religious dictums issued by qualified *ulama* or local *maulvis* (priests). Traditionally, among the bulk of rural Muslims, the *fatwas* preponderate over secular laws derived from the colonial civil and criminal procedure, and this has been so since the early days of the British *raj*. During the British period, the local and itinerant *ulama* played the role of the *mufti* (one who is entitled to issue *fatwas*) throughout the region defying the authority of the colonial courts, especially in regard to moral offences. Sometimes the *fatwas* also questioned and challenged the legitimacy of the British *raj*. Maulana Shah Abdul Aziz (1746–1823) of Delhi is famous for his various *fatwas*, including the one declaring British India to be an 'abode of war' or *Dar ul-Harb*.[8] The political culture promoting the defiance of authority and the occasional denial of the legitimacy of the Government is quite well-entrenched at grassroots level throughout the region. It seems that the tradition of defiance established by the legacy of *fatwas* along with the prevalent peasant culture of the masses, have been playing significant roles in this regard. Although etymologically *fatwa* in Arabic stands for a judgement or decree of *muftis* or *faqihs* (well-versed Islamic scholars), establishing the stand of the *Sharia* law with regard to any question about any problematic issue, the dearth of such scholars has led to the ascendancy of semi-literate *mullas* to the status of *muftis* throughout the country. It is interesting that during the Pakistani period, when the region was part of an Islamic country, the issuance of *fatwas* hardly created any controversy beyond the bamboo hedges of the village, yet in the 1990s the persecution of women with the sanction of *fatwas* has become an important issue for human rights groups, feminists, academics and politicians both within and outside the country.

Although some *ulama* have favoured women's participation in every sphere of life, including politics and the adoption of family planning measures, and more than 200 leading *ulama* of the country demanded 'exemplary punishment' for the *fatwa*-dispensing 'ignorant' *mullas* for tormenting women in the name of *Sharia* law,[9] the average *mulla* and his followers at grassroots level have not yet come forward with a similar stand over women's rights and privileges.

The reasons for such 'obduracy' on the part of the *mullas* are not far to seek. However, an appraisal of *mullas'* behaviour with regard to the Islamization of the polity, NGOs, Grameen Bank and the 'empowerment' of women requires an evaluation of some case studies portraying the plight of poor rural women due to the *salish*-verdicts, in order to highlight the level of obscurantism and persecution mania of the self-styled *'muftis'* of rural Bangladesh.

Salish, fatwa and victimization of women: case studies

In April 1992 a *salish* court in a village in the Dohar *thana* (administrative unit) in Dhaka district sentenced a young woman and her mother to 100 lashes each. Earlier, Shefali, the 14-year-old girl, had been raped by an influential village elder. After she became pregnant, local village elders convened a *salish*, to decide her case. The *mulla*, in charge of dispensing the verdict *(fatwa)*, asserted that since there had been no witness to the rape, the accused could not be held responsible, as under Islamic law four adult eye-witnesses of good repute are needed to convict someone accused of committing rape or adultery. However, as Shefali had admitted to the intercourse and as her pregnancy was obvious evidence for intercourse having taken place, she was sentenced to 100 lashes to be administered in public. Her mother received the same punishment for accusing the village elder of rape. Shefali's punishment was deferred pending delivery, while her mother's punishment was apparently carried out.[10]

There are many other case studies of rape-victims being caned in public due to *salish* verdicts. Some of them even committed suicide to save themselves from perpetual disgrace. Beauty Khatun from a village in Sirajganj district was raped by one Abdul Mannan when her day-labourer husband, Shukur Ali, was absent. Shukur Ali sought justice from the village elders but after getting no redress from them as they were under the influence of the rich and powerful Abdul Mannan, he filed a complaint against the culprit with the Raiganj police station. While the police refrained from arresting the culprit, influential village elders ostracized Shukur Ali and his wife. Afterwards a *salish* was held on 21 May 1994 to 'try' the victim, Beauty Khatun, for having 'illicit relationships' with various men. The *mulla* who presided over the *salish* sentenced her to 101 lashes and asked her husband to withdraw the case against Abdul Mannan. Beauty Khatun committed suicide not long after the judgment.[11]

Rozia Akhter Rina, a 19-year-old girl from a village in Feni district, killed herself in December 1994 after a *salish* falsely implicated her in adultery sentencing her to 101 lashes. Later on, an inquiry by several journalists, members of women's organizations, lawyers and human rights groups revealed that she was an innocent victim of a dispute over her father's property.[12] A woman named Zohra from a village in Ghior, Dhaka district, also killed herself by taking poison after a *salish* found her guilty of scolding an influential villager. She was sentenced to public beating and her husband, a poor peasant, in accordance with the verdict, had to beat her up in public.[13]

In another case, the wife of an alleged adulterer was lashed in public along with her husband in a village in Mathbaria, Pirojpur district, in March 1995. Reportedly, Razia Begum's husband eloped with her younger sister and after some time came back to his wife. Consequently village elders convened a *salish*, which sentenced both the innocent Razia and the 'adulterer' husband to 51 lashes each. The *mulla*, who presided over the *salish*, held that since Razia was no longer 'legally married' to her husband, she must marry someone else and only after getting a divorce from her 'second' husband would she be allowed to unite with her 'first' husband. Razia killed herself by taking pesticide.[14]

In early 1993, a young maidservant in Dhaka was given 25 lashes for maintaining a sexual relationship with her employer, by a *salish* consisting of neighbours and the local *mulla*. The employer did not receive any punishment but was forced to marry the girl although he had already been married. In a similar incident in Pabna district in May 1993, a local Quran teacher of a mosque, reportedly caught having sexual intercourse with a female student, was forced to marry her in accordance with the decision of a *salish*. They were also sentenced to 60 lashes each and a fine. In September 1993, another *salish* in Kalikapur village in Satkhira district sentenced Feroza, a 16-year-old girl, to 101 lashes for having an illicit relationship with a Hindu boy. She died shortly afterwards. Village elders and a human rights group investigating the death said she had committed suicide. Although police filed a case against the participants of the *salish* charging them with abetment to suicide, it is not known if anyone was arrested. The result of the post mortem has not been made public either.[15]

The most sensational and widely reported case, in which a *salish* unlawfully sentenced a woman to death by stoning for committing adultery, is that of Nurjahan, a 21-year-old woman of Chatakchara village in Sylhet district. On 10 January 1993, Nurjahan Begum was sentenced to public stoning to death by a *salish*. She reportedly died a few hours after she was partially buried in the ground and pelted with stones 101 times by villagers. She is said not to have died as a result of the injuries sustained during the stoning but to have later committed suicide out of a sense of shame. Some observers believe that Nurjahan's parents may have been put under pressure to make the statement that she committed suicide so that the possible charge against those responsible for her death would only be 'abetment to suicide and not murder', as the penalty for abetment is considerably less than that for murder. According to Amnesty International, Nurjahan's case (up to October 1994) was the 'only one case in which a *salish* unlawfully sentenced a woman to death has, to Amnesty International's knowledge, led to a conviction of those responsible for the offence'.[16]

Reportedly, the *salish* was convened to try Nurjahan, who was the daughter of a poor villager, Ashrobullah, of Chatakchara village, for the alleged commission of adultery with one Motaleb of the same village. According to her father, Nurjahan was first married to an expatriate Bangladeshi who later divorced her and formally sent her the *talaqnama* (divorce paper). Afterwards, she married a second time in December 1992, but according to Maulana Mannan, who presided over the *salish*, the second marriage had no legal validity. The *salish*, however, did not inform the couple why their marriage was considered illegal. During the hearing Motaleb, the second husband of Nurjahan, was reportedly slapped by members of the *salish* when he questioned the ruling that sentenced the couple to death by public stoning. He was told by members of the *salish* that the 'court's' word was law. Nurjahan's parents were held partly responsible for her 'un-Islamic' second marriage and were sentenced to 50 lashes each. Immediately after the verdict, Nurjahan was buried in the ground up to her chest and then stoned. Apparently her husband was also stoned and survived. Reportedly, Nurjahan's father had publicly to administer the flogging sentence to his wife as he would not let other villagers touch his wife on religious grounds.[17]

After the local press, human rights groups, women's organizations and Amnesty International gave wide publicity to and condemned the *salish* judgment leading to the death of Nurjahan, police arrested Maulana Mannan, the 'judge', and eight of his local accomplices, *mullas* and village-elders. They were charged under sections 306 (abetment to suicide), 504 (intentional insult) and 109 (abetment) of the Bangladesh Penal Code and tried at the District Magistrate's court at Maulvibazar. On 22 February 1994, each of them was sentenced to seven years' rigorous imprisonment and fined 2000 taka.[18]

In another case, another woman, also named Nurjahan, was tried by a *salish* on 5 May 1993 at Dokhin Sripur village in Faridpur district, some 80 kilometres west of Dhaka, and was found guilty of adultery. She was sentenced to death by fire. Accordingly, she was tied to a stake and after having kerosene poured over her was burned to death. After the Bengali language daily *Sangbad* carried the story on 20 May, seven alleged members of the *salish* were arrested on 24 May 1993. Despite the wide coverage of this public execution of a woman by a *salish* in local newspapers and in Amnesty International reports, the accused were acquitted by the Faridpur District Court judge on 22 June 1994, for 'want of evidence'.[19] It seems that the accused *salish*-holders in this case were much more powerful and influential than the convicted *mulla* and his accomplices in Maulvibazar, held responsible for the death of Nurjahan Begum of Chatakchara village. In September 1993, Feroza Begum, another poor village woman in Satkhira district, was sentenced to 101 strokes of the broom by a *salish* for having an 'illicit relationship' with a young man of her village. She also killed herself out of humiliation. Ten months after the incident, the police brought charges against the *fatwa*-dispensing *mulla*, Maulana Abdur Rahim, and ten accomplices including the chairman and a member of the local union council. Eight of them were later arrested by the police.[20]

By then, local human rights groups, women's organizations and Amnesty International had been condemning these atrocious acts against women, through reports in the media and representations to the government of Bangladesh, for quite some time. Amnesty International was very critical of the Government for not protecting poor Bangladeshi women from persecution through the *salish*. According to Amnesty International:

> To try people by a village *salish* violates the defendants' fundamental rights guaranteed by the constitution. Article 32 of the Constitution of Bangladesh says: 'No person shall be deprived of life or personal liberty save in accordance with law. . . . Articles 33 and 35 lay down safeguards regarding arrest, detention and fair trial, all of which are violated by illegal trials of *salish*. . . .

promising not to indulge in sinful acts again. Shahida, in her interview to the press, also narrated the same story. Neither she nor anybody else mentioned the use of a lash to discipline her in the *salish*.[27]

From the preceding account it appears that while some of the anti-government newspapers and women's organizations tried to vilify the government (Khaleda Zia of the BNP was Prime Minister at the time), citing its inefficiency with regard to the persecution of women by Islamic 'fundamentalists', the Government, on the other hand, became quite defensive and tried to take the wind out of its opponents' sails by sending a large police force to Savar to 'intimidate and punish' Islamic 'fanatics'.

Elsewhere, in outlying areas beyond the immediate area of the capital city, *mullas* and village elders continued to punish poor women through the *salish* for quite some time. It is noteworthy that while Shahida's case received wide publicity and government intervention to 'rescue and help' the victim (since the incident took place near Dhaka), another Shahida and her mother, Alimunnesa, from a remote village in Jessore district, were not as fortunate.

> From the testimonies of witnesses and survey of the locality it has been proven that the unmarried girl has committed adultery with Musharraf [son of a rich, influential villager]. As her mother is an accomplice, she should be given 39 lashes and asked to be repentant of her sin.

So goes the *fatwa* of Maulana Gholam Mustafa, a teacher of a local *madrasah* in Jessore. In accordance with the verdict and in absence of the 'main culprit', Shahida [who had an abortion and got married to a poor villager elsewhere], her mother received 39 lashes in public from a man, as directed by the *mulla*.[28]

After Shahida's mother (a poor widow) learnt about her daughter's pregnancy and the person responsible for it in February 1994 (Musharraf), she approached him, her neighbour and the son of a well-to-do expatriate Bangladeshi (based in Dubai), to marry her daughter to save her from disgrace. On his refusal to marry her daughter she sought help from village elders. Accordingly they decided in a *salish* that Musharraf would marry the girl, but very soon they changed their verdict and held Shahida responsible for her pregnancy. Acquitting Musharraf on all charges, the local chairman, members of the Union *Parishad* and other village elders decided to ostracize Shahida and her family for her 'sinful' conduct. Finally, they all agreed to hold another *salish* to be headed by Maulana Gholam Mustafa, a *madrasah* teacher from Jessore and in accordance with his *fatwa* Shahida's mother was caned in public. No action was taken against Musharraf as he could not be proven guilty. Local *matbars* and *member* Taijul Islam defended their action. Holding similar views, the Maulana further asserted that in accordance with *Sharia* law, fornicators and their abetters may even be stoned to death.[29]

Sometimes *salish* verdicts do not conform to the traditional pattern, dispensing flogging or stoning as modes of punishment, for example. In one case, reported by the Coordinating Council of Human Rights in Bangladesh, on 11 June 1994, Anjali Karmakar, an 18-year-old Hindu girl, was found guilty by a *salish* of 'violating social norms' of the village by 'chatting with a man' and (as punishment) was expelled from her village at Bagha Sadar in Rajshahi district. Her father was sentenced to perform humiliating push-ups in public while holding his ears for having failed to control his 'shameless daughter'.[30] In another case, Razia Khatun, a 22-year-old woman of Bara Chaimata village in Kishoreganj district, was made to drink her own urine after being found guilty of adultery by a *salish*.[31]

Traditionally, the issue of 'illegal cohabitation' by couples after the 'consummation of divorce' has been one of the most important subjects under discussion in the *salish*. Since Muslim men in the region can arbitrarily break the nuptial bond by merely telling their wives: 'I divorce you', three times in a row, the poverty-stricken countryside witnesses a large number of such divorces. In most cases, husbands utter the clause of divorce, albeit in unequivocal terms, out of anger and frustration and because of poverty. There are instances when regretful husbands, recanting or denying their pronouncements of divorce, continue to cohabit with their wives. If villagers learn about the prevalence of any such cohabitation in the village, which is not allowed by *Sharia* law, they convene a *salish* and punish such couples accordingly.

Sometimes influential villagers having an eye to poor villagers' young wives, spread rumours about their having 'illegal cohabitation' with their 'former' husbands, already said to have divorced them. As for the poor, there is hardly any way of disproving such allegations, they simply succumb to such pressures and agree to their wives' performing *hilla* or getting married to village elders, normally with the tacit understanding of waiting for their 'former' wives until they are divorced by their 'new husbands'. If and when someone is strong enough to resist such slanderous campaigns and does not yield to the pressure, he or she risks of being ostracized by the village community. The following examples may be cited to highlight the plight of such outcasts in the countryside.

Khatibullah and his wife, Sufia Begum, of Parajpur village in Dinajpur district were ostracized by a *salish* in 1976 and reportedly had been living in a state of total excommunication for 18 years. Khatibullah is said to have verbally divorced his wife out of anger and later changed his mind and the couple continued to live together and had four children after the 'divorce'. Consequently local *mullas* and village elders decided to ostracize the couple in the name of *Sharia* law.[22] There are instances of victims of rape and abduction being ostracized as well. Lovely, a poor orphan who worked as a maid in the village of Kellai in Manikganj district, was ostracized by a *salish*, after she had been lured into a physical relationship by a relative of her employer and became pregnant. No action was taken against the well-to-do lover, while the poor girl was reportedly living in total ostracism in the village.[33]

Despite the anti-*fatwa* and anti-*salish* campaigns carried out by various political parties, newspapers, NGOs, human rights and women's organizations, according to one report about 500 *fatwas* were issued in Bangladesh against individuals and groups (especially NGOs and newspapers) for their alleged anti-Islamic activities in the first six months of 1994. According to another report, because of *fatwas* about 50 women died at different places throughout the country in one year up to mid-1994 – 42 of them died because village elders and *mullas* barred them from getting treatment at NGO-run clinics in rural areas.[34]

Fatwas in the light of national politics

Thus, it is not enough to shed light merely on the conflict between *mullas'* orthodoxy-cum-misogyny and the ongoing process of 'female liberation' in the countryside. In order to understand the pugnacious behaviour of *mullas* and their opponents, it is important to keep in mind that:

1 *Mullas* and village elders do not necessarily always represent the aspirations of the rural masses, as the former are as subject to manipulation by urban *ulama* and other 'Islam-oriented' elites as the rural masses are subject to manipulation by rural elites.

2 NGOs and other advocates of female liberation are not necessarily motivated by a genuine concern to uplift those wretched of the earth, the poor rural women of Bangladesh, since most of them represent urban 'secular' and 'liberal democrat' capitalist classes.

3 This ongoing conflict in the countryside of Bangladesh is not solely a by-product of gender war but is an integral part of the conflict between ascending capitalist interests and receding pre-capitalist and semi-feudal ones – poor women have been simply sandwiched in between these rivals and are being used as disposable pawns.

However, the sudden re-emergence of *fatwas* against institutions and individuals and the rise in the number and intensity of persecution of women through the *salish* in the first half of the 1990s have other explanations as well. Before analysing these other contributing factors to the rise of 'Islamic resurgence' in relation to women's rights and status, we should consider some case studies regarding whether the dispension of such *fatwas* has a positive correlation with the persecution of women in Bangladesh in the name of *Sharia* law.

It has been widely reported in the local media as well as Amnesty International reports how *mullas* prevented women in a locality in Feni district from exercising their right to vote. However, the *fatwa* barring women from voting is an isolated example and the *fatwa* was not dispensed during the decade of the 1990s. In accordance with the *fatwa* of one local *pir sahib*, the late Alhaj Maulana Muhammad Ismail, who in the 1960s felt that 'women should not go to the polling stations for voting as this adversely affects the institution of *purdah'*, many women continued to refrain from voting at Mohamaya Union Council in the Chhagolnayya *thana* (administrative unit) in Feni district up to 1994. Reportedly, Maulana Muzammil Haq, principal of a local *madrasah* and (son of the late *pir sahib*), is said to have influenced all candidates from the locality in such a manner that they all agreed not to bring any female voters to the local polling stations to cast their votes, for the sake of *purdah*. Following the *fatwa*, women voters did not cast their votes in the Union Council elections of 1994. Reportedly, on the eve of the elections, local villagers campaigned against female participation in elections by distributing leaflets conveying a similar message, bearing the signatures of Maulana Muzammil Haq and three candidates for the position of chairman of the union council.

This campaign and the consequential non-participation of female voters in the local elections did not go unchallenged. One female voter filed a petition in the High Court charging that female voters had been intimidated by the *fatwa* and consequentially they had not exercised their franchise. In June 1994, the High Court directed the Union Council Chairman to show cause why the election should not be declared void.[35]

It is noteworthy that although the number of such incidents involving *mullas* and village elders forcing female voters not to cast their votes in local elections is very small, almost all the major newspapers representing the so-called liberal democrats and secular groups gave them wide coverage. Consequently even Amnesty International in its reports reproduced the reported incidents of women barred from voting. These newspaper reports, far from being objective, only reflected the viewpoint of the leading opposition party, the Awami League, and aimed at vilifying the ruling Bangladesh Nationalist Party (BNP), by portraying it as the protector of 'pro-Pakistani' obscurantist forces or the so-called Islamic fundamentalists of Bangladesh. By mid-1994, the expulsion of Taslima Nasreen, the controversial feminist writer, had also become a contentious issue among rival political groups. The 'Islamic' and secular forces were sharply polarized on the issue.[36] The subsequent narration of reported incidents of *mullas'* and village elders' attacks on NGOs and the Grameen Bank should also be taken with a pinch of salt, because almost all the newspapers which have been publishing such news items, garnishing them with exaggerations and sensationalism, suffer from a lack of objectivity. Their predisposition to the opposition parties, especially the Awami League, is made clear in these reports. They not only reflect the anti-government views of the 'liberal-secular' groups, so as to embarrass the government by projecting it as the 'defender' of the 'enemies of Bangladesh' or the 'Islamic' groups who collaborated with Pakistan during the Liberation War of 1971,[37] but also the pro-NGO sentiment of these groups.

The gulf between the opposition (led by Sheikh Hasina, daughter of Sheikh Mujibur Rahman, the founding president of Bangladesh) and the government of Prime Minister Khaleda Zia (the widow of President Ziaur Rahman) was further widened over a controversial by-election in 1994, which later culminated in a demand for the resignation of the Prime Minister. By mid-1994, Bangladesh politics had been sharply polarized between the pro-opposition (pro-Awami League) and pro-government (pro-BNP) groups. While 'Bengali nationalism' was the trump card of the former group, the latter was promoting 'Bangladeshi nationalism', apparently representing 'secularism' and 'Islamic orientation', respectively. With a view to dislodging the BNP government from power, the pro-Awami League newspapers highlighted the incidents of persecution of rural women by the *salish*, to 'prove' its incompetence and pro-*mulla* proclivity.

Islamic groups, especially the well-organized Jamaat-i-Islami (which had 20 seats in Parliament), were also targets of this vituperative campaign by the pro-Awami League newspapers, politicians and intellectuals. As the Jamaat-i-Islami support had been vital to the formation of the BNP government in the wake of the 1991 elections, the Awami League and its allies not only projected the party as 'communal and fundamentalist' but in 1992 also held a 'public trial' of Ghulam Azam, the supreme leader of the Jamaat for 'war crimes' allegedly committed by him during the Liberation War of 1971.[38] Various NGOs had been taking leading roles in vilifying both the BNP and the Jamaat-i-Islami throughout the period. Their anti-BNP stand was finally exposed during an intense opposition campaign to dislodge the government of Khaleda Zia in early 1996, as the Chairman of the ADAB (Association of Development Agencies in Bangladesh) openly sided with the opposition.[39] Consequently despite the Jamaat-i-Islami's withdrawal of support from the BNP government for various reasons by late 1992, the pro-Awami League opposition and NGOs continued their vitriolic campaign against the party and other Islamic groups.

Women, NGOs and popular Islam

According to an Amnesty International report, which is not solely based on subjective reports by 'opposition' newspapers, from early July 1993 to mid-1994 various 'Islamist groups' attacked NGOs engaged in women's 'development activities ... income generating projects, education and health services'.[40] The report also indicated that NGOs such as BRAC, Proshika, Nijera Kori and the Grameen Bank (Grameen stands for rural) were the main 'targets of Islamists' attack'. While some newspapers, mainly reflecting the views of the opposition, put the blame on 'Islamic fundamentalist forces' for attacking NGO-run schools, NGO staff and women working for NGOs, 'Islamist groups' vilified NGOs for alienating women from their 'proper' social roles and Islamic life-style and felt that 'anti-

Islamic, anti-people and anti-state' NGOs should therefore be banned.

The Coordinating Council of Human Rights in Bangladesh (CCHRB), which coordinates the work of various human rights groups, suggested that

> economic considerations may partly motivate clerics to issue fatwas
> against NGOs, as traditional religious schools are losing students
> to the non-formal education programmes of NGOs like BRAC.
> Similarly money lenders in villages, who together with the clergy
> and others are members of the local elites, are losing business to
> NGOs like the Grameen Bank which provide *low interest loans*
> [emphasis added].[41]

Some local pro-opposition newspapers have also held similar views. According to one such report, BRAC for example was targeted by *mullas* and *madrasah* teachers as it had been running more than 20 000 schools by early 1994, enrolling more than 600 000 students, mostly girls, in the rural areas of 49 districts of Bangladesh.[42]

It is, however, difficult to agree with such over-simplified assertions that village moneylenders and village *mullas* have been opposing the Grameen Bank and NGOs as these organizations lend money to poor villagers charging 'low interest rates'. Knowing how exacting and selective the Grameen Bank is with regard to its rate of interest (charging about 28 per cent), methods of collection of loan instalments and disbursing loans, I simply cannot accept the argument that *mullas* and moneylenders have been unitedly fighting the Grameen Bank and NGOs out of common economic interests: firstly because *mullas* in general do not approve of charging interest on any loan, as it is against the teachings of Islam; secondly, because the Grameen Bank and NGOs are not that competitive with regard to their rates of interest on loans. Had economic conflicts of interest been the main reason why *mullas* have been opposed to the Grameen-NGO lobby, there would not have been any *fatwa* against Taslima Nasreen and some leading 'leftist' and 'anti-Islamic' intellectuals, writers and journalists who compete neither with the rural nor with the urban *mullas, maulanas, pir sahibs* and *muftis*. One may also argue that had anti-NGO sentiment of intellectuals and the ordinary people been positively correlated with 'Islamic fundamentalism', intellectuals like Rajni Kothari in India would not have condemned NGOs at all:[43] Rajni Kothari's comments about NGOs highlight the non-religious dimension of the opposition:

The nation-state is disintegrating. We do not have self-reliant independent ruling elites. . . . There is an emerging crisis of both identity politics and alternative politics. Both have been hijacked by a new type of socio-political formations, namely, NGOs. . . . We need to distance ourselves from NGOised grassroots activities. . . . floated by the World Bank. NGOs have been coopted and corrupted. Large sums of money are flowing into the NGOs. These are failing to perform their functions. . . . The task is to enrich democracy, create a more assertive civil society. . . . South Asian states are in a bad shape, waiting for a new order to emerge.[44]

Some renowned Bangladeshi 'liberal-democrat' intellectuals, Zillur Rahman Siddiqi for example (poet, writer and a former vice-chancellor of a university), also feels that NGOs have replaced the traditional moneylenders in the countryside and some of them have been more exploitative than the moneylenders. Many other 'liberal-democrat' and 'leftist' intellectuals, Professor Anisur Rahman (economist) and Badruddin Umar (leftist writer) for example, have been critical of NGOs for their reliance on Western donors, including the World Bank and the IMF. Badruddin Umar considers NGOs and especially the Grameen Bank conspiracies to retard the process of industrialization in Bangladesh.[45]

Against this backdrop, we cannot assume that:

1   Conflicting economic interests between the *member-matbar-mulla* triumvirate (village elders and clerics) and the NGO-Grameen lobby, competing for control over the 'same group of people' as their clients, have been mainly responsible for the *fatwas* and attacks on NGO properties.

2   Islamic groups and rural *mullas* have been the only critics of the NGO-Grameen activities. However, one is tempted to draw conclusions establishing a positive correlation between such attacks on NGO-run establishments and the 'inherent economic competition' between village *mullas* and moneylenders on one side and the NGOs on the other. An elucidation of the situation prevailing in the countryside *vis-à-vis* the anti-NGO, anti-Grameen Bank sentiment and activities of a section of the people, may help us comprehend this state of affairs.

Between January and March 1994, more than 100 BRAC schools and schools run by other NGOs in the countryside were set on fire, teachers were attacked and teaching materials were destroyed. In January 1994, the parents of some 700 000 children attending

BRAC-run schools, 70 per cent of whom are girls, were asked by *imams* of mosques and *madrasah* teachers throughout the country to withdraw their children from such schools or to face a *fatwa* entailing social boycott. Consequently school attendance dropped for some weeks and recovered afterwards. In Sylhet and Rajshahi districts, several BRAC schools closed down by mid-1994 after *fatwas* had been issued against them. According to Professor Yunus, the founder of the Grameen Bank, by mid-1994 opposition to NGO activities and attacks on NGO properties were being intensified from local to national level.[46]

According to the report of a human rights organization of Bangladesh, 'following the publication of a leaflet written by an *imam*, Maulana Ibrahim, in November 1993 and its reprint in the daily *Inquilab* [representing "Islamists"] on 14 November 1993, widespread attack on NGOs in Bogra district began'. The leaflet portrayed NGOs as enemies of the Islamic way of life, engaged in converting Muslims into Christians and forcing women to act in an 'un-Islamic way'. Following the distribution of the leaflet and public addresses by Maulana Ibrahim, in February 1994, 25 BRAC schools were set on fire in Bogra district alone and families sending women and children to BRAC establishments 'were declared social outcasts and told that their dead would be denied an Islamic funeral'. Local *imams* directed villagers, using sermons given in mosques, to divorce their wives if they worked with NGOs. Maulana Ibrahim categorically attacked the Grameen Bank, BRAC and other NGOs for promoting promiscuity and inciting woman against men by lending them money while men were denied this privilege. It was alleged that consequently women were chanting slogans, taking a vow not to obey their husbands and not to live in poverty any more.[47]

According to a 'pro-opposition' (anti-BNP and anti-Islamist) newspaper report, the *fatwabaz mullas* (a pejorative expression, denoting *fatwa*-dispensing irritable *mullas*) were busy organizing their network at grassroots level throughout Bangladesh. They are said to have 'confused the ordinary masses by arousing their religious sentiment', especially in the interior of Bogra district. Maulana Mufti Ibrahim Khondker of Nimaidighi village under Nandigram *thana* in Bogra district is said to have organized a big gathering of *fatwabaz mullas* in the village in February 1994. These *mullas* are reported to have declared their intention of floating an organization called the Bangladesh Anti-Christian Organization, with a view to stopping the 'mass conversion' of Bangladeshi Muslims into Christians. Some *mullas* are said to have declared that: 'Although the total population of Bangladesh has not doubled from 75 million in 1971 to 150 million in 1994, the corresponding rise in the number of Christians in the country has been phenomenal – from bare 250 000, it has gone up to three million'. They allegedly held the Grameen Bank and NGOs responsible for the defilement of women and the society.[48]

Consequently, villagers in Bogra and elsewhere set fire to BRAC schools, cut down mulberry plants set up under a BRAC scheme to promote sericulture with women workers, urging everybody to boycott NGOs and the Grameen Bank. In April 1994, one Naziban Bibi, a young village woman in Bogra district, was divorced by her husband for working in a mulberry plantation set up by an NGO.[49]

While rural *mullas* were busy organizing anti-NGO meetings and rallies in the countryside, urging villagers to attack NGO-run organizations for their alleged promotion of 'sexual promiscuity' and 'unruly behaviour and insubordination' among women, urban *mullas* targeted 'liberal-secular' intellectuals and newspapers promoting their views. A section of the urban *ulama* asked the government to impose a ban on several Bengali dailies, including the *Janakantha, Ajker Kagaj* and *Bhorer Kagaj*. According to one *fatwa*: 'Unless Prime Minister Khaleda Zia imposes a ban on *Janakantha,* her impending performance of the *hajj* will not be acceptable to God.' By mid-1994, the incidents of *fatwa*-dispension had become common phenomena throughout the country both in the urban and rural areas. Various local anti-NGO and anti-Grameen Bank organizations were floated in different districts. Besides the Bangladesh Anti-Christian Organization, about a hundred grassroots organizations and movements, such as the Movement for the Protection of *Iman* (faith) and Motherland (*Iman Desh Bachao Andolon*); Islamic Youth Association (*Islami Jubo Sangha*); Association for the Protection of *Sunnah* or the Prophet's Traditions (*Anjuman-i-Mahisunnah*), have been actively engaged in mobilizing villagers against the Grameen Bank and NGOs throughout the country.[50]

Some of these organizations, having close links with the grassroots and reflecting peasant culture and popular Islam, have been dissuading villagers, especially women, from visiting NGO-run clinics for treatment. In some villages of Bogra and Rajshahi districts, it seems they were barred from getting medicine and treatment from these clinics, broadly classified as 'anti-Islamic Christian organizations' in the parlance of *mullas* and their associates. In early 1994, some patients in Bogra district were prevented by *fatwas* from con-

tinuing their treatment for tuberculosis at BRAC clinics, as that
NGO was allegedly converting people into Christians. Pregnant
women were also prevented from continuing their treatment in a
BRAC clinic. On 30 June 1994, the offices and clinic of Friends in
Village Development Bangladesh were set on fire by 'Islamists' at
Atgram village in Habiganj district. On the same day, another clinic
run by Bangladesh Women's Health Coalition was burned down by
a mob led by the sons of a local *pir* at Zakiganj, Sylhet district. The
mob apparently attempted to lock in and burn alive the clinic's
medical officer.[51]

Besides these reports of attacks on NGOs and clinics run by them,
there are indications that *fatwas* issued against women associated
with NGOs led to their being deserted by their husbands, being
ostracized or physically punished. By March 1994, 60 families were
socially isolated in Bogra district alone for having contacts with
BRAC and ten women were divorced by their husbands for similar
association with NGOs. Some village *imams* in Bogra district, reportedly, announced in Friday congregation prayers that women
who did not observe 'full *purdah*' would have their heads forcibly
shaved and those who attended NGO schools and clinics would be
beaten. Consequently several villagers, both men and women, were
beaten and some of them had to leave their villages in accordance
with the *fatwas*.[52] Some reports even reveal that village *mullas* in
certain cases declared pregnant women getting medical check-ups
in clinics as *haram* or forbidden in the eyes of Islam and that even
children being inoculated was opposed, because it was considered
an act of converting them into Christians.[53]

There are extreme examples of how in some cases even the dead
were not spared from the wrath of the *mulla* and village elders.
One Akali Begum of a village in Thakurgaon district could not be
buried in the village graveyard as she had been sterilized by a Family
Planning clinic run by the government. The local *mulla* and the local
Union Council chairman felt that by undergoing a ligature operation,
the woman had defiled Islam and thus forefeited her right of burial
in the village graveyard.[54] Reportedly, in some areas *mullas* did not
approve of taking videos of wedding ceremonies. In one case, local
mullas 'imposed a fine' of 5000 taka on one villager in Chittagong
district for using videos to record a wedding in the family.[55]

However, there are also examples of *mullas* and their followers
being harassed and persecuted by pro-NGO villagers and government
officials. According to one newspaper report, Maulana Ibrahim of

Bogra, said to have organized an anti-Christian and anti-NGO organization, was severely beaten up by some villagers in the presence of police. One of them is reported to have pulled his beard telling him: 'shave off your beard, it is not suitable for the modern age'. Reportedly, the *maulana* and his followers were attacked by local BRAC workers as he was trying to organize an 'Islamic' micro-credit organization to provide interest-free credit to local villagers in Bogra district.[56]

Fatwas, secularism and political Islam

It is noteworthy that despite the government opposition to such *fatwa*-dispensing *mullas* and its taking firm action against some of them, 'pro-opposition' newspapers and intellectuals representing the so-called 'liberal-progressive' groups were highlighting even minor cases of disputes between a section of villagers with local *mullas* and village elders as 'examples of flagrant violation of human rights by *fatwabaz mullas*'. These *mullas*, at the same time, were being branded as 'anti-Bangladesh' or 'pro-Jamaat fundamentalists' throughout the period 1991–5, while Khaleda Zia of the BNP remained Prime Minister. While on the one hand, the vitriolic campaign against the *'fatwabaz mullas'* had an anti-Jamaat and pro-Awami League demeanour, on the other, it had a direct bearing on the campaign against the BNP government by the Opposition, led by Awami League leader Sheikh Hasina, who wanted to overthrow the government in the name of restoring 'democracy' in the country. The movement gained further momentum with the mass resignation of most opposition members of parliament in December 1994 and finally they succeeded in toppling the Government by organizing countrywide general strikes for months from early 1995 to early 1996.

It is noteworthy that although the Jamaat-i-Islami, a former ally of the BNP government during and after the parliamentary elections of 1991 (up to the arrest of its leader, Ghulam Azam, in 1992), was also demanding the resignation of Prime Minister Khaleda Zia and the holding of fresh elections under a caretaker government during 1995 and 1996, the 'liberal-progressive' opposition leaders and newspapers continued their tirade against Jamaat-i-Islami and other Islam-oriented groups. Many NGOs joined hands with them against their common enemy, the Jamaat and similar Islamic groups. As it appears from different 'opposition' newspaper reports and writings of many 'liberal-progressive' and 'feminist' writers, includ-

ing those of the controversial Taslima Nasreen, that NGOs quite
often fail to differentiate between the followers of Jamaat-i-Islami
and those of other political and non-political Islamic and quasi-
Islamic groups, it often becomes difficult to understand the real
nature of Islamic resurgence in Bangladesh.[57] The state of confu-
sion is further compounded by the hyperbolical and sensational
accounts of the situation given by many 'liberal progressive' writers
and newspapers, along with their over-simplified analyses of why
mullas and many villagers have been opposing 'women's liberation'
and NGO-Grameen activities in the countryside. Consequently some
mullas' pronouncements against Taslima Nasreen and some other
Bangladeshi writers, condemning them to 'death' for committing
'blasphemy' against Islam or 'renunciation of the faith' and the
persecution of rural women by *mullas* and their patrons-*cum*-followers
during 1991–5, have been broadly portrayed as by-products of Jamaat-
BNP politics of 'communalism' and their 'anti-Bangladesh' or
'pro-Pakistan' conspiracy. One renowned 'freedom-fighter', Colonel
Nuruzzaman, who had been at the fore-front of the anti-Jamaat
Ghatak-Dalal Nirmul Committee (Killer-Collaborator Elimination
Committee) to try Ghulam Azam and other 'collaborators' of the
Pakistani armed forces (during the Liberation War of 1971), even
sarcastically portrayed the BNP, the then ruling party, as 'Bangladesh
Now Pakistan' (instead of the Bangladesh Nationalist Party), for its
alleged 'pro-Jamaat' and 'pro-Pakistani' stand.[58] The late Ahmed Sharif,
a retired professor of Dhaka University and a leading 'leftist' intellectual, indicted by several *fatwas* for his 'blasphemous and
anti-Islamic' writings and statements in 1994, also felt that the BNP
government had been an 'idle spectator' of the 'reign of terror'
unleashed by the *mullas* of Bangladesh. He felt that *mullas* were
virtually running a 'parallel government' in the country and blamed
the BNP government for its indifference to the *mulla raj*.[59]

As cited earlier, the over-enthusiastic 'liberal' newspapers simply
blew up several minor incidents of *salish* cases (incriminating local
women) out of all proportions and with sheer subjectivity. Their
pronouncing every Tom, Dick and Harry as *'fatwabaz mulla'* for
their own political interest has been quite widespread. According
to one such report the police arrested six *'fatwabaz mullas'* in a
village in Bogra district in May 1995. These so-called *'fatwabaz'*
people were actually ordinary villagers who had been involved in
fighting over a minor religious issue, concerning the correct way of
slaughtering a sacrificial animal on the day of the *Qurbani* or Eid

ul-Azha. Villagers had apparently been divided over the issue – some suggesting that the head of the animal should be in the northern direction while others had been insisting that it should be in the southern direction.[60]

Similarly, there is hardly any reason to give credence to all such reports and assertions establishing a positive correlation between *mullas'* anti-Grameen and anti-NGO *fatwas* and their economic interests, said to have been adversely affected by the Grameen-NGO activities. It would be difficult to establish that *mullas* have been primarily opposing NGO-run schools, as they have been driving away potential *maktab* and *madrasah* students to the detriment of village *mullas* who are employed by such religious schools. Secular education through schools and colleges predates the advent of NGOs in the region by more than a hundred years. Since *mullas* and their followers did not set fire to secular schools during the British period and afterwards during the heyday of *mullas* (*pirs* and *maulanas*), it is difficult to understand why they should encourage such destructive acts in the 1990s. Traditionally schools and *madrasahs* in the region have had different clienteles, and there has hardly been any competition between the two educational systems. Many villagers send some of their children to schools and some others to *madrasahs* for various reasons. Again, as we know, village *mullas* (*imams* and *madrasah* teachers) are not powerful enough to motivate village elders and other villagers to attack NGO-run schools. Since village *mullas* are not patrons but rather clients of village elders (*members* and *matbars*) in the rural hierarchy, the latter, who mostly send their children to local schools rather than *madrasahs* for education, have no reason to destroy schools. While government and private schools (and colleges in some villages) are being patronized by villagers, why should they not also patronize NGO-run schools?

It also appears that mostly BRAC-run schools were targeted by *mullas* and their followers. The reasons are not far to seek. From various reports and empirical studies it appears that not only *mullas* but also ordinary villagers do not approve of adolescent girls attending co-educational institutions and the mingling of the sexes in NGO-run projects in the countryside.[61] Another important aspect of BRAC schools is that more than 70 per cent of the students are girls, who again, do not attend *madrasahs*. So, the main reason why *mullas* have been opposed to BRAC schools is not an economic but a socio-cultural and religious one. Had economic factors been the main reasons behind *mullas'* objection to the Grameen-

NGO lobby, they would not have issued *fatwas* against some 'liberal-progressive' writers and those poor female victims of the *salish*, who had nothing to do with NGOs or any activity adversely affecting the *mullas'* economic interests.

Against this backdrop, it appears that the discourse on persecution of rural women by *mullas* and their associates becomes quite problematic if one relies only on the 'liberal-progressive' media and intellectuals of Bangladesh. It is necessary to fathom the grassroots reaction to the Grameen-NGO activities in the countryside, especially with regard to the involvement of women in such activities. With or without the *mulla* being present at the scene, villagers who have strong reservations about Muslim women working in close proximity to unrelated men would have reacted against NGOs who do not segregate the sexes. We should not lose sight of the average villager's anger and helplessness *vis-à-vis* what may be seen as the sugar-coated exploitative endeavours of the Grameen Bank and NGOs in the sporadic and disorganized movements against these organizations, sponsored and run by non-peasant outsiders. It is not difficult to decipher the 'hidden transcript' (to paraphrase James Scott) of the peasant who has been trying to get rid of the newly emerging mode of exploitation of labour by capital through the over-touted Grameen Bank and NGOs. One may cite the following couplet from a song composed by one villager (not a *mulla*) in Bogra district which reflects lower peasants' opposition to the Grameen-NGO activities in the village:

> *East India Company keno deshey?*
> *Yunus Abedi anchchey dekey.*

[Why has the East India Company arrived again? Because Yunus (of the Grameen Bank) and Abed (of the BRAC) have invited them in our country.][62]

The portrayal of NGOs and Grameen Bank as foreign agents is also used by some urban *ulama*, along with rural bards and leftist intellectuals. Mufti Fazlul Haq Amini, 'a leading fundamentalist *maulana* (religious teacher)' of the capital city, considered their activities as 'unnatural and insidious', especially with regard to their involving rural women in their projects. According to him, they were like the East India Company of Britain, who come to do business 'but stayed to become our rulers. They must be driven from the country'.[63] The *mufti*, it seems narrated a story of a woman in Bangladesh, who had to sell her gold nose ring as she could not repay her loan to the Grameen Bank and consequently 'this brought disgrace upon her family' and her 'embarrassed husband' had committed suicide.[64] The *mufti* is said to have told a Western journalist from *Time* magazine that the Grameen Bank had turned 'modest' rural women of Bangladesh 'unruly'.[65]

Without contesting his views or authenticating the source of this information about 'the embarrassed husband' said to have committed suicide, one may perceive why *muftis* like this man and other members of the traditional elites and their followers have been apprehensive in the event of a total replacement of traditional (both Islamic and pre-capitalist) values by those of the modern age. This, however, does not mean that the inherent conflict of interests between the traditional and modern elites and elements of class antagonism should be undermined because of the many allusions to people, things and events, as appear in the anti-NGO discourse of the *ulama* and their followers.

It is noteworthy that some empirical studies have revealed that villagers in several districts burnt down NGO-run schools not at the incitement of *mullas* but at the behest of teachers of government-run primary schools, said to have been losing students to NGO-run schools. It also appears that NGOs have alienated village elders and others who have vested interests in fallow land belonging to the Government (*khas* land). They did not want these tracts under mulberry plantation (for the silk industry) under the aegis of NGOs with local women as their clients. Consequently influential villagers having an eye on these lands incited villagers to uproot mulberry plants in several places in the countryside. The findings of these reports are very different from the pro-NGO newspaper reports.[66]

The clash of cultures: elite conflict in a peasant economy

A reappraisal of the underlying conflict of interests between the Grameen-NGO lobby and the traditional elite (both urban and rural) establishes that while the former group has been trying to establish the predominance of capitalist relations in the 'transitional society' of Bangladesh, the latter has been resisting this transformation with a view to going back to the 'traditional society' of peasant economy with more or less unchanging production relations and methodology. Rostow's model of 'the stages of economic growth' is quite helpful in understanding the stages Bangladesh has been going through for quite some time. The application of Rostow's model also helps us understand the stage of the economy and the corresponding level of socio-political culture of Bangladesh.

According to this model, there are five stages of economic growth: (1) traditional; (2) transitional; (3) the 'take off' stage; (4) the 'drive to maturity' and (5) the age of high mass consumption. While in the 'traditional' stage the economy is mainly agricultural, having more or less unchanging production methodology; the 'transitional' stage connotes the phase when due to external influences, either through elites or disadvantaged groups, the possibility of economic progress is recognized. In the 'take off' stage, there is high economic growth and per capita income due to rising investment, changes in production techniques and institutional changes; the 'drive to maturity' stage is said to be attained when 10–20 per cent of national income is derived from the application of modern technology and when output exceeds population growth and old values are replaced by modern ones; and stage 5 when real income goes up to such an extent that people spend a lot on consumer goods and services and resources are allocated to social welfare and the security of the people.[67] Rostow's classification of societies on the basis of the stages of economic growth indicates that Bangladesh has not yet reached the 'take off' stage and that the 'drive to maturity' and the age of high mass consumption are not attainable in the near future. However, one must not disregard the inter-regional and inter-class differences with regard to production methodology and the consumption patterns of the people. The gulf between the rural and urban sectors, and the contrast between the traditional/transitional stage of the economy and 'the age of high mass consumption' (attained by a small section of the urban population) are quite visible in the country.

Parsons divided social evolution into the Primitive, Advanced Primitive, Intermediate and Modern stages.[68] From his classification of societies on the basis of social evolution, the bulk of the population of Bangladesh may be categorized as representatives of the Advanced Primitive culture, while a tiny minority has been on the threshold of the Modern stage.

It seems, the process of socio-economic changes gradually transforming Bangladesh society from pre-modern to modern and its economy from pre-capitalist to capitalist, has been due partially to historical reasons and partially to external factors. What we have been witnessing in the anti-NGO campaigns of *mullas* and their supporters is partially the reflection of the clash of cultures – conflict between the adherents of pre-modern/pre-capitalist and modern/capitalist ways of life. The waning influence of traditional elites and the loss of monopolistic control of leadership and ownership of the means of production have also aggravated the situation. One may agree with the view that 'modernization theorists' often fail to understand that what they decry as 'parochial and primordial values' could be very dear to the 'traditional' people, and consequently there is resistance to modernism from traditional elites. Many 'modernists' fail to see that the secular and rational may benefit some groups in society much more than other. It is quite pertinent to our understanding of the conflict between *mullas* and the Grameen-NGO lobby, that modernization theory could appear 'elitist and in contrast to the experience of the masses'. Modernists' depiction of religion 'as a less real' ideology is problematic as religion has remained 'a source of popular mobilisation, alternative notions of legitimacy, resistance and even insurrection' in many developing countries.[69] Secularization of society by elites is often resented by Muslims in various countries, as materialism and immorality are associated with modernism and secularism. Last but not least, we may agree with the view that 'there may be very "modern" reasons, such as economic exploitation or political discrimination, for conflict between groups identified by reference to "traditional" attributes and perceptions'.[70]

As discussed earlier, the nature and extent of the apparent Grameen-NGO exploitation and their selection of women and Christians (in the case of some NGOs) as the main beneficiaries of their projects have created tension in the village community, owing to misgivings about the short- and long-term impacts of these extraneous organizations on the culture, traditions and economy of the people; nor should the underlying elements of class conflict and 'peasant wars' in the anti-Grameen and anti-NGO sentiment of ordinary villagers be forgotten. The incidence of violent attacks on NGO properties is reminiscent of such attacks on village moneylenders by indebted peasants of the region under the leadership of local and itinerant *mullas* in the 1930s and 1940s.[71] Bangladeshi *mullas* in the 1990s are not very different from their counterparts in the first half of the century. With their plebeian backgrounds and solidarity with the masses, *mullas* in both periods fought well against what they saw as 'enemies of Islam' and 'agents of exploitation' often with selfless dedication and zeal.

Village elders' anti-Grameen and anti-NGO feelings are not necessarily reflective of their fiendish nature and misogynous exposition. They do not always represent the rich and landed classes in the village. Economically, they are much weaker than the newly emerging rural elites which have links with urban areas, NGOs or those villagers who work abroad as expatriate workers. Although they retain some influence over ordinary villagers, traditional village elders have been worried about their waning influence and economic clout due to the advent of NGOs in the countryside. With the substantial diversion of foreign donors' aid to the NGO channel in the recent past, village elders who have been serving as 'gatekeepers for the influx of national and international resources into the rural areas and control access to local resources',[72] have been hard hit. Hence their opposition to NGOs and the Grameen Bank.

This, however, does not mean that village elders do not share the *mullas'* and other villagers' concern about the involvement of rural women in the Grameen-NGO activities, which violate the norms of their tradition and popular Islam. So far as trials of women by the *salish* court under the aegis of the village elder are concerned, there is nothing striking about these other than the wide publicity they receive in local and national press. Western government media, aid agencies and human rights groups have shown a post-Cold War tendency to point a finger at Islam as the adversary of the West, and this is also responsible for such wide publicity of *salish* courts' persecution of poor women in remote villages of Bangladesh, as these courts dispense 'justice' in the name of *Sharia* or Islamic law. The recent phenomenal growth in the number of newspapers and periodicals in Bangladesh, which has more than 200 dailies, and the development of telecommunications are also responsible for the wide coverage of such sensational news about the persecution of poor women by village *mullas* and their associates. As we have seen, 'opposition' newspapers had been too eager to publish such news, often with exaggerations, in order to undermine the BNP government, projecting it as the benefactor of 'Islamic fundamentalism'.

The discourse on the persecution of Bangladeshi women in the name of Islam not only exposes the feud between the 'liberal-secular' and 'Islam-oriented' groups, respectively represented by the Awami League and BNP, but also highlights how the new world order of the post-Cold War era has emerged as the champion of 'human rights' and 'women's rights' (if not feminism), especially in Muslim countries. Consequently while 'human rights/women's rights in danger' and 'Islam in danger' have become the popular slogans of the rival groups (both globally, and locally in the context of Bangladesh, for example), both women and Islam have emerged as the new scapegoats of the 'post-modern' era. Meanwhile, what might be seen as the exploitation of cheap labour of women by NGOs, garment factories and others, has failed to emerge as an issue of grave concern in the main stream of (Western) human rights literature, alongside its *'mulla*-bashing' vitriols.

One wonders why the fact that village-elders and *mullas* (along with other upholders of Islamic tradition) have reservations about Muslim women's working side by side with men, in accordance with the ethos of the institution of *purdah,* should become such an important issue, when strict *purdah*, as observed in post-*Taliban* Afghanistan, Iran or Saudi Arabia, has never been imposed in Bangladesh. Since *purdah* has been a symbol of respectability, the *izzat* or honour and dignity of Muslim women, anyone suggesting that it is useless is most likely to encounter adverse reaction from Muslim villagers, even the poor who cannot afford to keep their women in *purdah*. Consequently after the creation of Bangladesh, 'the interpretation and the observance of *purdah'* have become quite different from that of the 1960s, as war, famine, landlessness, inflation and unemployment have forced women to seek employment outside their homes.[73] It is, however, noteworthy that while all sections of villagers, including *mullas*, have accepted the reality, turning a blind eye to poor women working outside for subsistence, the Grameen Bank and NGOs must have gone 'too far' in their pursuit of 'liberating women' to antagonize *mullas* and many villagers.

The 'persecution' of women through the *salish* is also a reflection of the ongoing, universal conflict between 'community' and 'society' or *gemeinschaft* and *gesellschaft*, as defined by Ferdinand Tonnies in his seminal work, *Gemeinschaft und Gesellschaft*. Robert Redfield may also be cited in this context. His 'folk society' is very similar to the village community of Bangladesh, which is also 'isolated, nonliterate, homogenous grouping with a strong sense of solidarity having simple technology', and where group members do not question 'traditional acts and objects . . . hence they are sacred'. In accordance with Durkheim and Tonnies, Redfield also thinks that the 'folk society' is the polar opposite of the urban society,[74] and so much so that, Tonnies feels, someone who travels from *gemeinschaft* (village community) to *gesellschaft* (urban society) is effectively going 'into a strange country'.[75] It is interesting that in *geimenschaft* (like the village community in the region of our study) women remain 'confined to the inner circle of home life', and that there are three types of authority in the community – authority of age, force and wisdom or spirit – but 'the authority of wisdom surpasses all others as sacredotal authority'. Since kinship is very important in the formation of the village community and within kinship 'all natural authority' is concentrated in 'paternal authority', women perpetually remain subservient to men and confined to home. 'No reason to go out can ever be as good as the reason to stay in', is the norm for women in *gemeinschaft*.[76]

What is pertinent to our understanding is that *gemeinschaft* promotes isolation, which leads to fixation of habit and neophobia. This fear leads to the resistance of all attempts to transform the 'community' into a 'society' and 'possibly nothing is more characteristic and important in the process of formation of the Gesellschaft and destruction of Gemeinschaft than women earning their own living'.[77] It is interesting that Tonnies' analysis of why women in the *gemeinschaft* commit suicide is useful to our understanding of why some persecuted rural women commit suicide in Bangladesh. He ascribes this to rural women's concept of shame and its relationship to fear and anger.[78]

Conclusions

In sum, this discourse on the persecution of rural women through the *salish*, with *mullas* playing the role of 'belligerent judges' in association with village elders and ordinary villagers, claiming to establish pure Islam, remains incomplete without comprehending what people at the grassroots feel about the whole thing. The harsh treatment of women, and especially their persecution in the name of 'Islamic' justice, are actually reflections of how the ordinary peasant, the *narod* or the 'untainted folk', behaves as a judge and he alone preserves the essence of the folk tradition 'in all its purity', like his Russian counterpart in the nineteenth century.[79] From the behaviour of *salish* judges, who mainly represent the *narod* culture of Bangladesh, hardly anything Islamic about the judgements can be found. It is interesting that peasants as judges in nineteenth-century Russia through their verdicts left 'evidence of the arbitrary, illegal, and

primitive nature of the peasant's approach to law'. One finds striking similarities between the nineteenth-century Russian and
late-twentieth-century Bangladeshi peasant behaviour *vis-à-vis* law
and women. Very similar to Bangladesh, 'frequency of corporal
punishment as a sentence, *especially when the guilty party was a woman*
[emphasis added]', was the norm in Russia. 'The preference for flogging
over fines and arrest pointed to the peasant's bestiality. . . . the peasant
judged cases less according to the evidence before him than according to his and the community's longstanding acquaintance with
the accused', reveals one study on Russia.[80] In view of this, it would
be unfair to put the blame on the shoulders of the *mulla*, implicat-
ing him solely in the acts of persecution of women in the name of
Islam, while (as in Russia) mundane factors and ordinary people
played the vital roles in the offensives against women, NGOs and
other perceived adversaries of the village community.

Last but not least, a proper evaluation of the so-called *mulla*-
women and *mulla*-NGO conflicts demands an appreciation of the
period (1990–5) in Bangladeshi society and politics, when:

1 Islam had already become the 'state religion'.
2 BNP and Jamaat-i-Islami were co-operating with each other and
   the BNP was installed to power with the tacit support of the
   Jamaat in 1991.
3 The leading anti-Jamaat forces held a public trial of Jamaat leader,
   Ghulam Azam, in 1992.
4 The polity was sharply polarized between pro-BNP and pro-Awami
   League, 'pro-Islam' and 'pro-secularism' respectively.
5 Many NGOs openly sided with the 'secular' groups.
6 Taslima Nasreen and some other writers provoked Islam-oriented
   groups and many Bangladeshi Muslims.
7 Jamaat-i-Islami and other Islamic groups were organizing themselves as an alternative force.

Against this background, one may regard the incidents of attacks
on NGOs and persecution of rural women as symbols of the inevitable
conflict between Islam (both political and popular) and 'secular'-
cum-ultra nationalist forces, mainly represented by the Awami League
and some like-minded groups. However, as some observers have
assessed, the *fatwabaz-mullas* and other opponents of women-
liberation simply cannot retard the process of 'liberation'; their ag-
gression is like the 'last flicker of the dying flame'.[81] It may be
concluded that 'Islamic' forces and other opponents of the Grameen-
NGO lobby and 'women liberation', seem to have lost the first round

of the bout to the 'liberal-secular' groups, backed by the Grameen-NGO lobby and their local and non-local patrons, but it is too early to say if the latter would continue to dominate.

Meanwhile one may surmise, poor Bangladeshi women, especially those working for NGOs, garment factories and Grameen Bank, will continue to suffer, not as victims of *fatwas* but as underpaid wage labourers and recipients of microcredit at exorbitantly high interest rates albeit in the name of 'empowerment of the poor women'. By late 1998 the dormant *mulla*-NGO conflict had again been activated by various Islamic groups. The Jamaat-i-Islami and the ultra-orthodox *Islami Oikko Jote* (Islamic United Front) have been in the forefront. In late 1996, these groups had jumped on the BNP bandwagon to topple the 'anti-Islamic', 'pro-India' and 'pro-NGO' government of Sheikh Hasina. Hence the revival of the anti-NGO movement. In December 1998 these groups attacked NGOs at Brahmanbaria (150 kilometres east of Dhaka). On 25 September 1999, they gave an ultimatum to all NGOs in the district to wind up their activities. Otherwise, they threatened to launch a civil disobedience movement from 20 October 1999.[82]

5
NGOs and Empowerment of Women: Some Problematic Prognoses

The real frustration comes from knowing that despite all the les-
sons learned we had managed to change nothing in the conditions
of the impoverished women there [rural Bangladesh].
                                          Ciba-Geigy Foundation

Can you really fight the whole society, Chachiamma [auntie]? I
somehow do not think you will win. This social order has been
there for thousands of years, like an old banyan tree which has
stretched its roots deep into the earth. Storms will not be able to
uproot it. The only way is to cut the tree down. Can you do that?
                                          A Bangladeshi village woman

Introduction

'Empowerment' is a loaded concept, suggesting a process as well as
an accomplished stage in human civilization where people are entitled to certain rights, having the licence and freedom to do things
in accordance with their desire or free will to improve, change or
modify the prevalent socio-political and economic order. Since this
sort of power and freedom of the individual are only attainable in
a civil society, where the rule of law and socio-political (if not economic) egalitarianism are well-established, Bangladesh, along with
scores of other Third World countries, does not provide the proto-
type of a society promoting equal opportunities and rights for
everyone. While the average Bangladeshi man lives below poverty
line and a few thousand members of the civil and military oligarchy

134

govern in the name of different brands of nationalism, democracy and even socialism, whilst upholding patriarchy and an urban bias, the notion of empowerment of women, especially in rural areas, seems quite out of place. Generally, the empowerment of women is conceived in terms of their 'growing self-confidence' and 'ability to act' or power to do, rather than women 'taking power' from ('having power over') men.[1]

However, despite the incongruity of the notion of empowerment of women with regard to Bangladesh, many local and foreign observers think that since the 'discovery of women' in Bangladesh by Western donors during the tenure of General Ziaur Rahman (1975–1981), 'women's issues' have become tagged to 'development issues'.[2] Consequently it may be argued that the pace of development has accelerated the process of empowerment of women in Bangladesh. Since NGOs started taking interest in the promotion of women's rights not long after the emergence of Bangladesh as a state, they think that as the 'harbingers' of democracy and civil society in Bangladesh,[3] they may also share the credit of helping the process of empowerment of women in the region. By now there are more than a thousand local and foreign NGOs in Bangladesh, many of them with close links to the grassroots in rural areas through their development projects such as schools, training centres, clinics, credit centres and other organizations oriented towards growth and development.

This constitutes an attempt to correlate rural women's participation in various NGO-sponsored activities at the grassroots level with the perceived notion of 'empowerment process' of these women in Bangladesh. Although the Grameen Bank is not an NGO as it is partially financed by the Government, its activities may be evaluated, especially with regard to providing credit to rural women, in juxtaposition with some NGOs engaged in not-so-dissimilar activities, dealing with the same 'target group', the rural poor. This book is not, however, a comprehensive study of all NGOs *vis-à-vis* their growth-, production- and development-oriented activities among the poor rural women in the region.

NGOs as mobilizers of women

The proliferation of NGOs in the region took place in the wake of the emergence of Bangladesh in 1971. Most of them came into being with the blessing of foreign donors who actively took part in rebuilding the war-ravaged economy and socio-political structure of the country. At the outset, we must bear in mind that unlike most Indian NGOs, those in Bangladesh and the widely acclaimed Grameen Bank have been financed by overseas aid agencies and governments. In short, their success or failure in eradicating poverty, especially raising the status of rural poor women in the region, are not different from those of any country perpetually dependent on foreign aid. Let us see what some experts and observers of some leading NGOs, such as the BRAC, *Proshika*, *Nijera Kori* and the Grameen Bank, have to say in this regard.

From the keen observations of one foreign scholar, Martha Chen, we learn that by the mid-1980s rural women's groups, organized by the BRAC (Bangladesh Rural Advancement Committee), in certain districts learnt how to improve their lot by defying the conservative and reactionary village elders and *mullas*. Their defiance is reflected in the following assertion of a group of poor rural women in a village in Jamalpur district:

> Before we were scared to talk to any outsider. Now we talk freely. We can write our names. . . . We have learned how to keep accounts, grow vegetables, rear poultry. . . . we eat thrice a day, wear good clothes, go to the cinema, send our children to school. . . . Before we were illiterate and could not talk with others. . . . If we go to other houses they give us chair to sit on. If there is a wedding, they call us.[4]

We further learn that these 'free' and organized rural women groups live in a society, thanks to the BRAC programme, almost free from conflicts, misery and suffering – nothing short of one's perceived utopia. It seems revolutionary changes have taken place in villages under the supervision of the BRAC. According to some of these women:

> If any member of the group goes hungry, we give them rice as loan to be returned later. . . . No member goes hungry. . . . Before there were quarrels among the villagers. . . . But now we keep ourselves busy with work and do not have time for quarrels. . . . Now everyone's things are the group's things. If anything is lost, then we feel for each other.[5]

Although the BRAC-sponsored women groups' accounts sound too good to be true, there is no denying that economically independent rural women are more assertive and free than those perpetually dependent on their husbands and other male members of the family for sustenance. However, this newly found independence of rural women has not been accepted gracefully by all the male villagers. Village elders and *mullas* have been their main adversaries. These groups of male villagers may be brought under the broad category of the *member-matbar-mulla* triumvirate.

The *members* of the Union Parishad (the lowest electoral unit) are elected officials, in charge of the disbursement of public goods and relief materials among the poor villagers, are the most powerful in the triumvirate. They are often connected with the ruling political party or other influential power-brokers in the neighbouring towns or group of villages. The *matbars* (*matabbars*) or village elders, who also sit on the *salish* (village court), are next in the hierarchy, having vested interests in the village economy as rentiers and moneylenders. They often get shares in misappropriated relief goods along with government officials and *members-chairmen* of the Union Perishads. The *mulla*, associated with the local mosques and *maktabs* (elementary religious schools), are sometimes quite influential as they endorse the activities of village elders albeit in the name of Islamic or *Sharia* law. They often sit on the *salish* and issue *fatwas* in support of their patrons, the village elders. The rural poor, often women, are victims of these *fatwas*.

Some BRAC-sponsored women's groups have pointed out how the *member-matbar-mulla* triumvirate, as their patron, used to advise and control rural women (and men), especially when the latter needed loans, food, work and security. These groups of women have also indicated how under the influence of the BRAC, gradually the rich and powerful in the villages have begun to lose control over their clients as women have become self-reliant and independent. Nevertheless, they have pointed out, the rich and powerful in the villages have been interfering in the affairs of the women while at the same time the latter have been resisting such meddlesomeness on the part of the triumvirate.[6] In some areas, *mullas* and other conservative elements have been spreading anti-NGO rumours, focusing on the religious consequences of women's participation in NGO activities. The women are accused of being *be-purdah* (without *purdah* or seclusion) and the BRAC is accused of spreading Christianity and promiscuity in society as men and women have been working in close proximity to each other in NGO projects. Sometimes the *mullas* spread rumours that the NGOs are secretly recruiting local women to work as maids in the Middle East. Village elders and *mullas* have also been threatening women NGO workers with banishment from society or total ostracism. In case female NGO workers do not stop talking to men on the street or going out of their homestead, village elders threatened: 'You will not be allowed to take water from the tubewell. If you go into the field, your legs will be broken'. *Mullas* often threatened that female NGO workers would be denied religious services at birth, marriage and death ceremonies and that *mullas* would not pray for their salvation. The threat of trying the 'disobedient' women through the *salish* courts has been another mode of intimidation.[7]

Some empirical studies suggest that organized village women-groups successfully resisted the anti-NGO forces in certain sub-regions in the 1980s and that rich villagers have been annoyed with NGOs for restricting the supply of cheap female workers to work for them by providing them alternative employment opportunities. However, it also appears that many poor rural women have been hesitant to join NGO groups, apprehending ostracism from village elders.[8] In some extreme cases, however, instead of being intimidated by such threats, some women's groups, with NGO support, resisted the village elders, defying verdicts of the *salish*-courts and even holding their own *salish*. Some of these assertive women did not even wait for their male guardians to 'represent' them in the *salish* run by local village elders.[9]

Besides the BRAC, some other NGOs, such as the Rangpur Dinajpur Rural Service Programme (RDRS) and the *Gonoshangathan* (People's Organization), for example, have also made villagers, both men and women, assertive enough to organize their own *salish* or arbitration courts to settle disputes within their communities. In some cases, rapists are forced to pay compensations to their victims. However, in general, influential villagers are beyond the reach of NGO-sponsored grassroots groups and organizations. According to one observer, female groups organized by NGOs are mostly very preoccupied with economic hardship, and are often abandoned by their husbands when a dowry is not forthcoming, and NGOs are hardly effective in abolishing the institution of dowry which, according to Bangladesh law, is illegal.[10] There are, however, cases where women organized by BRAC workers have asserted that they would not allow their husbands to marry for a second time. One group of rural women asserted: 'We will not allow that. Already he has got a wife, so why should he marry again? The way we will punish him, he will give up notions of marrying again. We will also call a "*shalish*".'

When asked 'are not *shalish* convened by the men?' they replied: 'A women's *shalish* will be convened by women. And from now on, we will hold our own *shalish*.'[11]

Rural Bangladeshi women, organized by NGOs like BRAC, are no longer fatalist and subservient to the village *matbars*, chairmen and *mullas*. Many of them are defying village elders and elites who seek their votes in local and national elections. It seems these organized women are aware of the hollowness of pre-election promises made by candidates and many of them do not cast their votes at all. There is a growing class consciousness and alienation from the village elders and elites who manipulate and rig elections and exploit the poor. Some of them portray all the rich as 'bad', expressing their liking for the fellow poor villagers only. When asked how they have learned to be so assertive they simply reply: 'Words come from the stomach.' They also revealed that this awareness was due to their exposure to the BRAC. It is noteworthy that under the influence of NGOs many illiterate women have acquired the courage to speak to the local village councils. One woman was found addressing the council in the presence of the President of Bangladesh who was visiting her village. In short, as a result of NGO activities, women in rural areas have acquired knowledge about their rights and how these have been violated by rural elders who eat up the bulk of the relief materials meant for the poor, and deprive them of medicine and health care at local clinics. Some of them have also gathered the courage to challenge the rural superordinates. They openly admit that they have become wiser than before and that previously they were 'blind', although they had eyes, since they used to work for others without getting the 'correct wages'. With the coming of NGOs in rural areas women have become confident and brave enough to challenge the local agents of exploitation. One of them has explained that after joining the NGO group organized by BRAC, she has learnt what is right and wrong now. 'Now, if anyone says anything wrong I answer back, before I used to keep quiet. Where did I get my courage? From my self-confidence and wisdom', one of them asserted.[12] It seems NGOs have made them not only brave and confident but also taught them how to take initiatives to become self-reliant and independent.

A number of examples may be cited of poor rural women be-coming independent only after coming into contact with certain NGOs, who either provided them with credit or other means to become self-reliant. It is also instructive to juxtapose Bangladeshi villages without any NGO activities against those exposed to NGOs. Let us first look into the findings of some fieldwork done in villages with NGOs within their perimeters. According to an observer:

> Prior to joining BRAC many of the women had worked on either Food for Work Programmes or in others' houses, or both. Now, most were economically independent and managed well. Many of the women had obtained several loans. . . . One impressive case was a woman who had established a restaurant with BRAC loans. . . . This particular woman had recently arranged the marriage of her 18-year-old daughter to the son of a BRAC member in another village. The marriage was arranged without dowry. . . . One example is a woman abandoned by her husband . . . with a loan . . . has started a chicken business (rearing chicken). . . . to quote one women member: 'We are no longer harassed by our husbands. They cannot do what they want, because they are dependent on us for BRAC loans and our earnings. Through our strength *(shakti)* we can bargain with our husbands'.[13]

In several cases, owing to NGO involvement, poor rural men and women have succeeded in getting lease of *khas* land (government land) for tree plantation and cultivation. They also learn from some NGOs who provide legal aid about their legal rights, including minimum wage laws, rights to *khas* land, and about contracts, marriage, divorce, inheritance, and so on. Some of the NGOs pro-vide legal advice at a nominal fee (25 per cent of legal costs) to poor villagers. In one case, agricultural workers, who had been members of the *Gonoshangathan* group, went on a strike against rich peasants during the harvest season in order to increase their wages. The *Gonoshangathan* has even succeeded in returning candi-dates nominated by its members in local Union Parishad elections. However, traditional rural elites reacted violently against those poor villagers who worked for NGO-sponsored candidates in local elec-tions at various places.[14]

Despite this, there is no reason to believe that massive NGO-involvement in the 'voters' education programme' and 'poll monitoring' process throughout the country, during and before local and national elections, has significantly influenced the election results. One can hardly agree with the view that a number of NGOs played 'a significant role in these elections through voter education'.[15] What NGOs have achieved with regard to women's participation in local council elections does not go beyond nominating some women as candidates in the local council elections. Every local council or Union Parishad has three reserved elected posts for women members. In the 1997 Union Parishad elections in the rural areas, only about 10 per cent of the seats were won by poor men and women belonging to NGO-organized groups.[16] Out of 700 elected women members, around 38 per cent were NGO members. In many places women voters were not allowed to enter polling centres by local followers of *fatwa*-dispensing *ulama* and local NGOs and women's groups could not do anything about it.[17] This simply means that village elders have remained dominant in most villages under the age-old patron-client relationship. Only about 10 per cent of the contestants for the position of chairman in Union Parishads were linked to NGOs, in the 1997 elections.[18] Another study reveals that NGOs' 'voters education programme' did not contribute to the failure of Jamaat-i-Islami candidates in the 1996 parliamentary elections either. This empirical study reveals that only about 1 per cent of female voters blamed the Jamaat for its activities against the women development programmes. The Jamaat defeat is attributed to the disunity in the rightist camp. According to the study, NGOs had 'no influence' on the voters 'to vote for or against any candidate or party during the 1996 elections'.[19] Yet another study reveals that, 'NGOs' experience in grassroots democratization has not been very encouraging', and that 'despite all propaganda' their success has ramained 'rather limited'.[20]

Despite certain setbacks, NGOs in general have been successfully mobilizing rural women in different income-oriented pursuits by providing credit and job-opportunities albeit not on the best of terms. Consequently there has been substantial growth in the self-esteem among rural women who traditionally have an inferior position and passive role in the community. As Westergaard says, the upshot of NGO activities is that:

> Women walk freely outside their homesteads, and even outside their own villages. They no longer hesitate to engage in economic activities which expose them to strangers, and their increased income have improved their position within the family. Group

strength and solidarity within the women's groups have also resulted in a number of marriages being arranged without dowry. In some places, the women have become active in local level politics.[21]

One gets a similar picture of Bangladeshi rural women as the epitome of power, defiance and authority with regard to the superordinate groups in the village, from some foreign journalists' accounts. According to one such report, some low-paid female workers who had been engaged in rock-breaking, hammering away at rocks from morning to evening at construction sites, started asserting their rights for higher wages and defying *mullas* and village elders thanks to their exposure to *Nijera Kori* and other NGOs in Comilla district. 'Within the space of only a few years', the report reveals,

> the Comilla group has produced some startling results. Women got pay rise after setting road-blocks. . . . When they address a mullah . . . they do so with their backs to him. They now vote at elections, and organise their voting strategy in such a way that the mayor is forced to heed their views.[22]

We also learn from the same report that under the influence of NGOs, by mid-1995 women throughout Bangladesh had become assertive enough to defy patriarchy and *mullas* and that 'hundreds of Taslima Nasreens' had emerged everywhere in the country.[23] Before we agree with or refute such hyperbolical assertions, it may be useful to examine the prevalent situation with regard to the power and status of rural women whether or not exposed to NGO activities.

Are NGOs really empowering women?

It is not certain whether the poor women engaged in rock-breaking at construction sites at bare subsistence, or those slogan-chanting, poor borrowers of the Grameen Bank, BRAC or other NGOs, who attend weekly meetings in public places have been equally 'empowered'! The problem seems to be the way the term 'empowerment' has been defined both by Western journalists and by some Bangladeshi scholars. Hashemi and Schuler's view, that those poor women who attend public meetings, interact with male members of the society and raise slogans 'deviate from traditional norms' of Bangladeshi rural society, may be a reasonable one, but not the idea that by merely controlling their loans, taken from various microcredit institutions, these women have attained 'empowerment' and freedom from patriarchy. Most women borrowers, again, have no control over their loans and are totally dependent on male members of their families.[24]

One may well imagine the situation in the post-independence period when Western commodities flooded the market and the country was almost solely dependent on foreign aid: the bulk of the aid was intercepted (to paraphrase van Schendel) by 'primary surplus-takers' with state patronage. These groups of government officials, rich peasants and political workers, 'well-organized at the supra-village level, rarely faced concerted opposition to their extractive activities', and on the contrary 'were often seen as crucial defenders of the village political brokers, sources of credit and legitimisers of local custom'.[25] Consequently while the government has been more dependent on foreign aid and less dependent upon rural surplus by distancing itself from the rural order without withdrawing its support from the rural and urban 'surplus-takers', there has been further pauperization of the rural masses as a vicious circle of under-development and conflict over the surplus sealed their fate.[26] The traditional rural elite – the *member-matbar-mulla* triumvirate – may have started facing opposition from the newly emerging NGO-sponsored groups, but this simply signifies the emergence of a new conflict between old and new rural elites, which van Schendel has classified as the conflict between different groups of 'surplus-takers' inherent in the rural class structure of the region.[27] Throughout its recent history this conflict has often been misconstrued as the class struggle of the proletariat when in fact, the lower echelons of the rural society can do no more than take sides on behalf of the old or new 'surplus-takers', in the name of achieving their cherished goals.[28]

Although it is often claimed that with the arrival of NGOs a new dawn has emerged in the mental horizon of rural women as they began asserting their rights, it is equally true that even before the emergence of NGOs in the region many women harboured deep feelings of discontent against tradition, patriarchy and exploitations, as some scholars have observed:

> Whether a woman expresses these feelings or stifles them depends not only on her personality but also on the circumstances of her life. With less to lose, poor women are often more willing

to break with tradition. Economic necessity forces poor... to move beyond the village, and the resulting knowledge that they can operate without the protection of men gives them a strength which other women lack.[29]

It seems that, like rural men, rural women from peasant families only need an assurance from some quarter that they can operate without the protection of their patrons. NGOs in many cases have been providing this assurance to them. Contrary to the general assumption, poor rural women in Bangladesh go beyond asking the question, 'What did you cook today?' to other women. 'They regularly help each other in their work, cutting vegetables, husking rice or stitching a quilt while discussing the day's events. . . . they soon move beyond talk of rice and curry to deeper issues: village quarrels, marital disputes, scarcity of work and food'. Occasionally, their meetings erupt into spontaneous song and dance, observe Hartmann and Boyce. We also learn from them (and various other sources) how poor rural women rush to distressed women to offer solace and even sometimes join together to protect a friend from the brutal beating of her husband. However, fearing harsh retribution from men 'as they lack an independent means of livelihood and a broader social movement to back them', women only respond to male domination with small acts of self-assertion or, in extreme cases, 'by recourse to the ultimate weapon of suicide'.[30]

The Helplessness of Rural Women

Suicides by victims of rape, *salish* courts and the persecution of husbands or in-laws are quite common throughout the region. Poor married women's total dependence on their husbands and parents-in-law, leading to their utter hopelessness, is mainly responsible for their committing suicide. One young married woman sums up the situation quite succinctly:

> If I don't obey my husband or father-in-law, they will give divorce without further question. They threaten that they will send me to my father's place. If I go there my father will marry me again. They won't let me stay there forever. So I have to listen to all that they say.[31]

Poor rural women's state of helplessness in the region may be further comprehended by understanding the state of helplessness of their male counterparts, who in general, are dominant over women. Several studies of credit relations, transfer of land and the share-cropping system in Bangladesh have highlighted the situation of perpetual dependence of the rural poor on their rich patrons – rich peasants, moneylenders and absentee landlords.

Despite the abolition of the *zamindari* system (landlordism) in the region in the early 1950s, semi-feudal patron-client relation-ship, absentee landlordism, the sharecropping system under which 50 per cent of the yield is extracted by the landowner, and a usu-rious moneylending system which often leads to the perpetual indebtedness of the poor borrowers are still prevalent throughout the country. Sometimes the well-to-do supplier of credit with 'con-trol' over his client not only imposes strict conditions on the debtor but may also demand a piece of land on mortgage terms and even evict the debtor from his holdings. Creditors quite often mould political behaviour, including the voting pattern of their debtors. Sometimes rich landowners, realizing that peasants in deficit are coming closer to a more balanced household budget by reducing their deficits, resort to measures which include imposing sanctions on their clients by denying them employment as wage-labourers, withdrawing sharecropping contracts or refusing to sell rice except when the price is at the peak. Rich peasants often resort to violence with a view to restraining their clients from becoming economi-cally self-sufficient or politically articulate. Sometimes rich landowners can manipulate the wage system and force poor peasants and land-less labourers to work for them as *magna kamla* (labourer without payment).[32]

The state of misery and powerlessness of rural women can be gauged from various studies devoted to the position of poor rural women in Bangladeshi. Muhammad Yunus (founder of the Grameen Bank) has given a comprehensive idea about the state of poverty and helplessness of rural women in the region in his work, *Jorimon and Others: Faces of Poverty* (first published in Bengali in 1982). This contains case studies of destitute rural women of Bangladesh, many of whom out of total frustration pose the question: 'Do you really feel that we belong to this country?' For example, in the case-study of Jorimon of Beltoil Village in the district of Tangail, we find that:

> Jorimon toiled hard from her very childhood. . . . when other small girls of her age were playing with dolls . . ., Jorimon was herding goats in the fields. . . . She never had any decent clothes. . . .

Since her father was very poor, her family never ate good food. . . .
In 1962, ten-year-old Jorimon was married to twenty two-year-
old Rustom Khan. . . . The ten-year-old little girl had come to
her new home with a heart beating in fear and eyes filled with
rosy dreams. But within a few days, all her dreams faded into
thin air. I never had any wish fulfilled at my father's home,
neither did I have any better luck at my husband's, says Jorimon.[33]

Jorimon and her husband worked for a rich peasant, in return
getting two meals a day and twenty taka per month as salary. Jorimon
had to clean the house, wash the dishes and take care of the cow-
shed while her husband ploughed the fields, weeded the crops, looked
after the cattle and worked in the house and outside, doing all
sorts of chores from dawn to dark. However, finally they came across
the Grameen Bank in 1979 and by borrowing 600 taka from it
improved their situation and became self-reliant and happy. According to Yunus, while previously Jorimon's husband had to pay
an interest of 50 taka per week on a loan of 1000 taka from a local
moneylender (which was exorbitantly high), the coming of the
Grameen Bank improved their situation to such an extent that from
destitute day labourers they became self-sufficient farmers, living
in their own house and never going hungry. As Jorimon puts it:
'God has showed us that path of happiness through the (Grameen)
bank loan'.[34] The other case-studies in the work portray more-or-
less similar images of rural women in Bangladesh – one of their
state of total destitution and another of prosperity which we are
told, was due to the Grameen Bank.

In another study by Westergaard of rural women in Bangladesh,
sponsored by the Bangladesh Academy of Rural Development (BARD)
in Comilla, we get a picture of abysmal poverty and a state of utter
hopelessness among rural women in Bangladesh. This study reveals
how poor women, out of an instinct for survival, have taken up
employment outside their homestead for the sake of getting bare
subsistence, compromising with the ethos of *purdah* or seclusion.
This study also shows their lack of decision-making power despite
their taking off-*bari* (homestead) employment. Their inferior position in the gender hierarchy remained unchanged despite their taking
up employment outside. In short, the work concludes that 'there
are indications that the work possibilities of the majority of village
women are decreasing and their position deteriorating'.[35]

The limitations of NGOs

It is noteworthy that Westergaard in her later work on empowerment of Bangladeshis through NGOs (cited earlier) has eulogized
NGOs for promoting a civil society and working as alternatives to
political parties to uplift the poor in Bangladesh by providing credit
and job opportunities. One may assume from this assertion that
but for NGOs rural women in Bangladesh otherwise would have a
bleak future. However, Westergaard's field-work-based report on NGOs
should not be taken as an unmitigated endorsement of NGOs in
Bangladesh with regard to the eradication of poverty. Her reservations
and scepticism about the efficacy of NGOs in this regard are clear.

1 Poor women borrowers from NGOs sometimes are unable to repay their loans as they cannot make enough savings and that
  'like other NGOs, BRAC is unable to help the poorest of the
  poor.'[36]
2 The adult literacy programmes of some NGOs, 'is not participa-
  tory and does nothing to build up grassroots leadership' and the
  villagers who attended such literacy courses 'could not explain
  what they had learned, and they were unable to relate their
  awareness to their life situation.' From her field work, Westergaard
  has observed that villagers attending NGO schools 'learned their
  lessons, albeit primarily in the form of memorization'.[37]
3 With regard to rural women's participation in NGO activities
  Westergaard's scepticism is quite significant: 'In many instances
  the women had achieved considerable economic benefits, but by
  and large, observations showed that *the activities undertaken by
  women yielded less profit and less return to investment than those
  undertaken by the men. The group savings funds built up by the
  women's groups were thus smaller than those of the male groups,
  making profitable investments more difficult* [emphasis added]'.[38]
4 Although Westergaard highlights the positive aspects of NGOs,
  especially the decreased dependence on rich peasants and moneylenders by poor villagers due to NGO-sponsored credit facilities
  in rural areas, she thinks 'the decreased dependence on the rich
  farmers by no means implies that structural poverty has been
  eliminated'. She has also pointed out how in some areas NGO-
  sponsored political activities at the village level only empowered
  middle peasants who were elected on particular NGO tickets as
  officebearers of Union Parishads, while the poor elected members
  had no plans of their own and were dependent on NGOs for
  guidance. We also learn from her field observations that NGOs'

rural credit projects have replaced rich peasants/moneylenders, with NGOs making poor villagers dependent on them for credit and support. It seems reasonable to agree with her that as NGOs' work is dependent on external funding, it makes 'development problematic for the long-run process of democratization in Bangladesh'.[39] Last but not least, her field work reveals that local influential villagers have been the main beneficiaries of loans offered by the BRAC for example, some of them getting four loans at a time, 'three of which were used for herding, while one was used for investment in a deep tubewell (for irrigation)'.[40]

It is possible, however, to concur with the view that the various economic programmes undertaken by NGOs 'could be interpreted as *one step towards empowerment* of the poor [emphasis added]'.[41] How big is the 'step' and how many 'steps' are being taken towards development, are the pertinent questions.

An even-handed critique of NGOs, with special regard to their role in empowering poor women in Bangladesh, requires some understanding of how they operate in the Third World in general and Bangladesh in particular, and why many leftists and liberal democrats as well as extreme rightist religious groups are opposed to NGO activities in Bangladesh. NGOs function in various countries as alternatives to governments, distributing goods, capital and ideas with a view to enabling them to become self-reliant and/or free from hunger, disease, illiteracy and exploitation. Traditionally, international aid or development assistance has flowed from the developed North to the underdeveloped/developing South. In short, NGOs are not only by definition non-governmental but also independent of governments and not associated with the profit-oriented private sector, as they are non-profit-oriented.[42]

Local NGOs developed, either as the offshoot of the international ones or as independent organizations promoting similar values and programmes in many Third World countries. However, both international and local NGOs went through a process of transformation. While NGOs in the 1970s were 'welfare-oriented', by the 1980s they were becoming 'development-oriented', being involved in projects of training and providing technical assistance, jobs and market (for handicrafts and other goods) to the poor, especially women in the Third World. However, by the late 1980s, there had been a major transformation in the nature of NGO-activities – health, nutrition, family planning and other community development and welfare-oriented activities were soon replaced by market – and profit-oriented

– activities, 'because ultimately NGOs were playing at business rather than helping people meet the demands of a real marketplace'.[43] Consequently 'economic rationality' and 'financial sustainability', rather than concern for the well-being of the poor, determined NGO activities including microfinancing at high rates of interest.

In Bangladesh, NGOs are not only dependent on foreign donors to a great extent, they are also much more autonomous than their Indian counterparts. Even foreign organizations and their local clients (NGOs) dictate terms to the government of Bangladesh, publish materials and take part in political activities which at times amount to inciting a section of the population against others. Examples may be cited in support of this assertion:

Example 1 In the wake of the devastating cyclone in coastal regions of Bangladesh in May 1991, foreign aid agencies and donors refused to disburse any aid through the government machinery, implying that corrupt government officials would misappropriate relief goods. Consequently the Bangladesh government had to agree on the distribution of foreign humanitarian aid to the affected people through local NGOs, which theoretically implies that NGO-workers are free from corruption.

Example 2 The Canadian International Development Agency (CIDA) and some other foreign organizations have been openly urging Bangladeshi women to 'overthrow male-domination to establish the rights of women' in the country through their publications, banners and leaflets which are being displayed in public places and at the premises of some local NGOs, throughout Bangladesh. Examples may be cited of how NGOs and foreign organizations working in Bangladesh meddled with local politics during the peak of the 'Taslima Nasreen Controversy' in 1993–4 in the name of protecting a 'female victim of Islamic fundamentalism' and human rights in the country. Consequently not only are the amorphous groups of Islamic fundamentalists opposed to pro-Western NGOs but liberal democrats and leftists are also their bitter critics.

Some leftist intellectuals have portrayed the NGOs, funded by Western donors, as a means of exploiting the poor in the Third World countries by capturing their market. They also think that the 'neo-imperialists' do not want Third World countries like Bangladesh to become self-reliant and that NGOs have been 'neutralizing the class struggle of the exploited masses' with a view to

crushing social revolutions in the Third World. Some leftist intellectuals are critical of Islamic groups for their double standards.
While on the one hand, they promote 'Islamic NGOs' funded by
Middle Eastern countries, but single out other NGOs as 'exploitative' and 'anti-people'.[44] Some critics point out that despite the
growth in the number of NGOs in Bangladesh the number of landless peasants has been multiplying and that women's liberation,
being a political issue, cannot be resolved by non-political, superfi-
cial works by an unspecified number of NGOs. According to a leftist
politician, Rashed Khan Menon, poor peasants of Bangladesh have
been 'falling victims of vicious circle of creditors and NGOs these
days.'[45] From a local newspaper report we find that even the Grameen
Bank has been portrayed as 'a new Shylock with great clout' and
that instead of removing poverty the bank has been 'robbing whatever
resources people had' in the rural areas.[46]

As some observers believe, NGOs in Bangladesh are run by certain 'Western-minded', educated rich people having no links with
the grassroots, and that these people are in the 'NGO business'
only to make quick money. Large NGOs, they believe suffer from
the syndrome called 'oriental despotism' and have 'emerged as one
of the four bastards of. . . . civil society'. The other three, according
to them, are: (a) the military, (b) civil bureaucracy and (c) political
parties. They are also critical of the Association for Development
Agencies in Bangladesh (ADAB), a parent organization of NGOs,
for openly siding with the military government of General Ershad,
while on the other hand, the so-called champions of civil society
joined forces to topple the democratically elected government of
Khaleda Zia in 1995–6.[47] Syed Hashemi has similar views on some
of the leading NGOs of Bangladesh for taking part in anti-government rallies to topple the government in 1996. 'The irony of this
coalition of the oppressed at the grassroots with those who have
systematically plundered state funds, was not lost', he observes.[48]

While Hashemi is critical of NGOs for promoting 'donor hegemony' in Bangladesh, and Shelley Feldman argues in favour of a
strong Bangladeshi state to protect the under-privileged, portraying
NGOs as undesirable, Harry Blair eulogizes the role of NGOs in
strengthening democracy and civil society in the country. Hashemi
says that NGOs, mainly funded by foreign donors, cannot be
beneficial to the overall development process of the country. He
has rightly pointed out that foreign donors dictate terms, especially
with regard to the selection of projects in accordance with their

sense of priority, which cannot lead to an independent civil society.[49] Some NGOs have become too powerful to obey government regulations. In 1992, the government decided to deregister several NGOs for defalcation of funds and receiving money from a foreign embassy without the knowledge and authority of the government, only to revoke the order after less than three hours of issuing it under pressure of the 'patron embassy'. Some Western governments have even threatened to stop foreign aid to Bangladesh unless NGOs are given free rein to run their affairs. The Government not only had to withdraw the cancellation order against 52 NGOs and the powerful ADAB but had to remove the director general of the NGO Affairs Bureau (a government body) under pressure from the powerful NGO lobby and foreign donor agencies and governments.[50]

Debates over NGOs and various other institutions and organizations which involve poor rural women in the region, support the conclusion that although women's work in garment factories or as NGO workers has changed 'gender roles' in the last two decades (from the mid-1970s), 'there has not been a commensurate change in gender relations.' There are contradictions in the rural development programmes in Bangladesh: while, on the one hand, incomes from non-agricultural occupations have increased in the last twenty years on the other, a simultaneous polarization has taken place in rural Bangladesh signalling the ascendancy of landholding classes as members of the higher income group.[51]

It appears from a report of the Ciba-Geigy Foundation, which projects the prevalent disparities in wealth and power in rural Bangladesh, that well-to-do peasants holding five acres or more land per family, account for about 8 per cent of the rural population and yet control 48 per cent of all arable land. Given the situation, it might be expected that economically powerful sections would also control whatever foreign aid comes to the rural areas. The report is also critical of the system which allows dominant groups running NGOs with foreign donors' money in the name of 'empowerment of women' and 'participation of target groups.' Pointing out the lack of control over NGO activities by the rural poor, the report reveals that: '*When decisions are made, the poor are under-represented, but when the actual work has to be done they are conspicuously strongly represented* [emphasis in original]'.[52] According to the report, NGOs in fact have been benefiting not the 'target groups' but women belonging to groups other than the poor. The height of disenchantment of the Ciba-Geigy foundation is reflected in the following assertion: '*The real frustration comes from knowing that despite all the lessons learned we had managed to change nothing in the conditions of the impoverished women there*' [emphasis in original].[53]

It is, however, interesting that although most NGOs initially did not have any gender bias, various NGOs started espousing 'women's issues' as they represented potential sources of funds from overseas donors, especially in the 'decade of women'.[54] There is also a symbiosis between NGOs and rural women. As NGOs took advantage of the 'women's development issues' to gain access to new sources of (overseas) funding, in many cases, women also took advantage of the new opportunities provided by NGO-sponsored (profit-making) labour-intensive sectors such as handicrafts or poultry rearing. It cannot be denied, however, that 'amongst the NGOs there are some impressive examples of women's mobilization' enabling them to save themselves and their families from poverty, unjust legal cases, threats of divorce or demands for dowry and violence against women.[55]

The BRAC: an Appraisal

The BRAC, established in the early 1970s with a view to rebuilding the war-ravaged country, is the most well-known NGO in Bangladesh and claims to be the 'world's largest national private sector development endeavour'. Its programme includes rural development, improvement of health and population control, spread of non-formal primary education and support of training, research and publications. It also runs a chain store, *Aarong*, in Dhaka and some other cities to provide a 'marketing outlet to rural artisans and reviving traditional handicraft heritage of the country'.[56] In its rural development programme, according to BRAC's own estimate, by March 1996 it advanced more than 9 billion taka to 1.7 million BRAC members, one from each household in over 35 000 villages (out of the total of 68 000) in Bangladesh to promote poultry farms, vegetable cultivation, fisheries, sericulture, small trade and the like. Most of its beneficiaries are said to have been 'landless poor, particularly women in the rural areas'. The BRAC claim to have enrolled more than a million children in 34 000 BRAC-run free primary schools throughout the country. As many as 70 per cent of the students are girls and 96 per cent of the teachers women. BRAC's own estimation about its educational programme is 'perhaps the largest private sector education programme in the world'.[57] By early 1997, BRAC claims to have employed about 50 000 regular and part-time workers to work in 50 000 villages in the country. It is estimated that by the turn of the century, two million families will be covered by the rural development programme of the organization.[58]

Besides undertaking rural development projects, BRAC has also been trying to educate the rural masses, including women, especially with regard to the social norms, culture and belief systems at the grassroots level. In one of its publications, *Desh-Kal-Samaj* (Country, Space and Society), for example, the BRAC has tried to give a comprehensive idea about Bangladeshi society, culture, people, their ways of life, production system and relations, land system, poverty and disparity between people, socio-economic and political problems, urbanization and development problems and so on. Women and their status, along with problems of exploitation of poor men and women by government officials and other superordinates, are important sections of the book. It is also critical of the urban bias of the government's development programme, which according to the author, has only benefited a parasitic class of urban rich and their rural collaborators.[59]

Some of the teachings and ideas, as expressed in this BRAC publication, go against the views of the traditional *mullas* and village elders, as they challenge the traditional hierarchies in the rural areas as well as the prevalent theory of inevitability of poverty. It has pinpointed corruption and lack of aspirations or fatalism of the masses as the main reasons of poverty in Bangladesh. According to the BRAC, 84 per cent of Bangladeshis live below the poverty line and most of them lack equal opportunities to improve their lot. The work quite boldly pointed out that due to the lack of ethical teachings in the sermons of *mullas*, who only glorify charity and the seclusion of women or *purdah*, the average Bangladeshi fails to identify lack of morality in a person unless that person is involved in an illicit sexual relationship. It has pointed out embezzlement of public funds, issuing false medical certificates by doctors, taking bribes, indulging in black marketing, smuggling, favouring one's own kith and kin to the disadvantage of others, casting fictitious votes in elections, evading taxes and abusing power, and so on, as immoral acts. As a solution, the BRAC advises the rural poor, through its publications and the training programme run by its workers, to organize themselves at grassroots level though village-based institutions against all modes of exploitation and corruption perpetrated by the rich and powerful. It puts counter-arguments to those who justify corruption as inevitable and hence acceptable. With regard to a Union Parishad Chairman, for example, who embezzles the wheat he is supposed to distribute among poor villagers under the 'food for work' programme of the government, many villagers would justify the corrupt practice of the Chairman arguing: 'One who can procure the wheat from the government is also entitled to misappropriate a portion of it as well.' The book describes how the same person who defends the corrupt Chairman would possibly argue: 'Let this chairman stay, because once he is fully saturated (after embezzling enough from public funds) then he would not steal any more, but if another person takes over as the new chairman, he would start stealing and it would take much longer to reach his saturation point.' This BRAC publication rejects such arguments as faulty.[60] BRAC believes that the educated middle and upper classes of Bangladesh are the most immoral sections of the population. Citing Professor Ahmed Sharif's work, the BRAC publication stresses that: 'Nothing positive has taken place in Bangladesh in the wake of independence. . . . The middle class has lost faith in morality and ethics.'[61]

This BRAC book has also brought feminist issues and questions about women's rights and status in society to the fore. In its critique of the Hindu and Muslim scriptures and laws, which advocate the subjection of women as natural, it has condemned those who misinterpret the *Sharia* law and texts of the Quran and *hadis* to undermine the position of women. In short, it has advocated equal rights and opportunities for women in every sphere of life. It is highly critical of child-marriage, polygyny, the dowry system, arbitrary divorce by husbands, wife-beating and the injustices which cause women to suffer from malnutrition and have to work more and earn less than men.[62] Last but not least, BRAC has been urging its workers, and through them the rural masses, to establish 'solid village institutions' as opposed to the 'evil institutions of the state'. It has also advocated the creation of village courts of justice, 'free from the interference of outsiders', to settle their disputes, in the 'sovereign' and 'self-sufficient' villages.[63]

Although BRAC is primarily not an organization of women, its programme has been mainly devoted to promoting or empowering poor rural women in Bangladesh. While 70 per cent of the 160 000 children attending BRAC-sponsored primary schools are girls, 64 per cent of the 400 000 landless poor covered by its education, training, credit and income-generating activities are also women. Sixty per cent of the Village Organizations formed by the BRAC are women's groups and 74 per cent of those who graduated from BRAC's Functional Educational Programme and another 74 per cent of the borrowers of small loans are women as well.[64]

Although the BRAC literature is full of anti-urban, anti-exploiter rhetoric, there is no mention of exploitation of cheap labour, especially of rural women and children, in its publications. One does not have to dig very deep to find out the nature of this exploitation of the poor of which the various BRAC projects, undertaken in the name of alleviating rural poverty and the empowerment of women in Bangladesh, are guilty. From a survey of wage and salary structures of BRAC employees, especially women, working at its marketing outlets, the *Aarong* shopping complexes in Dhaka and elsewhere, it is evident that most female workers are part-time employees earning between 900 and 2000 taka ($25 to $50) per month. From interviewing *Aarong* employees as well as rural female workers, producing different kinds of handicrafts – embroidered sarees and quilts, leather products, garments, jewellery – it is clear that there is a huge gap between the prices of these products at *Aarong* outlets and their actual cost of production, including labour. While a rural female worker, for example, receives around 300 taka (less than US$ 7) for embroidery work on a saree (for about a month's labour) from the BRAC, the average selling price of each is 6000 taka at BRAC shops. It is noteworthy that BRAC also buys up garments from Bangladeshi manufacturers to export them to north America. These garments are marketed in north America in specially labelled packets bearing the message, 'manufactured by poor Bangladeshi women', with a view to drawing sympathy of the consumers and thus sell them duty-free with the support of US and Canadian governments. This eventually further raises the profit-margin for the BRAC.[65]

What one finds in BRAC literature and publications is often counter-productive, if not seditious. The very concepts of 'sovereign villages' and 'independent village courts', as found in its book *Desh-Kal-Samaj*, are indicative of the defiant attitude of the authors of the work towards the Government. How is it possible, by weakening the already shaky and weak structure of the Bangladesh government, to alleviate poverty and empower the poor, rural women of the country!? While patriarchy and both government and non-government agents of exploitation are well-entrenched in society, it is not clear how by mere defiance of socio-cultural norms and institutions poor rural women of Bangladesh will be able to accelerate the process of their empowerment. The lack of harmony in rural areas, as reflected in the occasional but violent attacks on BRAC properties – schools, training centres and the like – and male and female BRAC group members throughout the country by different disgruntled groups and individuals does not appear to indicate that the process of alleviating rural poverty and empowerment of women has been accelerated and NGO-sponsored projects are bringing about an era of peace and development in the countryside. The unbiased reader must have reservations about the BRAC assertion, as reflected in its publications, that only village elders, touts and government officials in Bangladesh represent the corrupt and greedy sections of the population, while the NGO-organizers and workers are immune to such vices and temptations.

As NGOs adopted 'profit-oriented' rather than 'welfare-oriented' policies in the late 1980s, they emerged as financially viable 'neomoneylenders' at the expense of the diminishing 'social return' at grassroots level. Consequently a great many micro-loan recipients have enormous difficulty making productive use of these small loans when 'the real issue here should be the return to the borrower'.[66] The BRAC in Bangladesh is not an exception in this respect – it also emerged as a micro-credit institution, driven by 'economic rationality'. However, BRAC's track-record with regard to reaching the poorest with its 'pro-poor' credit schemes is not altogether different from those other micro-credit organizations in Bangladesh or elsewhere – 'the poorest remain difficult to reach'.[67]

I want to highlight here the adverse effects of peer group pressure on BRAC borrowers, who borrow on one-year terms and whose loans are repaid in weekly instalments at 20 per cent interest. Borrowers hardly have any formal influence over savings and credit policy as all deposits and 'Group Trust Fund' are controlled by BRAC staff. BRAC's 'rigid' and 'top-down' Rural Development Programme 'is maintaining high repayment rates, but at the cost of a section of its membership and its original social development objectives'; and there is a significant drop-out amongst its membership at grassroots level as they lack access to savings and are unable to cope with rigid repayment schedules. Finally, BRAC's transformation into a top-heavy bureaucratic institution is evident from the shift from a *bhai* (brother) culture to a 'sir' culture – 'nowadays, field staff are more likely to be called "sir"' by the poor villagers.

So far as BRAC's shift towards a 'women only' recruitment policy, it seems this policy has been instrumental in perpetuating male supremacy over female as 'most field staff are men; the real "power" of (male) field staff over (female) members may therefore be reinforced by cultural norms of higher male status'. In sum, it appears that BRAC's rigid, credit-focused financial service system, with an emphasis on discipline is possibly 'disciplining' rather than 'protecting the poor'.[68] It is astounding that while the NGOs are not accountable to the Government, some large NGOs are nothing short of profligate profiteers. The BRAC, for example, earns more than 700 million *taka* per year alone by charging each 'group member' 5 *taka* (returnable after 20 years) as the 'saving component' every month. Had this mega-NGO not been involved in any other profit-generating project, its net profit would still have been in the region of 400 million *taka* per year, after setting aside around 300 million *taka* which it spends as the employees' salary.[69] It is also noteworthy that the BRAC, like most NGOs, was not registered as a social welfare trust but as a joint-stock company under private ownership.[70] This means that, if the organization goes into liquidation, the Government cannot simply take over its assets, as happened with those of the *Gano Sahajya Sangstha* (GSS), another NGO, which was liquidated in early 1999, without the Government being able to take over its assets.

NGOs in the empowerment process

What about other NGOs, engaged in similar activities as those of BRAC in rural areas of Bangladesh? Unlike BRAC, *Saptagram Nari Swanirvar Parishad*, the Seven Villages Women's Self-Reliance Movement (Saptagram), is a grassroots organization of women, founded by history professor Rokeya Rahman Kabeer in 1976. By 1994, it had spread over 900 villages, reaching 22 000 members. Saptagram is the first NGO to have introduced a gender-oriented syllabus for girls in its schools in the mid-1980s, soon to be followed by other NGOs in the country; and it has been hiring its own graduates as teachers in its schools. One of the achievements of this NGO is making its members (exclusively women) aware of the prevalent social prejudices against women. Lily Begum, a member of the group, who has become conscious of her rights and status as a woman, narrates how naive she was before her exposure to the Saptagram: 'We have been told all our lives by the Mollahs, our mothers, aunts and grandmothers that according to the Koran, our heaven is at the feet of our husband, and that when our husband beats us, the portion of our body which has been hurt will go to heaven'.[71] Saptagram's *modus operandi* as well as its composition are different from BRAC's and that of many other NGOs, run by men. Rather than adopting a short-term, welfare-biased programme, Saptagram has taken a long-term plan of empowerment of its members. Its main aims are:

1 To work among women in poor rural areas.
2 To make women aware of the causes of their socio-economic deprivation and give them the means to gain more control over their lives.
3 To initiate non-traditional income-generating activities on a co-operative basis and give women some control over resources.
4 To provide education to groups of women, with emphasis on book-keeping. The gender-oriented syllabus also reinforces women's knowledge of their rights. The education programme grew from the women's demand for classes as they came to realize the links between education, employment opportunities and basic human rights.
5 To provide knowledge of health and nutrition.

Saptagram's programmes are mainly funded by Oxfam, the Swedish International Development Agency (SIDA) and the Norwegian Agency for Development Cooperation (NORAD).[72]

Although in both government and non-government organizations 70 per cent of training curricula in women's programmes are oriented to embroidery, sewing and knitting, and only a few like the BRAC and Grameen Bank have been integrating women into development by providing them with credit and technical support to start up small businesses and other productive activities. However, unlike Saptagram, BRAC and Grameen Bank are mainly organized by men and are not solely geared towards women.

Saptagram's target groups have been women from very poor families and mostly those 'who have been deserted, divorced or widowed'. Although Saptagram has distanced itself from village elders and *mullas*, not provoking them unnecessarily, Rokeya Kabeer received death threats from some rich villagers who had been against the emergence of self-sufficient and independent women in rural areas. Some Islam-oriented political groups, especially the Jamat-i-Islami, have been the main rivals of Saptagram because they are asking women to come out of *purdah* or seclusion.[73]

Saptagram, through its women organizations or *andolon* (movement)

at grassroots level have been serving female victims of dowry ex-
tortion, divorce threats by their husbands and rape. One woman,
Dalim Begum, for example, resisted her husband Bokkor Ali's attempts to prevent her from attending the adult literacy programme
run by Saptagram in her village, as Saptagram field staff and other
female members warned the husband that 'if something happened
to her', they would turn him over to the police. Another group
member, Rahima Begum, a mother of four and widow, recovered
her deceased husband's property from her in-laws with the intervention of Saptagram at Pangsha in Faridpur district. After Saptagram
intervention offenders were forced to pay hefty fines to victims of
rape in a village in Kustia district. In another case, the son of a
well-to-do family was forced to marry a poor girl whom he made
pregnant, giving her a dowry of 25 000 taka. With each case, women
gained a moral victory and a sense of power. By the mid-1980s,
rural women associated with Saptagram had become brave enough
to come outside to meet and talk to strangers about what had been
happening in their lives and their families. By the mid-1990s,
Saptagram group members had the advantage of having access to
basic education and some capital to run their own enterprises. Under
the aegis of Saptagram, rural women have learnt that they can do
everything men can and consequently they have been doing earth
work and selling their own products in the village market like male
villagers throughout Bangladesh.[74]

The way Saptagram adult-schools are run following its gender-
oriented syllabus is also quite impressive. For example, teachers use
flash cards with an illustration of a veiled woman walking with her
husband and a boy, to denote seclusion or *purdah*, and dowry is
portrayed with the drawing of a scale with a woman on one side
weighed against a bicycle, a radio, a watch and other goods. Early
marriage, violence against women, divorce and so on are also illus-
trated this way. One of the pictures, entitled 'Address', shows a
postman handing in a letter to a woman, signifying the independent identity of women, who in general are only addressed as
someone's wife, daughter or mother. 'Now my husband talks to me
and asks my advice', says one Saptagram group member. This is
reflective of women's attaining the status of an individual which
hitherto was lacking.[75]

The overall picture that emerges out of Saptagram activities among
rural women is that on the one hand, they have shown resilience,
persistence and courage, and on the other, many of them have

also become creative thinkers about the *modus operandi* to improve their lot. This is reflected in the following assertion by a Saptagram group member:

> Can you really fight the whole society, *chachiamma* [auntie]? I somehow do not think you will win. This social order has been there for thousands of years, like an old banyan tree which has stretched its roots deep into the earth. Storms will not be able to uproot it. *The only way is to cut the tree down. Can you do that?* [emphasis added][76]

In view of the above, one may agree with the UNESCO observer that: 'When women are brought together, they begin to question their lives, gain strength, overcome their fears and step into action'.[77] However, the question remains: Can you really fight the whole society without cutting down the 'banyan tree'? Some NGOs, Saptagram, *Gano Shastho Kendro* and *Nijera Kori*, for example, have started the process of empowering poor rural women of Bangladesh, not by providing them with easy credit but by training them to be self-reliant.

However, as some observers have pointed out, although participation in NGO-sponsored income-generating activities by poor women may have changed their behavioural patterns – the observance of *purdah*, for example – this change is not an entirely liberating experience for women, as 'new patterns of social control defining the behaviour of rural women come to hold sway'. Criticisms may be made of the 'strong social welfare bias and a simplistic feminist bias' on the part of donor agencies in assuming that 'all women are sisters', ignoring the class interests of women.[78] Various NGOs' income-generating activities among rural women do not benefit the poorest women in the region, who are 'excluded from participation' in home-based 'factories' to produce handicrafts as 'home resources are unavailable to them'. It also appears that those who manage to work for NGO-managed 'factories' (who sell their products in shops, such as Aarong, Karika and Shetuli, for example), on average earned only 340 taka a month ($17) in 1983, which was 'only sufficient to cover the costs of basic food needs of the main worker and only half the needs of an additional person'. There is, again, no positive correlation between the training that these women receive and the income-generating activities they undertake, as independent production by them is 'highly unlikely to succeed without the institutionalized program network'.[79] The institutions (NGOs) are, again, highly exploitative of female labour in the countryside.

The Grameen Bank, Micro-credit and Women

The Grameen Bank, although started in the 1970s, evolved as a fully-fledged bank in 1983 to provide credit to the rural poor owning 0.5 acres or less cultivable land per family. While the government of Bangladesh owns 15 per cent of the shares, the bank's borrower-shareholders own the remaining 85 per cent. The unique aspect of the bank is that loans are issued without any collateral to poor villagers, both men and women. By late 1993 women constituted 94 per cent of its members, holding 90 per cent of its total cumulative disbursement of US$768 million, and accounted for 74 per cent of all savings mobilized by the bank. The loan recovery rates for men and women in 1992, for example, were 89 and 97 per cent respectively. The credit network of the bank is much wider than any other NGO in Bangladesh. However, the bank's rate of interest on loans is very high – with membership fees and other charges it is almost 28 per cent. Small amounts (3–15 000 taka – US$75 to 375) per head are borrowed by villagers from the bank. By early 1997, about two million rural women had borrowed by becoming Grameen members throughout the country.[80]

For adopting various innovative measures, with a view, as believed by many, to 'empowering rural women', the bank is said to have 'substantially changed' the lot of many poor Bangladeshi women, for example by means of its housing programme. If the housing loan for building, repairing or upgrading is taken by a married woman, the bank ensures that the homestead must be registered in her name, so that in case of divorce she is not evicted from the house.[81]

Besides providing credit, the Grameen Bank has a social development programme called the 'Sixteen Decisions' to imbue members with discipline, unity, hard work, cleanliness and the like. Most loans are taken by women to raise cattle, goats or poultry, or for paddy husking, bamboo work and setting up grocery shops. Although the net return from such activities is very low, a little over 6 taka per hour (or less than ten cents), many observers believe that this additional income has been a factor in improving rural women's socio-economic condition, especially in regard to their attaining independence as a result of their sense of self-sufficiency.[82] It is often said that the most important effect of the bank on women borrowers/members is the increase in their decision-making power, especially with regard to fertility, voting in elections and working outside the homestead, side by side with men.

However, according to a recent study, religion and patriarchy have been the dominant factors in determining rural women's decision-making power with regard to fertility, work and voting in elections. Hindu women members of the bank in general, are said to have significantly more decision-making power than Muslim women, and religion seems to be a 'negative resource for Muslim women', as their close proximity to non-relative males is considered sinful. So far as rural women's participation and voting in elections are concerned, religion and husbands' level of education are determining factors.[83]

Mere availability of easy credit does not empower illiterate and poor rural women, as 'cultural norms override the effect of such resources. . . . Because the ascribed status of sex legitimizes men's power in society, they retain more power than their wives'. However, a wife's income, even though it is meagre, gives her some leverage in power relations; and that while patriarchy is more powerful in extended families, women enjoy increasing power in nuclear families.[84]

In view of the above, and since Islam as understood and practised in the country has a

> depressing effect on women's decision-making power. . . . In order to dispel . . . misconceptions . . . the government should solicit help from religious experts who could give appropriate interpretations. Such efforts could be the beginning of questioning the norms that disadvantage women'.[85]

On the other hand, some observers are not even prepared to acknowledge any negative aspect of the Grameen Bank's micro-credit scheme. Para Teare from the Genderwatch feels that:

> In the midst of all the Third World's problems, one success story seems to be talked up time and again. The Grameen Bank in Bangladesh is widely applauded for its policy of lending money for self-help projects . . . especially to impoverished women. . . . Hillary Clinton expressed her appreciation for the bank's role. . . . The Grameen model is now being emulated elsewhere.[86]

The problem is further compounded by the fact that the world-wide publicity of Grameen Bank has led to the deification of Professor Muhammad Yunus (the founder of the bank), both within and outside Bangladesh, among academics, politicians and laymen, establishing the myth of the 'success story' of his micro-credit scheme. Professor Yunus has contributed to establishing the myth of 'Grameen Bank as the permanent and only cure of poverty' by his hyperbolic, self-congratulatory statements.[87] One observer argues, contrary to 'a rosy view of some feminists about the bank', that, since the female borrowers are totally dependent on the bank and as they do not want their children to become Grameen Bank members, one should not buy the bank's success story. According to this observer,

> a major reason for the Grameen Bank's success is that its strategy makes hard-headed business sense for the financiers. . . . Professor Yunus argues that the rich can always abscond with loans; the clear implication of his remarks was that the poor, on the otherhand, will always be there to repay.[88]

According to another critic, the bank is similar to the evil dwarf in the story of Rumpelstiltskin, who saves the life of a king's bride by spinning flax into gold, but the price is high for performing the miracle – the bride must give the dwarf her first-born child. 'Like the king's bride', Jeffrey Tucker observes, 'these borrowers might regret that they ever made the original deal with Yunus. But Bangladesh's legendary poverty makes it appear that our Rumpelstiltskin offers the only way out of a desperate situation'.[89] Whether the bank is an 'evil' institution with 'ghoulish' financial and social plans for the poor rural women of Bangladesh or not, I believe that there is no 'economic miracle worth copying' in the Grameen's 'femino-socio-financial engineering'.[90]

Since 'livelihood enterprises' are usually secondary or tertiary rather than the primary source of household income, these 'seasonal, intermittent and part-time' (and uncertain) sources of income from subsistence-oriented, livestock-rearing or paddy-husking projects for women, cannot be long-term solutions of poverty. Although 'livelihood enterprises' might lead to accumulation of capital, there is always an inherent risk in such enterprises – the poor often consume their surpluses to raise their living standard. In addition 'the inherent unprofitability' of these livelihood enterprises and the constraints and dangers of market saturation cause more difficulties.[91] As these activities require no special skills and lack competitive advantage in the market, growth is not their main consequence. In the long run, as T.W. Dichter suggests, the outcome of such micro-credit-based projects is stagnation and decline in growth as after the second or third loan cycle 'either people stop borrowing, or they stop increasing the amount they borrow. There is simply little or no absorptive capacity'.[92]

Contrary to the assertions of Grameen and NGO supporters, various studies have shown that many poor villagers in Bangladesh opt out of micro-credit schemes as the rate of return on loans is lower than the cost of borrowing,[93] and the average income of a household which has taken loan from BRAC thrice is less than that of a household that has taken loan once.[94] Habib Ahmed has shown that

> microfinance schemes entrap the poor in a perpetual debt cycle (vicious cycle)... as the number-of-times credit taken increases, total net-income of the households declines... [it is no longer possible for poor borrowers] to increase their income to levels that would graduate them into the non-poor status... longer association with micro-credit institutions can, in fact, lower income levels [as investments in low-return projects by borrowers do not pay for the interest and loans].[95]

Contrary to the assertions by Grameen-supporters,[96] no miracles take place for the poorest among the poor Grameen-borrowers to enable them to start repayment of debt-instalments immediately after borrowing small amounts to buy cows, for example, as the likelihood of buying milch cows from anybody is very rare, since nobody normally sells off a cow which is still lactating. Consequently it may be argued that since getting quick returns from cattle or poultry is highly unlikely, the poorest women cannot afford to borrow from the Grameen Bank. Only those with enough subsistence and alternative sources of income (or credit) to repay the debt instalments (at high interest) and other charges of the bank, are the real beneficiaries of the micro-credit scheme. One study reveals that there is a 'natural process of selection' when Grameen Bank borrower groups are formed at the grassroots level. 'The poorest of the poor are not asked to join groups', as the maintenance of the relationship with the bank is a 'predominant consideration'.[97] This simply implies that only those who can afford to repay their loans should join the Grameen loan-groups.

David Bornstein although an admirer of the bank, has shown in his empirical study that all those who borrow money to buy milch cows, for example, are not living in comfort but rather are struggling to survive. He illustrates a case-study of one Aleya, a poor village woman, who borrowed 3500 takas to buy a cow which stopped lactating after six months, leaving her owing 1700 takas to Grameen Bank. As under bank rules the cow could not be sold until the loan was repaid, Aleya had to work in the houses of wealthier villagers and cut down on the family's eating and put everyone, even her seven-year-old daughter, to work to repay her debt-instalments.[98] Every now and then local newspapers come up with stories of how poor rural women are forced to sell off their cattle, household goods and even homesteads in order to repay Grameen loans.

What is missing in the over-simplified assertions by the Grameen-supporters is that, while more than 50 per cent of the population of Bangladesh live below the 'extreme poverty line' of 1805 calories per person per day and about 80 per cent below the poverty line of 2122 calories per person per day,[99] the average Bangladeshi is too poor to consume milk and eggs produced by Grameen borrowers. Consequently the over-production of dairy products, poultry and eggs would eventually benefit the rich and urban consumers to the detriment of the rural poor. It is difficult to give any credence to the assertion that due to the concerted efforts of NGOs and Grameen Bank, out of the total 'nine million families' who had been living below the poverty-line in Bangladesh, about 50 per cent of them have managed to cross the poverty line and can no longer be considered poor.[100] While one study on Dhaka city alone indicates that there are about three million slum dwellers and squatters in the city, living in abject poverty, how could Professor Yunus come up with the absurd figure of only 4.5 million families or 27 million Bangladeshis living in poverty in the whole country of 120 million people! Had micro-credit been so successful in alleviating poverty, hundreds of thousands of poor Bangladeshis would not have gone overseas, spending more than 100 000 takas each after selling off their properties, to work as labourers in harsh conditions.

It is noteworthy that Grameen admirers such as Hashemi and Schuler have finally admitted that Grameen Bank cannot overcome the inherent obstacles to poverty alleviation in Bangladesh:

The greatest obstacle Grameen Bank faces in providing targeted credit for poverty alleviation is poverty itself. Economic stagnation in rural areas limits the potential for productive investments such that the poorest of the poor often are unable to use credit productively and may even worsen their situations by taking loans from Grameen Bank. Although some borrowers succeed in using credit to pull themselves out of poverty, for many the benefits are more modest. Lack of social services for the poor in rural areas leaves Grameen borrowers highly vulnerable to health crises and natural disasters, which can quickly reverse the economic gains from credit.[101]

Depriving the rural, poor men from credit facilities, and viewing them as 'petty criminals' and 'touts', would intensify the fragmentation of society by further deepening the cleavage between men and women. Providing credit facilities to women again is not an 'empowering experience, this situation only points to the degraded status of women in Bangladeshi society', as their selection as the beneficiaries of the bank and NGO credit reinforces all the traditional notions of poor, rural women as 'conservative, passive, submissive and gently persuasive'. There is every reason to condemn the Grameen Bank for accepting the traditional values which demand that women stay at home doing the 'cooking, cleaning and caring, worrying about the health and education of their children'. Such observations along with the following ones are quite thought provoking:

(a) Grameen loans do not open up brave new worlds for the women of Bangladesh. Instead they invest the money in traditional small-scale tasks like paddy husking, petty trade and livestock rearing. *The fact that women are still trapped in such home-centred drudgery suggests that Grameen Bank loans act more as affirmation of the status quo than a breakthrough for female emancipation* [emphasis added].

(b) Far from being a people's movement, the Grameen Bank's policies can only help to fragment and deepen the divisions between men and women in a place like Bangladesh ... the bank's focus is on redistributing wealth and power between men and women within the impoverished households of rural Bangladesh. The result is to mystify the wider causes of the problems which these communities face.

(c) More [Bangladeshi] men have found that there are fewer jobs and there is less money to go around ... the intervention of banks and NGOs which prioritise giving resources to one section of the population women – can only exacerbate tensions. . . . Redistributing income from men to women, sharing out the misery of a shrinking cake, is not going to solve the people's problems. While the Grameen Bank claims to empower women against men in Bangladesh, its policies actually help to reinforce the power of outside agencies to control the lives of rural poor. . . . Not only can they be in debt to the bank for the rest of their lives, but they also have to conform to rules laid down from above.[102]

There is possibly some truth in the assertion that male-female conflicts have been mystifying the wider causes of the class conflicts inherent in an inegalitarian society with perpetual scarcity of goods and services. It seems that the long-term consequences of ignoring poor men and treating them as 'petty criminals' and 'touts', both by the bank and many NGOs, would be disastrous, as horizontal gender war and vertical urban-rural conflicts would further polarize society to the detriment of the rural poor, especially women. The inherent contradictions of Grameen Bank and its profit-oriented motives in the name of uplifting the poor (women) have also drawn the attention of some renowned scholars and political thinkers to Bangladesh. Badruddin Umar has rightly pointed out how since its inception, the founder-director of the bank has been confusing people with a jumble of words about the reality of the institution. According to the Grameen Bank Ordinance of September 1983, while the Bangladesh government owned 60 per cent, 40 per cent 'ownership' of the bank lay with landless villagers. In accordance with the 1986 Ordinance of the bank, landless villagers 'gained' 75 per cent shares of the bank while 25 per cent remained with the government. Umar has emphatically affirmed that:

1. The Grameen Bank is nothing but another profit-making institution and exploitative of the poor villagers, especially women;
2. If the borrowers are simultaneously the 'owners' of the bank then all clients of other commercial banks should be classified as such, in accordance with the definition of 'ownership' by Professor Yunus;

3. Grameen Bank is not different from other NGOs and garment industries in Bangladesh who also employ poor women as their workers with a view to exploiting them in the name of 'liberation of women';

4. Despite the 'balderdash and bluff' of the Grameen Bank organizers, local and foreign agents of imperialism have been glorifying the bank because the institution is a by-product of 'imperialist conspiracy'.[103]

However, there is hardly any point in only criticizing the dominant North for promoting the Grameen Bank as the saviour of poor rural women in Bangladesh. Many Bangladeshi promoters of the bank also think that as Hillary Clinton and Queen Sofia of Spain along with other Western dignitaries have been impressed with Grameen Bank, and especially with its female members/borrowers in rural Bangladesh, the bank must be achieving its goal – the empowerment of poor rural women in the country through its micro-credit scheme. While highlighting the level of 'self-reliance and freedom' of Grameen borrowers (94 per cent of whom are women) at a civic reception at the Royal Melbourne Institute of Technology on 23 March 1997, Professor Yunus narrated several anecdotes about poor rural women of Bangladesh. In one account, he mentioned the village woman who asked Hillary Clinton (visiting her village in early 1995) if she lived on her own income or on her husband's, while another village woman enquired about the number of cows the First Lady had at her residence. Yet in another account, we hear from Professor Yunus how Queen Sophia of Spain relished a glass of warm sweetened milk offered by a village women while she was visiting her village in Bangladesh. The queen is said to have also enjoyed the home-made cube of date-sugar (*khejurergur*) offered by another village woman. How does the portrayal of poor village women as objects of curiosity for the rich and powerful of the developed world establish the 'empowerment thesis', correlating Grameen Bank with the empowerment process of rural women in Bangladesh!?

Some micro-level empirical studies of Grameen Bank activities in rural Bangladesh also give us a somewhat abysmal picture of the bank. One study shows (fulfilling Para Teare's apprehensions) that instead of empowering poor women, the operation of the bank programme 'produces various levels of domination over women', generating new forms of female dependency in society and causing the growth of tension among household members, thus aggravating gender relations and leading to an increased level of violence in rural areas.[104]

What is revealing in the study is that:

1 The bank extends credit to women 'but it is mostly men who use the loans' while the women remain as surrogate borrowers, with the knowledge of the bank.

2 Women are preferred to men as clients because of their shyness, passivity and submissiveness. Many bank workers regard women's passivity and submissive nature as qualities which are lacking in men and take advantage of the vulnerable honour or *izzat* of women, which gives the bank 'an unwritten guarantee' of getting back regular instalments from female members. A women's failure to repay her loans in time would bring shame to her entire family.

3 Over 90 per cent of women are directly influenced by their male guardians in becoming Grameen Bank members (borrowers). 'In many cases male members in the household are directly approached by bank workers to send their female members to join in women groups, and they are promised loans for their (males) own use'.

4 Since the bank lends money to two members of groups of five at a time, who are supposed to repay the loan in 52 instalments to the 'loan centre' (six to eight groups/30–40 members constituting a loan centre), subsequent loans to other members in a group are not sanctioned until the individual accounts of each group member are settled. In this micro-credit network peer-pressure works as the collateral for the bank.

5 If someone fails to maintain regular weekly payment of a loan instalment, other group members 'are forced to sit on their bare feet on a mud floor for several hours until all instalments are collected'. If the defaulter is not available in her village or is unable to make her instalments, peer members either take her saleable household items or personal assets such as her jewellery and sell or mortgage them out to collect the instalment.

6 The members repay all their loan instalments within 50 weeks after borrowing. Two per cent of the capital amount must be paid every week. Besides the 20 per cent interest on loans, borrowers have to pay 25 per cent of the calculated interest amount or 12.5 times greater than a member's weekly instalment within the remaining last two weeks (out of the total 52 weeks) in order to qualify for the next new extension of credit. Over 95 per

cent of all members (in the surveyed area in Tangail district) pay the interest and emergency fund through short-term emergency loans from other sources.

In many cases, members of a particular loan-centre lose their entitlements to further credit from the bank due to 'the loss of credibility' of their centre because of irregularities of any other member or 'due to a woman's adverse personal relations with other members or with the centre chief [bank employee] who also has authority over approval of the loan proposal'. The non-availability of a new loan for a woman who has paid off her outstanding loan often leads to her facing verbal and physical abuse from her husband or male relatives. Sometimes irregularities of a member lead to feuds and fights among members of a centre.[105]

Some studies reveal that the Grameen programme has led to an increase in violence against women in the home and that possibly 'the violence represents men's struggle for the maintenance of certain fantasies of identity and power'.[106] One empirical study informs us that in certain sub-regions men resort to polygamy to get more micro-credit from the Grameen Bank through their numerous wives.[107]

It is noteworthy that despite the continual flow of foreign and government capital into the coffer of the bank, 'the more developed is the local economy and the more alternative income-earning opportunities, the higher is the dropout rate of Grameen Bank members'. Villages under the government's Rural Electrification Programme, or which have branches of commercial banks, witness an accelerated rate of dropout of Grameen Bank members.[108] This suggests that it is poor villagers of backward localities without alternative sources of credit and power who are drawn to the Grameen Bank. Owing to various other factors, including the high transaction costs of membership for potential borrowers, the bank is attracting only about 25 per cent of the target households in its area of operation. In agreement with the empirical findings of a World Bank study, it may be assumed that the returns from Grameen Bank-financed and subsistence-oriented projects 'are likely to decrease, given demand constraints, as more and more people join the bank and undertake similar productive activities [rearing milk cows or a couple of goats, for example]'. This, in the long run, would threaten the viability of both the bank and the borrowers, since this depends on the disbursement of loans for growth-oriented (not subsistence-oriented) projects or 'technology loans', which are larger in amount than general loans and are mainly borrowed by men. Subsistence-oriented collective loans by Grameen Bank, mainly offered to women, are not going to transform the socio-economic condition of the poor rural women of Bangladesh radically, some argue.[109]

As discussed earlier, various empirical studies on NGOs and Grameen Bank have shown that, for the borrower, the rate of return from micro-credit is lower than the cost of borrowing: 'microfinance schemes entrap the poor in a perpetual debt cycle (vicious cycle)', and that most female borrowers do not have control over their enterprises and incomes. Hence the ineffectiveness of the micro-credit scheme as a source of alleviating poverty and empowering rural women in Bangladesh. Since NGOs and Grameen Bank are only accessible to a small proportion of the rural poor, and most NGOs have been 'facing difficulties with strategies for expansion', government intervention and its sharing of the responsibility to raise standards for the rural poor are essential.[110]

The garment industries and exploitation of women

The impact of the 2000-odd garment industries employing more than a million poor rural women in urban areas of Dhaka and Chittagong on the overall socio-economic conditions of the women workers is very complex as well. On the one hand, these industries have been providing employment to thousands of poor women, who previously had no succour other than working as domestic maids at bare subsistence, begging, resorting to prostitution in ex-treme cases or remaining as unwanted dependants on near or distant relatives; and on the other, they have been exploiting the cheap labour of these helpless women who have no right to organize unions to demand better wages and working conditions. Their social in-feriority is exploited by the rich and powerful and consequently many poor women 'are forced into employment by poverty, and these jobs do not fulfil any emancipating role at all'.[111] According to an ILO report, these working women are a form of underpaid drudgery, often carried out under deplorable working conditions.[112]

Some recent studies have shown the state of misery, powerless-ness and uncertainty undergone by the average female garment factory worker in Bangladesh. They are not only grossly underpaid – the average salary being 640 taka or US$16 per month, which is much below the minimum a woman needs to sustain herself and her family – but also have to suffer terrible working conditions and environment. They are often victims of physical abuse – beating, rape and molestation – not only by male employers and supervisors but also by members of the police force. Most of the female workers are, again, malnourished and overworked.[113] The lack of fire exits and overcrowded workplaces take scores of lives of female factory workers; in 1997 alone, more than 30 workers were burnt alive in Dhaka.[114]

According to the report of a Canada-based human rights organization, by 1992 there had been approximately 1.2 million women employed as domestic servants and another half a million as garment factory workers, subject to cruelty and 'widespread abuses' by their employers.

> Women have been forced to work overtime for no pay and 'many' have been sexually assaulted, either in the work place or on their way to or from work. . . . The *Toronto Star* reports that 10 per cent of all female garment factory workers have been beaten or tortured by an employer and in some factories women are forced to 'stand on their heads for extended periods as punishment for flaws in their work' (5 July 1992).[115]

The same report reveals that iron bars are used to lock the doors of many of Dhaka's 885 garment factories and that working conditions are 'slave-like', female workers being 'shut into their workplace . . . the iron gates stay sealed until the male shop bosses say it's time to leave'.[116] Some local observers feel that while the female factory workers spend most of their earnings on food, clothing, housing, medicine and support of extended family members, married ones are forced to part with the entire salary as it is surrendered to their husbands.[117] One recent study has portrayed production-relations in these factories as 'wage slavery' for women workers and has compared the working conditions with those Marx referred to with regard to British industries in the early nineteenth century, including violations of the 1965 Factory Act, denying workers certain basic rights and forcing them to work for 13 hours a day. The study has shown how male workers have retained their dominance within a factory's 'sexual hierarchy' by insisting that their work be defined as 'skilled' (better paid) and women's work as semi- or unskilled.[118]

However, despite all these constraints which undermine human dignity and rights, garment industries have opened up a new world for female workers. Some critics of the exploitative garment industry have acknowledged the positive aspects of women working on their own, and agree that women's participation in wage-employment empowers and liberates women 'by introducing changes not only in the life-pattern but also the values held by the workers and their families regarding women's role and position'. Even those workers belonging to the lowest income bracket manage to save themselves and their families from starvation, and their entry into the urban labour market in the long run will 'make themselves more indispensable for industrial capital', eventually leading to empowerment and freedom of women.[119] The signs are already there, indicating the gradual transformation of labour law, including female factory workers' right to have trade union organizations, which will eventually turn women workers into agents of 'organised and active social force'. As Marilyn Rock says,

> Regardless of the tradition and perpetuation of cultural Islamic constraints on Bangladeshi women – influenced as much by patriarchal social arrangements as by religious ideology – the garment workers have become incorporated into new structures in their struggle to respond to globalisation and concomitant forms of restructuring.[120]

It may fairly be assumed that some sort of class solidarity has developed amongst garment workers.[121]

Last but not least, Naila Kabeer has rightly assessed the significance of the garment factories which helped the creation of a first-generation female industrial work-force in a society where *purdah* had existed as an almost impenetrable barrier to the flow of female labour into the public sphere. She has correctly pointed out how the poverty-stricken rural women, who have been forced to emigrate to urban centres to work as garment workers, have attained freedom from the village community (*samaj*) or from the 'surveillance and face-to-face contact' of village elders and *mullas* who insist on the observance of *purdah* and the perpetual servility of women. These factory workers, living in 'urban anonymity' and protected from the so-called Islamic ethos of the *samaj*, have on the one hand been uprooted from the village and on the other have become bold enough to question the authority of the *samaj*. To them '*samaj* is made up of people who are educated, who own houses and cars and work in government jobs. *Samaj* is for them, not for us'. In short, the female garment workers have found a new interpretation of *purdah* or modesty, which they believe is not more important than the obligatory (*farz*) task of saving oneself from starvation. They have also learnt to associate themselves with male workers as their brothers. Despite the problems of sexual abuse and harassment at the workplace, female factory workers' newly found freedom and higher self-esteem have led to the 'de-sexualization' of the workplace.[122] This has substantially empowered female garment workers and they are most definitely more independent and better off than the 'disciplined' and 'domesticated' female NGO workers and clients of the Grameen Bank.

NGOs, social change and conflict

Despite their limitations and their profit-oriented exploitative nature, the Grameen Bank, NGOs and garment industries have brought about changes in Bangladesh society, especially with regard to the gender-relations and roles of women in the society. The institution of *purdah* or seclusion of women has also been jolted by these changes. Although *mullas* in particular and many conservative villagers in general have been alarmed by the process of change, eroding the institution of *purdah* and their power-base at the village level, many other villagers, both men and women, have welcomed the changes, justifying men and women working together for the sake of progress and development (or survival).[123]

Despite some positive response from a section of the poor villagers towards NGO activities, *mullas* and other opponents of NGOs have remained unconvinced of any positive aspects of these organizations. Consequently the Grameen Bank and NGOs may be held responsible for further polarizing the already factious and divided Bangladesh society. Gender issues, along with those of class and religion, have simply led to further aggravation of the situation. In view of this polarization between the pro- and anti-NGO groups, it would be too easy to brush off the ideological aspect of the anti-NGO discourse of both the Islamic and liberal/leftist opponents.

For the average *mulla*, the issues of women working side by side with men, adopting family planning and receiving secular education are of fundamental importance, as to him, they amount to the loss of *iman* or faith of the Muslims, endangering Islam. His misogynous exposition and understanding of Islam as a promoter of patriarchy are also important in this regard. The *mullas'* dependency on rural and urban elites for sustenance, nevertheless, plays a significant role in promoting the patriarchal, age-old vested interests of their patrons. The coming of the NGOs in the countryside in juxtaposition to village elders and *mullas*, in the name of protecting the interests of the poor, especially women, has led to the clash of NGOs with the *member-matbar-mulla* triumvirate, as both the parties have a common clientele in the poor men and women in the rural areas. The upshot is the protracted conflict between the indigenous and external elites in the countryside. While the NGO-Grameen lobby has been vilifying their opponents as obscurantist proponents of male supremacy and enemies of progress and development, the latter has been portraying the NGOs as 'agents of neo-imperialism' and 'enemies of Islam'. NGOs are often depicted as 'foreign agents' engaged in spreading Christianity in Bangladesh. They are often criticized for preferring local Christians to Muslims so far as allocation of jobs and distribution of credit and relief-materials are concerned. Consequently NGO-run schools and other projects have been burnt down or damaged by villagers in some places.[124]

In sum, while the NGO-Grameen lobby and its opponents have been engaged in acrimonious discourse, maligning each other as 'enemies of the people' (anti-NGO *mullas* often being portrayed as *razakars* or quislings of the Pakistani military junta, responsible for killing Bengalis in 1971, or as supporters of the radical Islamists belonging to the Jamaat-i-Islami) both rural and urban women have been mobilized by political activists, NGO workers and feminist groups in the name of establishing their rights through secularism, democracy and Bengali nationalism.[125] Consequently under the aegis of NGOs, feminist groups and proponents of Bengali Nationalism,[126] thousands of poor, backward and subjugated women have been mobilized throughout the country in the name of defending 'secularism' and the 'sovereignty of Bangladesh' from the clutches of 'pro-Pakistani Conspirators', who incidentally have been opposed to the NGO-Grameen activities in the country.

Since the adherents of the NGO-Grameen lobby and their fellow-travellers belonging to several feminist and 'secular-Bengali nationalist' groups have been identifying only the Islamists and opponents of NGO-Grameen activities as the main enemies of and obstacles to the process of female-empowerment in Bangladesh, poor rural women have remained vulnerable to the exploitation done in the name of generating wealth and power at the grassroots level.

Unless we subscribe to the view that only through the availability of credit to the poor is a nation saved from the scourge of

poverty, there is no reason to be subdued by intellectually intimi-
dating assertions about the 'success story' of the Grameen Bank
and other NGOs providing credit to the rural poor of Bangladesh,
nor to be overwhelmed by assertions (by Yunus) such as 'We can
remove poverty from the surface of the earth only if we can rede-
sign our institutions – like the banking institutions', or swerved by
such flippancy as: 'credit is a human right. . . . If credit can be accepted as a human right, then all other human rights will be easier
to establish'.[127]

Mass empowerment and elite hegemony

Empowerment is not simply derivative of the economic self-sufficiency
of an individual, group or polity, but is also conditional on the
level of socio-political autonomy and freedom available to individuals, groups and communities. With regard to the empowerment
of the poor rural women of Bangladesh, one may assume that it is
not attainable only through the help of certain external forces. The
process of empowerment from above is much more difficult (often
unattainable) than that of empowerment from below. Unless both
the urban and rural, rich and poor, men and women in a given
society have mutual understanding, trust and most importantly, a
meeting ground of their respective aspirations, not even poor men,
let alone poor women, have any hope of attaining the power to
regulate their lives in accordance with their wish. Unless there are
concerted efforts from every direction – including both government
and non-government institutions – it would be too early to expect
that relatively backward and illiterate Bangladeshi men and women
would strive for the empowerment of women. While even urban
Bangladeshi men think that working women are taking over male
professional roles, threatening men's sense of patriarchal power,[128]
it is easy to imagine why rural Bangladeshi men, mostly illiterate
and under the influence of misogynist and conservative *mullas*, would
oppose women working and earning side by side with men.

It appears from a recent empirical study of several villages in
Faridpur district that more than 70 per cent of men object to women
working outside. Most villagers think that 'women are not suitable
for employment outside home'. About 70 per cent of men also do
not want their women to work side by side with men outside home
in order to earn income. About 75 per cent of rural men do not
approve of granting equal status to women, especially with regard

to outside activities. A similar proportion of men think that women should not participate in decision making in 'off-*bari*' (outside home) matters either. Most rural women – 90 to 97 per cent (depending on their economic background) – do not regard themselves as equal to men in respect of 'off-*bari*' activities. Again, about 90–9 per cent of rural women are opposed to imparting higher education to girls and about 90 per cent of them prefer literacy for a male child rather than a female child. It is noteworthy that while the majority of upper class rural women prefer secular to *madrasah* education for their daughters, 60 per cent of landless women seek religious education for their daughters, while more than 80 per cent of Muslim men and women in the countryside prefer religious men *(mullas)* as their 'social leaders' than Western-educated men.[129] Hence the need for interventions either by the state or by a well-entrenched civil society for the empowerment of women.

Since it may be argued that development-oriented projects and institutions, initiated both by governments and NGOs, lead to the 'emancipation', and eventually 'empowerment', of the clients of such organizations, poor Bangladeshi women as beneficiaries of NGOs have already been empowered or are in the process of acquiring complete empowerment. Although Marx thought that power has a positive correlation with the ownership of means of production, implying that only the capitalist classes exercise power in a bourgeois state, Gramsci has widened the scope of power by including those classes who establish their hegemony over the masses by controlling religion, education and means of communication.[130] However, both Marx and Gramsci have excluded the notion of gender-domination from the discourse of power. Foucault by contrast explains gender inequality and the problem of female empowerment. According to Foucault the power of the superordinate is not always repressive nor is the penal system (maintained by the bourgeois state) always 'an apparatus of prohibition and repression of one class by another'. 'If power were never anything but repressive, if it never did anything but to say no', he argues, 'do you really think one would be brought to obey it?' He thinks that 'it does not only weigh on us as a force that says no, *but that it traverses and produces things, it induces pleasure, forms knowledge, produces discourse*' [emphasis added].[131]

We may further assume, with Foucault, that only through the 'insurrection of subjugated knowledges' ('a whole set of knowledges that have been disqualified as inadequate to their task', or 'naive knowledges located low down in the hierarchy') would the power-less be empowered.[132] He believes that only through the union of 'erudite' and 'popular knowledge' or 'local memories', 'a historical knowledge of struggles' is established and the masses in alliance with intellectuals are able to challenge the existing knowledge favouring the *status quo*. However, it is pertinent to our under-standing of the power-discourse that power is neither given to someone nor exchanged with someone. It only 'exists in action'.[133] Are NGOs, Grameen Bank and garment factories generating 'a his-torical knowledge of struggles' by sharing their knowledge with that of the poor women of Bangladesh? That is the pertinent question.

Conclusions

The assumption that various NGOs and the Grameen Bank (through its 16-Point Programme) have been disseminating a new discourse or knowledge among Bangladeshi women with a view to challeng-ing the grassroots-based traditional or 'historical knowledge' nourished by both the village community and popular Islam. The 'new knowl-edge' or the 'emancipatory' movements initiated by the NGO-Grameen lobby are not necessarily aimed at empowering the poor women of the region, nor are they aimed at destroying the patron-client rela-tionship. As is well-known, emancipatory movements often benefit the elites instead of those for whom the theories are formulated. So, one may assume that the concerted efforts by the NGO-Grameen lobby to enlist poor rural women support are nothing but new ways of establishing urban elite hegemony over the rural poor by replacing the rural elites – the *member-matbar-mulla* triumvirate – in the name of empowerment of women. While on the one hand, the new dis-course is telling women how to defy their rural superordinates who are protective of patriarchy and popular Islam, on the other, it is ignoring the grassroots-based perception of 'moral' and 'immoral' which throughout history has taught the masses how to fight both local and external agents of exploitation. The core of the problem *vis-à-vis* the process of female empowerment in the region lies in the unfulfilled dream of the poor, illiterate village woman, who felt that the only way to fight patriarchy and exploitation was by cutting down the age-old 'banyan tree'. Neither the rural elders nor the NGO-Grameen lobby are prepared to do so.

Finally, as some 'developmental feminists' have pointed out, male-dominated international institutions who finance 'development' projects in the Third World are biased against women and tend to ignore their contribution to economic growth. The class-divided, patriarchal Bangladesh society benefits from these projects by retaining their control over property, income and women's labour. Poor Bangladeshi women's problems are further aggravated by the patriarchal bias of many 'working-class theoreticians', who (a) advocate women's participation in wage labour employment as the basis of their social liberation, and (b) overlook these same women's domestic labour.[134]

6
Militant Feminism, Islam and Patriarchy: Taslima Nasreen, *Ulama* and the Polity

*Men admire the tea a woman makes for them, not their poems or
literary works. . . . No man is good enough for me in this city.*

Taslima Nasreen

*While a man is at liberty to take his shirt off on a hot summer
day, why should a woman not take off her shirt in similar situation? . . . Women should no longer be 'eatables', they should take
the role of 'eaters', treating all men as 'eatables' and as nothing
more than lumps of flesh.*

Taslima Nasreen

Introduction

It is generally assumed, both in the East and West, that Islam and
feminism have extreme negative correlations, because Islam is supposed to have sanctioned polygamy and an inferior status to women
in comparison to men in all spheres of life – socially, politically
and economically. Scholars as well as laymen cite examples from
Afghanistan, Iran, Saudi Arabia and Pakistan, where laws of evidence, the *hudud* law, the seclusion of women (especially in
Afghanistan and Saudi Arabia) and the laws pertaining to marriage,
divorce and inheritance are not always up to the levels of acceptance and expectations of a modern individual. Since the rise of
Islamic militants – often wrongly subsumed under the ill-defined
category of 'fundamentalists' – Bangladesh has often been portrayed
by many as another 'Islamic country' in the offing.

The militant Jamaat-i-Islami's success in the parliamentary elections of 1991 and their decisive role in the formation of the Khaleda Zia government (headed by a female Prime Minister) are also important indications that Islam has been emerging as a political factor in the country. This is all the more interesting, because the Jamaat-i-Islami and some other Islamic groups who have at least established a prominent niche in the socio-political structure of Bangladesh since the mid-1970s were thoroughly discredited and not allowed to function as political organizations in Bangladesh up to 1975 because of their active collaboration with the Pakistani occupation forces during the Liberation War in 1971. But what was unthinkable in the early 1970s has happened. The 'pro-Pakistani' Islamic groups became quite powerful throughout the country, with support across cross-sections of the population, including university teachers and students, professionals and businessmen. Most supporters of these groups are not trained in *madrasahs* or Islamic seminaries.[1]

By the late 1980s Islamic militants, especially those belonging to the 'fundamentalist' and politically ambitious Jamaat-i-Islami, had become so active, posing threats to secular groups and individuals throughout the country, especially at the Chittagong and Rajshahi universities, that even the Government was forced to adopt means to counter their growing influence by championing the cause of Islam. Consequently the corrupt and hedonistic military regime of General Ershad declared Islam the 'State Religion' of Bangladesh in June 1988. This act of appeasement, with no commitment whatsoever, alarmed many liberal democrat, socialist, secular and feminist groups and individuals in Bangladesh as they apprehended further persecution in the name of Islam as the 'State Religion' for ideological reasons. Many feminist groups opposed the act, anticipating the imposition of *Sharia* and *hudud* laws to undermine women's rights and status in society as had happened in Pakistan under General Zia-ul-Haq, who also Islamized the polity.[2]

As discussed earlier, not only politically organized Islamic militants have been in the ascendancy; non-political *mullas* or village clergy, under half-educated, near-megalomaniac leadership, in alliance with influential village headmen, prone to roguery and thuggery, have also emerged as a force in the rural areas. Their main victims have been poor women. The persecution of these women has alarmed intellectuals and the government machinery in general and women's groups in particular.

Taslima Nasreen, a medical doctor by training and an activist by choice, also wrote against the persecution of rural women by rural thugs and their accomplices, the *mullas*. She, however, also pointed out how women in general were persecuted, humiliated and discriminated against in 'Islamic' Bangladesh. Her main targets of attack were: all religions, especially Islam; the *mullas* and the *ulama* (Muslim theologians); educated Bangladeshi Muslims; and all men in general.[3] Her comments on the Quran and Islam, which will be discussed later, provoked all sections of Muslims in Bangladesh, including a large section of the liberals. This chapter aims at shedding light on the nature of Islamic resurgence in Bangladesh and its impact on the women's movement, with special reference to the solitary and controversial writer, Taslima Nasreen. It also aims at highlighting the impact of Nasreen's writings and activities on the feminist movement, Islamic resurgence and Bangladeshi society in general.

'Desecularization' of the polity and the rise of Islam

The adoption of the four-pronged state ideology – Nationalism, Democracy, Socialism and Secularism, also known as 'Mujibism' – not long after the emergence of Bangladesh, is regarded by many as the last nail in the coffin of the 'Two Nation' theory held by Jinnah. However, they ignore the facts: that what is Bangladesh today was once the eastern part of an undivided Bengal, up to 1947, which took a leading role in espousing the cause of Muslim separatism in the sub-continent; that about 90 per cent of the population are Muslims, but about 70 per cent are illiterate, having incomplete knowledge of the Islamic scripture, hence their gullibility with regard to revivalist and communal propaganda in the name of Islam. Last but not least, in a peasant economy like Bangladesh, where almost 60 per cent of the population are landless peasants, suffering from malnutrition, while viewing from a far the corruption, inefficiency and hedonic life styles of the ruling elites and the *nouveaux riches*, those peasants vulnerable to ideologies that promise revolutionary improvement of their lot.

Secularism and socialism were only incorporated in the constitution in 1972, for which the bulk of the people were neither mentally prepared nor possesesd of any ideological commitment to such alien concepts. They were never the *raisons d'etre* for the liberation struggle of Bangladesh. Both secularism and socialism developed in the industrialized West (not in peasant economies) in the post-Renaissance, post-Industrial Revolution periods of history. This also explains why Islam emerged as a socio-political force in Bangladesh not long after the emergence of the nation concept; both secularism and socialism, having no congenial breeding grounds, therefore only created misgivings and apprehensions about these ideologies among the bulk of the population. The concepts were also associated in the popular mind with godlessness, corruption and the inefficient management of the polity.

While the average Bangladeshi, who had few illusions about Mujib's administration (1972–5), was angry with his government, he also despised India, supposed to be responsible for all his problems – for being instrumental in the creation of the nation and for supporting the existing government which failed to deliver the goods to him in the promised 'Golden Bengal'. Consequently not long after the formation of the polity, this average Bangladeshi, unhappy with the mishmash of secularism and socialism, joined hands with the anti-Mujib (and at times, both anti-Bangladesh, anti-India) forces, which included radical leftists with pro-Chinese inclinations as well as orthodox and communal clandestine Islamic groups. Since all the political parties with any sort of Islamic identity were banned by the Mujib government (examples include the Jamaat-i-Islami, Nizam-i-Islami and Muslim League) for their collaboration with the Pakistani military junta, their supporters found it convenient to support the anti-Mujib/anti-Indian Maulana Bhashani during the 1972–5 period. Although this marriage of convenience between the anti-Soviet/anti-Indian leftists and the adherents of political Islam did not last, the marriage succeeded in producing offspring committed to anti-Indian if not pro-Pakistani policies, communally anti-Hindu and firm believers in Islamic resurgence to capture political power.

For the sake of convenience, these groups with some commitment to an amorphous or well-defined Islam may be categorized as: the militant reformists ('fundamentalists'), mainly represented by the Jamaat-i-Islami and some other militant groups; the fatalists, mainly represented by the puritan, non-militant and non-political Tabligh Jamaat; the 'Anglo-Mohamedans', who are only interested in using Islam for political reasons, and the orthodox groups, which included *pirs* and *sufis*, often with an escapist mentality. However, the above categories do not necessarily imply each respective group's unalterable commitment to a particular ideology. They may shift their allegiance from one group to another.

Despite their mutual differences and enmity, especially those between the orthodox *uluma/pirs* and the Jamaat-i-Islami, or between the 'Anglo-Mohammedans', and the Jamaat-i-Islami for example, with the exception of the 'Anglo-Mohammedans', all the the groups in general are opposed to female liberation, the Western code of conduct, law and ethic, dress and culture, and in favour of establishing the *Sharia* or Islamic law as understood and interpreted by the Sunni *ulama* of the sub-continent. They are apparently committed to the notion of an 'Islamic State', but this notion is often more vague, abstract and utopian than concrete and explicable in terms of modern social sciences.

Beside these four categories of Muslims espousing political or mystic/non-political Islam, there is a fifth category which may be classified as the Liberal Muslims, often indifferent or hostile towards any sort of Islamic ideology, who at times involve themselves in issues concerning the nation, society, including women's affairs and position *vis-à-vis* Islam in Bangladesh. Since most 'Anglo-Mohammedans', militant reformists and many orthodox *pirs* sided with the Pakistani military junta during the war of liberation for Bangladesh in 1971, liberal Muslims have been critical of the Islamic groups' political activities, legalized by General Ziaur Rahman after the military takeover in 1975. Liberal Muslims have been also critical of conservative Muslims' attitude towards the liberation of women, including co-education and equal opportunities in all spheres of life.[4]

Liberalism, women and the polity

Despite conservative Muslims' attack on women's liberation and their advocacy of the seclusion of women and the abolition of co-education and free mixing of the sexes in the workplace, the liberals have been successful in resisting the former group. Both liberal men and women, including the bulk of the 'Anglo-Mohamedans', have been in the forefront of resistance to all attempts to turn Bangladesh into another Iran or Saudi Arabia. It is, however, easier to understand the problem of women's status in Bangladesh society, and especially the ongoing controversy over the radical 'feminist' writer Taslima Nasreen, if we shed light on the prevailing situation in the country.

Legally Bangladeshi women have been accorded equal status in comparison to men in almost every sphere of life. But the reality is somewhat different: women have very limited power and opportunities *vis-à-vis* men, and women's work (in the sense of domestic chores) is still not considered as 'work' by men and by women themselves. Their work is either regarded as 'assistance to the husband or effort to supplement family income'.[5]

Bangladesh is not the only Muslim country (or Third World country, for that matter) where women do not enjoy equal status and opportunities *vis-à-vis* men. Taslima Nasreen is not the first Bangladesh woman to point out the inequalities prevailing between men and women in the country. Begum Rokeya (1880–1932), for example, championed the cause of women's liberation throughout her career as a school teacher and writer, mainly writing against the seclusion of women, and demanding equal status for women in all spheres of life. Although some *mullas* were critical of her activities and writings for espousing the cause of women's liberation, she had the support of the bulk of the 'Anglo-Mohemadan' and the liberal Muslim men and women of Bengal. However, unlike Taslima Nasreen, she did not antagonize every section of the Muslim community by her writings and activities. She understood that it is important to be first of all acceptable to a society before trying to reform or transform it.

Qazi Imdadul Haque (1882–1926), the author of *Abdullah* (a popular Bengali novel), pointed the finger at the superstitious *mullas* for the general backwardness of the Muslim community. He also advocated higher status for women. The famous Bengali poet Qazi Nazrul Islam (1899–1976), known as the 'rebel', pointed out (quite boldly for his age) that 'If the offsprings of an unchaste woman are illegitimate, those of an unchaste man are illegitimate as well.' In another poem by him we read:

> Whatever is a great achievement and an act of eternal piety, the half of them have been accomplished by women and the other half by men.

What we find in the writings of Begum Rokeya, Imdadul Haque and Nazrul Islam is a reflection of Bengali Muslim writers' quest for equality between the sexes. But these writings, with the exceptions of some by Rokeya, did not challenge the social structure and religious scriptures, as hindrances to the attainment of the total freedom of Muslim women in Bengal.

Moderate reformist and some vocal women's organizations since the early 1960s had been active in promoting the interests of women in the region, which is now Bangladesh. But their efforts were mainly confined to Dhaka and some other urban centres. Women's organizations such as the Women for Women; *Mahila Parishad* (Council of Women); *Naripokkho* (On the Side of Women); *Nari Unnayan Shakti* (Front for the Upliftment of Women) and the Women's Development Forum are no exceptions to this. Since their activities are mainly confined to the urban areas and are not critical of Islam and the Quran, neither the *mullas* nor the other Muslim parties in Bangladesh take much notice of these groups. They are tolerated and often ignored by men as nothing more than women's voluntary organizations, promoting birth control and literacy among women. But of late these women's organizations have been facing opposition from conservative forces after Taslima Nasreen made controversial comments about Islam and the *sharia*.

This, however, does not mean that women in Bangladesh have not achieved anything through these organizations. Ever since the introduction of the Muslim Family Law Ordinance of Ayub Khan in 1961, which granted legal protection to women against the right of men to divorce at will and practise polygamy, women's organizations have continued to defy the conservative *ulama*. From the 1960s onward, women in the region also came forward to express their solidarity with various cultural and political movements, especially with regard to the singing of Tagore songs and wearing *bindi* (the vermilion spot on the forehead, traditionally worn by Hindu women), which were regarded as being 'un-Islamic' by the Pakistani government in the late 1960s. Bengali women also took part in political rallies and meetings asserting the rights of East Pakistan, which eventually led to the formation of Bangladesh in 1971.[6]

Not long after the creation of Bangladesh, the 1972 constitution recognized the equality of the sexes, but reserved certain jobs exclusively for men considering those 'unsuitable' for women.[7] The Government, however, reserved 15 parliamentary seats for women (later raised to 30) under Ziaur Rahman (1976–81), who took special measures to improve the condition of women. The creation of the Ministry of Women's Affairs; the reservation of 10 per cent of jobs for women; the allocation of funds for the Women's Rehabilitation Foundation (especially in the rural areas) and family planning programmes; the induction of women in the police force; and the establishment of the *Jatiya Mahila Sangstha* (National Women's Organization) in 1976 to mobilize women in production and development-oriented programmes, all had positive effects with regard to the overall condition of women throughout Bangladesh.

The military regime under General Ershad (1982–90) continued the previous government's policy in this matter. The Ershad government took some measures to give legal protection to women with regard to divorce, abduction, rape and murder.

One may, however, find loopholes and limitations in these government measures and may even reject them as politically motivated, inadequate and instrumental in promoting the interests of the dominant classes in the village power structure. Some observers have rejected the Women in Development project promoted by the Government as a temporary measure to meet the immediate needs of poor women.[8]

Although government measures could not bring about 100 per cent improvement in the lot of Bangladeshi women, these measures have certainly made a positive, albeit slow, contribution towards promoting the women's cause by safeguarding their interests. The Women in Development project has reached 'a fairly broad spectrum', observes Naila Kabeer. She has also pointed out that despite the illiteracy and backwardness of the bulk of the population, government family planning programmes managed to reach more than 10 per cent of women.[9]

To date, although the government measures have played an important role in promoting women's advancement (if not liberation) in Bangladesh, they have never been decisive in this regard. The government declaration of intent to make Islam the state religion in 1988 also could not stop women from participating in the public sphere, despite the misgivings and apprehensions this act created among a large number of intellectuals and women's groups.

Some of the women's ogranizations are affiliated to political parties while others are connected with women voluntary groups and NGOs. The *Mahila Parishad*, for example, which had been an offshoot of the pro-Soviet Communist Party, with more than 30 000 members in 1989, is still operating with a vague socialist inclination. It is the best-managed women's organization in the country, is committed to the implementation of the 10 per cent quota for women in the job market (as promised by the government) and is opposed to any reserved seats for women in parliament, which it points out is an anti-democratic ploy to strengthen the position of the ruling party. Naila Kabeer has rightly pointed out that although the *Mahila Parishad* denounced male violence and subordination of women in Bangladesh, it lost the support of other women's organizations by linking the struggle for women's rights with the wider struggle for socialism and democracy during the Ershad regime.[10]

The numerous women's voluntary groups, such as the Federation of University Women, the Federation of Business and Professional Women, *Naripokkho* (On the side of Women), Women for Women and *Nari Shanghoti* (Women's Collective), for example, together with the women NGOs, such as *Proshika, Nijera Kori* and Saptagram, have been organizing women's groups with long-term programmes to raise the status and conditions of women in every sphere of life. Despite opposition from powerful landowners who appropriate government lands in collusion with corrupt government officials, *Nijera Kori* group members have taken action against these men and have started settling disputes among themselves without relying on traditional power brokers in the rural areas. In some cases, *Nijera Kori* groups have fielded their own candidates in local elections.[11] Besides *Nijera Kori*, several women's groups are engaged in providing legal literacy to Bangladeshi women, especially *vis-à-vis* divorce and inheritance. The Bangladesh Women Lawyers' Association (established in 1986) is pre-eminent among them. These volunteer members (female lawyers) go out to different districts conducting sessions to spread legal literacy among women groups and NGOs. They also broadcast radio and television programmes and publish booklets on women and law. Their achievement is not negligible as they have been safeguarding women's interests in accordance with the existing Family Law and Muslim Law of inheritance.[12] Besides the NGOs and organizations committed to liberate women from subjection, many Bangladeshi intellectuals have been publishing research monographs, books and articles projecting the plight and sufferings of women in Bangladesh and suggesting their remedies.[13]

The emergence of a newly developed female working force, both in the garment industries and elsewhere in Bangladesh, is well reflected in the change of attire and lifestyle of the working women. *Saris*, not convenient for outdoor work, have been replaced by *shalwar-qameez*, hitherto worn by unmarried girls and often despised as Pakistani or non-Bengali by many Bengali nationalists. Some urban and upper-class women have also been wearing jeans and trousers. The bulk of rural women have neither taken up the trendy *shalwar-qameez* nor are they as independent as the garment workers and other urban women. However, as discussed earlier, orthodox and conservative elements in both the urban and rural areas have refused to accept gracefully the phenomenon of women taking up jobs with garment factories, NGO-sponsored projects, nor their borrowing money from the Grameen Bank and other NGOs.

Women and the eclipse of liberalism

It has been pointed out earlier that the Jamaat-i-Islami and other Islamic groups had been gaining ground since the late 1970s and more specifically, since the early 1980s. Their student factions captured the Chittagong University Student's Union and terrorized all their opposition groups – secularists, socialists and liberals. They exert substantial strength in Rajshahi and some other northern and western districts of Bangladesh, especially in regions close to neighbouring India. The Jamaat-i-Islami and some other rightist Islamic groups became so powerful both among students and intellectuals (by mid-1994 the Jamaat had as many as 141 supporters among Dhaka University teachers) that in early 1992 some 'pro-liberation' intellectuals organized the 'public trial' of Professor Ghulam Azam of the Jamaat-i-Islami for his alleged collaboration with the Pakistani military junta in 1971. However, despite their concerted efforts and the verdict of the 'peoples court' held in a park on 26 March 1992 which suggested the death penalty for his 'war crimes', he finally won back his citizenship on 22 June 1994, as decided by the Supreme Court, and he was legally restored as the *amir* or chief of the Jamaat-i-Islami. It may be mentioned here that he had been living in Bangladesh from 1978 to 1994 as a Pakistani national without any valid visa to stay in Bangladesh.[14]

Another example indicates how powerful the Islamic militants have become in urban centres as well. On 12 May 1994 a certain Shamsuddin published an article in a Bengali daily, *Janakantha*, depicting the plight of rural women, especially with regard to the *fatwabaz mullas'* activities. While condemning the rustic, half-educated *mullas*, he cited a well-known story about how *mullas* dispensed *fatwas* citing the verses of the *Quran*.[15] It is interesting that almost a month later someone pointed out that the said article had hurt the religious feelings of many Bangladeshi Muslims. He wanted the author of the article along with the editor and owner of the daily to be arrested in accordance with the law of the land for outraging the religious feelings of many Bangladeshis. Consequently four journalists associated with the newspaper were arrested on 8 June 1994.[16]

The growing influence and strength of the Islamic militants in the country, especially those of the best-organized group, the Jamaat-i-Islami, was well reflected in their militant demonstrations in Dhaka

and other urban areas demanding the execution of Taslima Nasreen
in the wake of her going into hiding in early June 1994. The Jamaat-
i-Islami, who had been relatively indifferent to the controversial
feminist writer up to mid-1994, as the illiterate masses had no access to her anti-Islamic writings, started taking an interest in the
matter when other Islamic groups (some being very obscure and
with very little organization, or following among the masses) had
arranged country-wide protest rallies and meetings demanding the
execution of the writer. In asserting its demands, The Jamaat supporters clashed with supporters of the anti-Jamaat *Sammilito Sangskritik
Jote* (Alliance of Cultural Forums), an alliance of secular, liberal and
leftist groups, opposed to Islamic militancy.[17]

By 1996 the Jamaat-i-Islami were no longer been in alliance with
the ruling party (BNP) of Prime Minister Khaleda Zia (widow of
Ziaur Rahman). The Jamaat felt slighted as the BNP government
abandoned the party not long after winning the 1991 elections
and forming the Government with its support. The Jamaat MPs
played the decisive role in electing 28 female MPs (out of the 30
seats allocated to women) for the BNP, which was vital for the
latter in acquiring a majority in parliament. Yet they did not receive 'most favoured' treatment from the BNP government, who at
one stage arrested Ghulam Azam, the controversial Jamaat leader,
in 1994. Consequently by early 1995 the Jamaat had joined the
opposition bandwagon led by the Awami League under Sheikh Hasina
(daughter of Sheikh Mujib) demanding the resignation of the BNP
government and fresh parliamentary elections. Finally, the BNP had
to resign in March 1996 and fresh parliamentary elections under a
'caretaker government' (the concept was first formulated by the
Jamaat), in June led to the installation of Sheikh Hasina as the
new prime minister. Although the Jamaat played an active role in
the overthrow of the BNP government, it lost its clout in parliament,
barely managing to win three seats in the parliament of 330 members.

However, this does not mean that the Jamaat and other Islam-
oriented political parties, groups and individuals have lost ground
in the political arena of Bangladesh. The process of Islamization,
started by Ziaur Rahman and further accentuated by General Ershad,
had already impacted on the country politically. The influence of
Islam in society and politics is reflected in the way the constitution was modified under Ziaur Rahman who replaced 'Secularism'
with 'Absolute trust and faith in the Almighty Allah shall be the
basis of all actions' in the preamble. Another amendment of the

constitution had *Bismillah-ir-Rahman-ir Rahim* in Arabic (In the Name of Allah, the Beneficent, the Merciful) inserted at the beginning. The impact of Islamization of the polity was further felt during the 1991 parliamentary elections (by then the country had officially had Islam as the state religion since 1988). During the 1991 elections almost all the candidates, including those belonging to the communist parties, had to show their commitment to Islam through their speeches, banners, manifestos and slogans. The Awami League's most popular slogan of the 1970s, *Jai Bangla* (victory to Bengal), was hardly audible during the election campaigns in 1991. Islamic slogans such as 'Allahu Akbar' (God is Great) and 'Bismillah' (in the name of God) were raised by most candidates. 'Bismillah in the Constitution' became so important that even Sheikh Hasina, the Awami League chief, had to declare in public that her party had 'no quarrel with Bismillah'. Despite her assertions that the Awami League was not against Islam, Sheikh Hasina and her allies did not get the majority in the elections. The Islam-oriented parties, the BNP, Jamaat and the Jatiya Party of Ershad, got 54.13 per cent of votes, as against 34.81 per cent by Awami League-led alliance.[18]

Islam had become so important as a political factor that both Khaleda Zia and Sheikh Hasina had to adopt 'Islamic' dress code by covering their heads. Both of them performed the *haj* more than once. Sheikh Hasina, representing the relatively secular Awami League party, even wore black head-gear and a long-sleeved shirt on the eve of and immediately after the 1996 parliamentary elections. The leading women politicians of the country have to conform to the so-called Islamic dress-code for the sake of legitimacy.

What is noteworthy about the changes in attire of women, especially politicians, and the political programmes, rhetoric and style of politics in Bangladesh (all smacking of Islamic revival) is that the polity has been substantially Islamized since the second half of the 1970s. With the violent removal of the one-party rule of Sheikh Mujibur Rahman in 1975 – which apparently had commitments to secularism and socialism – Islam emerged as a political factor in the country. As religious intolerance has been institutionalized in the post-Bhutto Pakistan (since 1977) under the aegis of military rulers and their protégé, Bangladesh is not altogether different in this regard. In both Pakistan and Bangladesh, the Jamaat-i-Islami is neither in power nor is likely to come to power through democratic means in the near future, but political Islam is very much in the ascendancy. In short, politicized Islam has simply Islamized politics in Pakistan as well as Bangladesh. Economic sufferings of the masses along with political chaos and uncertainty have accentuated escapist and fatalist tendencies among every sections of the population. Hence the tremendous rise in the activities of *pirs*, mystics and the Tabligh movement in Bangladesh. The biggest congregation of the devout (albeit escapist) followers of the Tabligh movement is held every year at Tungi, not far from the capital city of Dhaka.

Consequently, as it appears, neither is 'political Islam' any longer the monopoly of the Jamaat-i-Islami and other 'Islam-loving' political parties, nor is Islam any longer irrelevant to the day to day affairs of the government and the people. The Islamization of the polity has another dimension in Bangladesh. It has signalled the ascendancy of the rural and petty bourgeois culture in the arena of politics. The morale of the adherents of a pre-modern culture of escapism and fatalism in Bangladesh was further boosted by the military rulers, Ziaur Rahman and Ershad, who badly needed legitimacy.

In view of the above, it would be easy to assume that the BNP, Awami League or any other political party would be able to go too far in the opposite direction and de-Islamize the political culture of Bangladesh. Granting equal rights and opportunities to women, in the changed circumstances, has become more challenging because of the ascendancy of the 'Islam-loving' culture. Although the Jamaat has been routed in the 1996 parliamentary elections, Maulana Delwar Hossain Saidi, one of the leading demagogues of the party, who had strong misogynous opinions,[19] was elected an MP.

Besides the so-called 'Islam-loving' misogynists, many 'secular' adherents of partriarchy have also been opposed to granting equal rights and opportunities to women, especially with regard to inheritance and employment opportunities. The Taslima Nasreen episode can be understood only through an understanding of the dynamics of the society and politics in Bangladesh. As Taslima Nasreen has rightly pointed out, not only the so-called 'Islam-loving' people are responsible for the overall backwardness and sufferings of women, the so-called 'liberal democrats' are also responsible for circumscribing women's rights in Bangladesh. The *Sharia* is frequently cited by both Islam-oriented as well as secular and agnostic/atheist Bangladeshi Muslim men in justification of unequal inheritance rights of Muslim women. It is interesting that when one female MP from the ruling BNP party, Farida Rahman, during the tenure of Khaleda Zia as prime minister, tried to table a bill in parliament to prohibit polygamy in Bangladesh, both BNP and opposition MPs opposed the move as an encroachment on the *Sharia* law. This incident is instructive on the implications of Taslima Nasreen's ultra-feminist and anti-Islamic tirades in a backward, patriarchal society like that of Bangladesh.

Before evaluating the controversial feminist Taslima Nasreen with regard to the rights of women, Islam and other supposed impediments to the growth of a liberal, secular society in Bangladesh, we should consider why Islamic militants are feared by Bangladeshi liberals and leftist forces, and why the liberal/secular forces opposed to Islamic resurgence have not been strong enough to oppose them.

A closer observation of the programmes and activities of the Islamic militants, especially the Jamaat-i-Islami, reveals that their cherished 'Islamic state' means much more than a mere change in the name of the country as 'Islamic'. What the liberal and secular groups apprehend in the Jamaat's Islamic utopia is authoritarian rule of the *ulama*, who are opposed to:

- democratic institutions
- equal rights and status for women and the non-Muslim minorities
- co-education
- women's involvement and participation in politics
- women's appearance in public places without a veil.

Other habits, institutions and ways of life associated with the West or the syncretic Bangladeshi culture (often ridiculed as 'Hindu' by most Islamic groups and individuals), developed in the course of history, also arouse their opposition.[20]

On the question of the activities of liberal, secular forces *vis-à-vis* those of the Islamic militants it may be pointed out that despite the Jamaat-i-Islami's success in capturing 18 seats and 12 per cent of the votes in the 1991 parliamentary elections,[21] liberal-secular forces are dominant in every sphere of Bangladesh society and politics. Some empirical studies indicating the rural as well as urban Bangladeshi Muslims' political orientation and temperament suggest that they prefer the 'Islam-loving' Western-educated to the *mullas* as their favourite candidates in elections.[22] What the liberal-secular groups and individuals have attained in the last century or so with regard to freedom and a higher status for women is not insignificant at all. In view of the way Muslim women have achieved higher status in society, rights to modern education (including at tertiary and post-graduate levels), and opportunities to come out of *purdah* or seclusion since the late nineteenth century,[23] there is no reason to believe that Islamic militants will be able to reverse the process of women's liberation in Bangladesh.

It is important here to note that unlike Muslims in Iran, Saudi Arabia, Afghanistan or some other Muslim countries, Bangladeshi Muslims in general, including those in the rural areas, are not accustomed to the complete seclusion of women. Muslims in Bangladesh are not regulated by Islamic culture. Their culture is very syncretic (if not secular), very similar to that of Indonesian Muslims. Parts of Sylhet, Comilla, Noakhali, Chittagong, Barisal and Khulna and some pockets in north-western Bangladesh, which were relatively free from the dominance of Hindu *zamindars* (landlords) and elites throughout history, are more 'Islamic' than the rest of the country, but in the limited, cultural sense of the term. The Islamic revival, in the true sense of the term, is not well-entrenched in Bangladesh society.

Taslima Nasreen and her controversial writings

Islamization of the polity is more symbolic, with Islam as the 'state religion' since 1988, than real. However, the political use of Islam by the two successive military regimes between 1975 and 1990 has overshadowed liberalism and secularism by promoting intolerance and militancy in the name of Islam.

In the light of this, there is no reason to believe that Taslima Nasreen is the first crusader to liberate Bangladeshi women. Since she is not the first one to point out discriminatory practices against women in Muslim and Bangladeshi societies, for our understanding of Islam and feminist movement in the country, we must explain why she has emerged as the most articulate champion of women's liberation in Bangladesh. Taslima Nasreen was born in 1962 in Mymensingh (northern Bangladesh). An anaesthetist by training and a poet and writer by choice and temperament, she entered the limelight after starting writing a column for a Bengali weekly, *Khabarer Kagaj*, in 1989. These 'columns' were later published in a book, entitled *Nirbachito Column* (Selected Column) in early 1991. Meanwhile she published her collections of poems in Bengali. Her initial writings were about the rights of women and their violations in Bangladesh. Soon sex emerged as the most important theme and issue in her works. The next phase of her writing portrayed Islam in particular, and Hinduism and other religions in general, as manmade tools for the exploitation of women. Meanwhile, she continued writing erotic poems and prose depicting men as the meanest creatures on earth. For novelty and sensationalism, her writings were among the best-sellers in 1991–2.[24] Her *Nirbachito Column*, which soon catapulted her to fame, fetched her the Ananda Award from the Indian media-mogul, the *Ananda Bazar* group of Calcutta. She was the first non-Indian to receive this award.

The award, however, not only brought her fame but also the stature of one of the most controversial persons in Bangladesh. Many Bangladeshi writers and intellectuals associated the award with anti-Muslim Hindu chauvinism in India. It was also pointed out that the award was a slap in the face for the nation because many well-established Bangladeshi writers had not been considered suitable for the award, and it was awarded to Taslima Nasreen's *Nirbachito Column*, sections of which appeared to have been taken from Indian feminist writer Maitreyi Chatterjee's book (recipient of Ananda Award in 1988). It has also been pointed out that famous Bengali writer Sunil Gangopadhyay had introduced Nasreen to the *Ananda Bazar* group, who later awarded her with the Ananda Award.[25]

No sooner had Nasreen received the Ananda Award in 1992 than a well-organized opposition called 'Taslima Nasreen Suppression Committee' was formed. This group, mainly formed by liberal-secular students of Dhaka University having nothing to do with Islamic militants, vehemently attacked her writings. In February 1993, these students set fire to her books in the Bangla Academy book fair. Some of them even physically assaulted her. They threatened all Bangladeshi publishers with dire consequences in the event of their publishing any work by Taslima Nasreen. Not long after, Islamic militants followed suit by condemning her for defiling Islam. It is interesting that even a professional group like the Doctors' Association of Bangladesh to which Nasreen belonged as a practising doctor working in a government hospital in Dhaka, urged the government of Bangladesh to transfer her from Dhaka to a rural hospital to 'stop her activities'.[26]

A cross-section of educated Bangladeshi Muslims were not very comfortable about Taslima Nasreen's activities. Apart from her personal life – married and divorced thrice, and not leading a conformist lifestyle – her writings and interviews with local and international media, full of attacks on male chauvinism and religious texts and practices, which were alleged to have supported male supremacy in the society, antagonized them.

An examination of her writings indicates that initially they were mainly critical of male supremacy and chauvinism as reflected in the socio-political economic spheres and also in the adages/proverbs and literature. The next phase was devoted to attacks on Islam, especially on popular Bengali books on Islamic teachings and ways of life (that includes women's/wives' duties towards men/husbands) written in the early twentieth century. In the next stage, she started writing against the Quranic texts and *hadises*.

Her award-winning *Nirbachito Column* begins with the story of how her arm was burnt with the fiery end of a cigarette by a teenage boy outside a cinema in Mymensingh, when she was 19 years old. In her account of the incident she tells us that she did not ask for any help from the people nearby as 'not only illiterate but even literate' people in Bangladesh treat women as being less than human. Then she goes on to tell us that high-heeled shoes for women were designed so that women could not run away when attacked by men; 'why girls are not supposed to travel on their own', 'why men cannot accept that a woman's writings could be better than those of many men', 'why only women should be "chaste" not men'. 'Many wives are getting venereal diseases from their husbands', 'why many (Bangladeshi) wives refer to their husbands as *sahib* or *karta* (lord and master)', 'why Bangladeshi women, raped by Pakistani soldiers during the Liberation war in 1971, are disgraced and not rehabilitated in the society', 'the incidents of rape of women by their husbands are very common in Bangladesh', 'men admire the tea a woman makes for them, not their poems or literary works', 'women are very lonely, some of them are aware of their loneliness and some are not', 'marriage for Bangladeshi women is similar to lottery – only the very lucky ones get good husbands', 'women were better off in the Soviet Union, capitalism is bad for women', 'if wearing of bangles is disgraceful for men (bangles are associated with women), why is wearing of men's attire not bad for women?' These questions and statements are hardly either offensive or far from the truth.

However, her most provocative writings include the following: 'while a man is at liberty to take his shirt off on a hot summer day, why should a woman not take off her shirt in similar situations' and 'women should no longer be "eatables", they should take the role of "eaters", treating all men as "eatables" and as nothing more than lumps of flesh'. She has also suggested that women should rape men in retaliation. She also thinks that men are running after women 'only to have illicit sex with them' and to bring them under male subjugation. 'No man is good enough for me in this city', goes her assertion. She has also advocated the 'freedom of the uterus' for women, rejecting the age-old notions about chastity and virginity. In short, she has openly advocated promiscuity and free sex, without taking into account the cultural outlook of the average Bangladeshi.[27] Some of her poems and newspaper articles, especially in the Bengali weekly, *Jaye Jaye Din* from Dhaka, are full of erotic expositions and vivid descriptions of how women and young girls are molested, in most cases by elderly Muslim men. There is no dearth of pornographic descriptions of sexual acts in her fiction either. At times, the plight of the raped female characters of her novels is overshadowed by the vivid descriptions of rape.

In an interview with me, Enayetullah Khan, a renowned journalist and intellectual of Bangladesh, who also edits *Holiday*, described Taslima Nasreen as 'the epitome of vulgarity', 'a liar', 'an agent of the BJP (a Hindu revivalist political party in India)' and 'one who was after cheap popularity'.[28] In an editorial, *Holiday* has portrayed her as 'the hard porn poetess', who has 'pathological and libidinous distaste' for Bangladesh society.[29] Not only Muslim men, with both Islamic and liberal-secular orientations, but also modern, educated women in Bangladesh do not support her writings and activities. Some Bangladeshi feminist leaders feel that she has done great harm to the women's liberation movement, as many people have been misled into equating women's liberation with the demand for free sex and promiscuity.[30]

Among her anti-Islamic writings and statements, excerpts may be cited from her *Nirbachito Column*, press and TV interviews and a four-hour interview with me in November 1993, to show how she relates problems of women's liberation in Bangladesh with Islam. She has been, however, critical of all religions, including Hinduism and Islam, as 'man-made devices to exploit women'.[31] However, what appears from her tirades against Islam is the reflection of her grossly inadequate knowledge of the religion and bias against it. She failed to differentiate between the *hadises* (which are not universally accepted by all Muslims as authentic) and the Quran. She has often cited the ways half-educated *mullas* and others practise and perceive Islam in Bangladesh in order to substantiate her arguments against the religion, portraying it as supportive of male supremacy.

Since her criticism of Islam has been based on second-hand information, literal translations of the Quran, unauthentic *hadis* literature and above all, on a complete lack of knowledge (or even vague

ideas) of how many Muslim intellectuals throughout history have
been critical of the backward-looking *mullas*, suggesting major changes
in the *Sharia* law, by re-interpreting the Quran and de-emphasizing
the *hadis*.[32] Taslima Nasreen's invectives against Islam may be rejected as lop-sided arguments put forward by a lay person without
any knowledge of Islam. Her writings censuring Islam, including
the Quran and *hadis* did not go unchallenged. It is interesting that
the 'threat on her life' which will be discussed later, did not come
only for her anti-Islamic writings, but for her 76-page novelette,
Lajja (Shame), depicting the plight of the Hindu minority community
in Bangladesh. Some Bangladeshi intellectuals with an Islamic orientation reacted against her anti-Islamic writings, branding her an
ignorant, uninformed person. Some *mullas* and Muslims from the
wider community demanded her trial, if not execution, in late 1993.

One of her critics has rejected Nasreen's claim that the Quran
has allowed husbands to torture their wives. He also holds that
hadises do not consider women as 'commodities', or 'objects of
enjoyment', as Nasreen has perceived, but as a 'human resource'
and very precious. He has cited other *hadises*: 'Be kind and nice to
women'; 'The best among you is the one who is also the best person to his wife'; to contradict Nasreen's assertions. He has quoted
the Quran to substantiate his argument: 'And behave nicely with
your wives and lead an honest life'.[33] Another critic rejects Nasreen's
view that the Quran is 'unscientific'. He rejects Nasreen's assertion
that the Quranic teachings include: 'The sun moves round the earth';
rather, he points out, there is no such verse in the Quran, but on
the contrary, the Quran suggests that all planets including the Earth
are not static.[34] Others have attacked Nasreen's claim that Islam
allows rape of wives by their husbands. They cite the following
hadis in this context: 'If too much of sex between the husband and
the wife is not good for the latter, the husband is not allowed to
force his wife to have sex'. They also cite a Quranic verse to show
the equal status of men and women in Islam: 'What rights men
have on women, women have the similar rights on men'.[35]

Despite the bitter criticisms of Nasreen's writings by Islamist intellectuals and politicians she remained undaunted, and continued
her tirades against Islam and male supremacy. Her major confrontation with the Government and the bulk of liberal Muslims started
with the publication of *Lajja*, published in February 1993, which
explored the plight of Hindus in Bangladesh in the wake of the
BJP movement against the Babri Mosque at Ayodhya in 1990. Her

book is not typical fiction. Many of the characters are fictional, but some are real. This book not only portrays the plight of Bangladeshi Hindus who lost their property, had their temples and idols destroyed, their women abducted and raped by Muslim hooligans, but it also suggests a total helplessness of Hindus in the country. No Bangladeshi Muslim was shown as liberal, non-communal, and protective of Hindu life and property in Bangladesh.[36]

The government of Bangladesh proscribed the book after a few months in mid-1993. By then the book had received wide publicity throughout India. The BJP was using it to justify its anti-Muslim stand. The book has also been translated into some other Indian languages and into English, and Penguin (India) published it in 1994. By October 1993 Muslim intellectuals and others from all sections of the community had become aggressively anti-Taslima for her *Lajja*. Not only Islamist groups and individuals, but even liberal-secular Muslims, including some radical pro-Chinese communist politicians and intellectuals staged demonstrations against the book throughout the country.[37]

In September 1993, the anti-Taslima agitations assumed a new dimension. Three obscure Islamic groups of Sylhet (north-eastern Bangladesh): *the Sahaba Sainik Parishad* (the Council of the Soldiers of the Companions of the Prophet), *Hafizjee Huzur Sangsad,* and *Shah Waliullah Smriti Sangsad* (Councils of Committees as memorials to Hafizjee Huzur and Shah Waliullah, two Muslim leaders of the sub-continent), demanded Nasreen's arrest, the proscription of all her writings and her death for her anti-Islamic writings, especially *Lajja*. Only two relatively insignificant Bengali dailies published the *fatwa,* said to have been issued by the above-mentioned Islamic groups. It was alleged that the *fatwa* declared a price (50 000 taka or US$1200) for Taslima's head. However, the leaders of the said groups denied having issued such a *fatwa*. But by 11 October, Amnesty International took up the matter and world media, especially Indian and Western, started a campaign to 'save' Taslima's life.[38]

The Government granted police protection to the author. Most Bangladeshi intellectuals did not believe that the 'threat on Taslima's life' was real.[39] She even told me in November 1993, 'I am not scared at all'.[40] Meanwhile, her passport had been impounded on 23 January 1993, for concealing her identity as a doctor working with a government hospital. (Incidentally her passport was impounded before the publication of *Lajja* and was returned after her resignation from government service.)

Not long after the alleged *'fatwa* to kill' gained wide publicity throughout the world, Nasreen returned to the limelight in early May 1994. After recovering her impounded passport, she went to Paris and Calcutta. The trouble erupted with the publication of her interview in a Calcutta daily, *Statesman*. She was quoted by the daily suggesting that the Quran should be re-written to safeguard the interests of Muslim women. Islamic groups, as well as 'secular/ liberal' political groups, students and intellectuals demanded her arrest and trial for committing blasphemy against Islam. Many *ulama* and their supporters simply sentenced her to death.[41] This incident reminds us of what Ayatollah Khomeini of Iran and the Iranian government did to Salman Rushdie in 1989.

By early June 1994, Nasreen went into hiding for fear of her life. Meanwhile, she drew sympathy from different quarters of the world. Amnesty International and most of the Western governments and media came forward to protect her from the clutches of the 'fanatic' Muslims. Finally she surrendered to the judiciary in Bangladesh and was released on bail. On 3 August 1994, Nasreen left Bangladesh for Sweden, where she was well-received by the Swedish government and was later honoured with a literary award.[42] The episode did not end with Nasreen's self-imposed exile in Sweden. Various Islamic groups, including the influential Jamaat-i-Islami, mobilized mass support demanding the introduction of a 'blasphemy law' to protect the 'sanctity of Islam' throughout Bangladesh. Several general strikes were observed in support of the demand in various towns of the country.[43] These groups held the 'pro-Western' and 'anti-Islamic' government of Bangladesh responsible for allowing Nasreen to leave the country before the completion of her trial. Her short visit to Bangladesh to see her dying mother in late 1998 again aroused various Islamic groups who demanded her immediate arrest and trial for committing blasphemy. Although the Government did not arrest her, she was not able to come out of hiding during her short stay and had to leave the country after a couple of months.

The anti-Nasreen lobby in Bangladesh represented by both Islamists and secular groups having an anti-Western proclivity, soon 'discovered' links between her and the West. Some Western media reports depicting both the government and people of Bangladesh as intolerant and obscurantist strengthened the suspicion of these groups.[44] The Australian Broadcasting Corporation's portrayal of Bangladeshi women as the 'most oppressed in the world' in a documentary on Taslima Nasreen in June 1994, may be cited in this regard. President Clinton and the Amnesty International among others, also condemned the Bangladesh government for the 'violation of human rights', with reference to Nasreen.

Despite Taslima Nasreen's assertions condemning Western capitalism and *Hindutva*, she has virtually been trapped by them both. Consequently she has been identified as a 'BJP agent', 'CIA agent', 'Indian agent' and 'enemy of Islam', and also has been tarnished with epithets such as 'pervert', 'anarchist', 'sexually deprived and abused person', throughout Bangladesh. Not only the often-maligned and undefined Islamic groups but atheists and agnostics have derided her for her writings and activities.

Conclusions

The outcome of the Taslima Nasreen episode is both pathetic for the country and nothing short of a nemesis for the author. The issues with which Taslima Nasreen started – pointing out how women are discriminated against in our society, boldly illustrating our double standards, hypocrisy and irrational practices, beliefs and superstitions, could be very positive for the progress of Bangladeshi society. But then she lost her way. From her writings and other sources, her personality appears to be not only an odd combination of opposites but also that of an aggrieved, angry woman. However, her works (besides their vulgar, pornographic connotations) are indicative of her lack of knowledge and ideas about her subject matter, especially Islam and the rights of women in Islamic texts, and the society and people she was dealing with in Bangladesh.

Unfortunately for Nasreen (as well as for Bangladesh), instead of trying to find out the reasons she has emerged as a rebel, most Bangladeshi politicians, intellectuals, students and others have been lynching her for either committing blasphemy or for writing provocative prose and poems. She could have been portrayed as an effect of the prevalent social order or a by-product of social disharmony and lack of commitment among the bulk of the population – peasants, petty bourgeoisie and *lumpenproletariat*. The rampant, unbridled corruption of the *nouveaux riches* and members of the well-established elites; the mutual patronage of half-educated *pirs* and elites (administrators and businessmen); and last but not least, the advent of a class of half-educated *mullas* in both the rural and urban areas must have alienated many educated men and women in Bangladesh from Islam and other well-established norms and practices. Taslima Nasreen is no exception.

Taslima Nasreen could have been a positive force in promoting the interests of women in Bangladesh, especially the downtrodden rural and poor illiterate ones. Instead, she has antagonized all sections of the society, including feminist activists and progressive thinkers, writers and professionals. It was very unkind towards Indian and Bangladeshi Muslims to suggest that while communal riots in India have always been 'two-sided' conflicts between Hindus and Muslims, in Bangladesh they have been 'one-sided' – Muslims persecuting Hindus. Her depiction of the Babri Mosque as 'a symbol of discrimination' (against Hindus) and her refusal to accept the boundary lines drawn between India and Bangladesh are simply counter-productive, one-sided and even 'seditious' from the Bangladeshi viewpoint.[45]

In sum, Taslima Nasreen's works do not enrich our knowledge about the plight of women and minorities in Bangladesh and they are in no way useful in understanding the phenomenon which is wrongly portrayed as Islamic fundamentalism. What *is* pertinent to our understanding of Islam and women in Islamic and Muslim societies is that they are not monolithic. The concepts and customs relating to women's rights and roles vary from one generation or class to another, from one country to another. What is generally assumed to be the 'Islamic' persecution of women is in fact a by-product of patriarchal kinship arrangements and pre-capitalist ideologies, which often are more powerful than, and independent of, Islamic ethos and values. There is no basis in assertions made by Taslima Nasreen, and echoing those of many Western intellectuals and media, portraying the Bangladeshi government and people as obscurantist and Islamic 'fundamentalist' in the derogatory sense.

However, the statement made by Dr Kamal Hossain, Nasreen's main attorney, in the wake of his client's release on bail in August 1994, contradicts the assertions portraying Bangladesh as a barbaric polity.

> The grant of bail . . . has again established that there is a constitutional government in this country . . . Different fundamentalist and communal forces are engaged in conspiracies to tarnish the image of our society and country . . . They should realize that there is rule of law and free judiciary in the country.[46]

Yet this does not mean that the bulk of the population has much respect for rule of law, let alone the freedom of expression. The people in this region are by nature prone to violence, anarchy and factious actions. There is among them hardly any long-lasting commitment to any particular ideology or leader. The chaotic situation prevailing in Bangladesh in almost every sphere of life reflects the nature and political culture of the people. The marriage of convenience between the protagonists of political Islam and rustic masses (poor and exploited) is not a new phenomenon in the region. But since the 1820s such marriages have often led to dramatic and unpredictable results. Taslima Nasreen has unwittingly provided additional material to strengthen the tie between rustic anarchists and the protagonists of 'Islam in danger' in Bangladesh.

However, Nasreen does not agree that through her confrontational style she has provoked the 'fundamentalists'. According to her, religion is not the exclusive property of the fundamentalists. She thinks that she has the right to speak and is critical of many of the 'so-called progressive writers' in Bangladesh who, according to her, 'do nothing to give the fundamentalists an issue to shout about, so they keep their mouths shut'.[47] She is quite convinced that she should write about the plight of Bangladeshi women. 'Do you know what it's like to see a woman crying out in the delivery room when she gives birth to a girl, terrified that her husband will divorce her? To see the ruptured vaginas of women who've been raped? The six – and seven-year-olds who have been violated by their fathers, brothers, and uncles – by *their own families?*' She poses the questions and affirms, 'No, I will not keep quiet'.[48]

As we have seen, many Bangladeshi intellectuals who have sympathy for women, minorities and other under-privileged groups in the country, deride her 'irresponsibility'. According to one female social worker who works on women's programmes in the countryside: 'Taslima went for the jugular, and we're not ready for that. There's simply too much at stake. You have to learn how to deal with the situation . . . And that is something Taslima never understood.'[49]

Some observers believe that both the West and the 'fundamentalists' used Taslima Nasreen for their own political purposes. Shafik Rahman, the editor of weekly *Jaye Jaye Din*, which used to publish Nasreen's writings up to 1994, is one of them. He thinks that: 'The fundamentalists needed a symbol, the West needed a symbol ['a female Salman Rushdie'], and Taslima was the demarcation line. On both sides, she was catapulted into a political – not a literary –

sky'.[50] As Begum Sufia Kamal, an octogenarian female writer and social worker, has observed, while several other Bangladeshi writers, including herself, had simply ignored the *fatwas*, this did not happen in the case of Nasreen.[51]

However, this is equally true that while the *fatwas* against other writers and intellectuals like Ahmed Sharif, Shamsur Rahman and Sufia Kamal portrayed them as *murtads* or apostates, the *fatwas* against Nasreen brought more than 300 000 anti-Nasreen people on the street demanding her death and a 'blasphemy law'. One wonders why some other Bengali writers, such as Humayun Azad, did not have to face any *fatwas* for writing anti-Islamic, 'blasphemous' books! Azad's *Nari* [Women] may be cited here. Azad is much more critical of many Quranic verses and Islam than Taslima Nasreen is. Is Nasreen singled out because of her sex? Has patriarchy something to do with this? Nasreen is right in saying that the average Bangladeshi men, including the 'progressive ones', can at best be condescending to women. They may accept female writers who imitate the style and subject matter of male writers as long as they remain conformist. 'The problem grows up when a Bangladeshi woman wants to do some rally creative writing'.[52]

Last but not least, Nasreen's creativity combined with her courage, defiance and rebellion, as reflected in her writings, are too much for the average Bangladeshi man. As she antagonized the different sections of the population, especially the *ulama* and others who are too inclined to believe that she had asked for the revision of the Quran (despite her denials), she cannot preach her ideas in the country any more in the near future. She may be a 'symbol of freedom' for the women of the world,[53] not so in Bangladesh, as neither her admirers not her critics in the country are willing to identify themselves with her and her ideas, for various reasons. The former are apprehensive of reprisals from the various 'Islamic' and 'secular' groups and the latter are simply averse to associating with her because of her anti-Islamic and irresponsible writings.

7
Conclusions

*In every age and country, the wiser, or at least the stronger, of
the two sexes, has usurped the powers of the state, and confined
the other to the cares and pleasures of domestic life.*
> Edward Gibbon, The Decline and
> Fall of the Roman Empire, *ch. 6.*

As explained in the Introduction, this book has attempted to understand the dynamics of a predominantly Muslim and agrarian society
like Bangladesh in relation to the position of women in different
spheres of life. It has raised the question whether 'Islamic' societies
have necessarily negative correlations with feminism or any attempt
to promote women's interest. This study has tried to answer the
question by shedding light on various aspects of beliefs and practices
of Muslims in general and those of Bangladesh in particular in
relation to the rights and status of women. The reciprocity between
Islam (as understood and practised in the region) and patriarchy-
cum-misogyny of Bengali men has also been explored. Both the
'great' and 'little' traditions of Islam has been studied in juxtaposition with patriarchy as well. In short, this binary of Islam (both
the scriptural and the popular versions of the faith) and male
supremacy, may shed new light on the problem of subjection of
women in peripheral Muslim societies.

   This study has resolved some questions and raised many more
with regard to the problem of granting equal rights and opportunities to Bangladeshi women. The contentious issues of granting
equal inheritance rights to women and the institution of *purdah* or
seclusion of every sphere of life, as analysed in this study, might

disturb the conservative section of Bangladeshi Muslims, especially those with vested interests in properties. Nevertheless, this attempt to resolve the contentious issues does not seek alienation from the modernist-*cum*-reformist Muslims. Rather it aims at opening a dialogue between the two groups. The study has revealed that while there are semi-ignorant and misogynous people in the country, the so-called protagonists of women's 'liberation' and 'empowerment', including those associated with various NGOs, human rights and feminist groups, are not less opportunistic, dishonest and exploitative than the conservatives. While one may verbally lynch village elders (*matbars* and *mullas*) for the persecution of women in the name of *Sharia* law, one should not lose sight of the exploitative nature of some NGOs and micro-credit organizations, especially in the countryside. Contrary to the observations made by some Western scholars, donor agencies and their local clients, the bulk of Bangladeshi women who are subject to some sort of exploitation and persecution, are victims of patriarchy and secular institutions rather than those of Islam-oriented politics and social order.

Whether the 'transition' through which Bangladesh is said to have been going since the late 1970s and early 1980s – a by-product of 'globalization' and the market economy – has anything to do with the 'sudden rise' in the level of persecution of women in the region, is a question raised and resolved here as well. It is noteworthy that throughout modern history, from the advent of the East India Company to the emergence of Bangladesh in 1971, politicians and scholars have always discovered positive correlations between social changes and upheavals with the so-called 'transitions' the country has been supposed to be passing through. So there is nothing new about the so-called transition as the catalyst of social change in the region.

However, as discussed in this study, the emergence of NGOs and Western donor agencies and missionaries since the 1970s have brought qualitative changes in the modes as well as relations of production throughout the country. The phenomenal demographic pressure, coupled with the mismanagement of the polity in the quarter century following independence in 1971, have further accentuated the patron-client relationship, which is the norm in any resource-constrained peasant society. The advent of new patrons, mostly the pro-Western '*NGO-Wallas*', with new programmes and slogans to improve the conditions of the poor, especially women, has led to competition between the old and new patrons. While the former represent village elders – the *member-matbar-mulla* triumvirate – the latter represent more powerful, modern-educated, urban cronies of Western aid agencies and missionaries. So, the crux of the problem lies in the understanding of this elite conflict, which in a way, is a 'clash of the civilizations' in miniscule.

As this study has shown, both the traditional and modern elites have been vying with each other for power, influence and authority over the masses. This, however, does not mean that all the new patrons have ulterior motives behind their efforts to uplift and empower the poor women. What is questionable is not their integrity but their *modus operandi* and programmes. One may admire some of the grassroots-based NGOs and social workers for their efforts to eradicate illiteracy and poverty among women. However, this does not alter how futile and disruptive are (a) the attempts to empower only women leaving aside men and (b) to condemn Islam, especially the Quran, unwittingly for every malady afflicting society, including the subjection of women.

As analysed in this work, many NGOs and donor agencies have been vilifying the *mullas* and Islam-oriented political groups and people as the main agents of exploitation of Bangladeshi women. While village elders and NGOs fight over the control of the village community for mundane reasons, pro-NGO intellectuals, newspapers and Western donor agencies and media do not hesitate to portray the conflict as one between the protagonists of Islamic 'fundamentalism' and secularism. Their lack of understanding of the village community, Islam and the sense of dignity and honour of the people at grassroots level is partially the reason for such irresponsible remarks. The pro-Western, pro-NGO lobby are also prejudiced against anything remotely resembling an Islamic resurgence. Consequently some objective studies, portraying the NGO-villagers dispute in some districts as by-products of local conflicts over scarce resources, have not been acceptable to Western donor agencies. They are not yet prepared to accept the reality that nine out of ten intra-village conflicts, such as burning down NGO-run schools or destroying mulberry plantations by villagers, have nothing to do with Islamic resurgence or fanaticism. As some studies have revealed, some local primary school teachers incited villagers to burn down NGO-run schools who had been taking away students from their schools. Some villagers who have vested interest in government land, used by NGOs to grow mulberry for feeding silkworms, on the other hand, were behind the destruction of mulberry plantations.

However, as the study has shown, there have been endemic conflicts between rival groups, apparently between the 'protectors of Islamic values' and the champions of 'women's rights and liberation' throughout the country in the 1980s and 1990s. For someone who is not familiar with the history and traditions of East Bengali Muslims, these conflicts could be symptomatic of an impending change in the socio-political and economic structures of Bangladesh, which is supposed to be at the crossroads of the great transition between modernism and orthodoxy, or the market economy and pre-capitalist economy.

Those who *are* familiar with the history and traditions of the people are aware of the realities prevailing in the predominantly rural, peasant and illiterate/semi-literate society of Bangladesh, in which no substantial changes have taken place with regard to the beliefs, values, customs and norms of the rural masses (about 80 per cent of the population). Despite the cosmetic changes and some exposure to the world outside the bamboo hedges of the rural hamlet through education, radio and television networks and 'NGO-activities', the bulk of the rural masses, especially women, have remained illiterate, poor and dependent on patrons. The conflicts, in a way, are those between the supporters of new and old patrons, the former representing the NGOs and others extraneous to the traditional village community, which has *mullas* and *matbars* as its integral parts. The disputes are also reflective of the nature of the traditional village community of East Bengal, supposed to be run by 'the most quarrelsome, litigious and vindictive' people, and where harmony has been the exception rather than the rule.

In view of the above, this study has shown that neither factional squabbles nor the persecution of women at the hands of patriarchy in the name of Islam are novelties in the region. This is an attempt to understand why there has been a substantial rise in these disputes, and more open discussion and condemnation of such acts. On the one hand, the phenomenal growth of population, which has almost doubled since the 1960s, and the slow pace of development and growth have accentuated the competition for scarce resources among the people. On the other hand, the exposure of violent and discriminatory acts against women through the media, human rights groups, donor agencies and NGOs (who have proliferated in the post-Bangladesh period) have led to more discussion and studies of the problem than ever before. This book has also shown that despite the concerted attacks on NGOs and feminist/human rights activists, especially by conservative/Islamic groups, the former are well-entrenched in society. However, as the study has shown, various Islamic groups, both political and socio-cultural, have remained entrenched as well. Consequently radical/anti-Islamic feminists like Taslima Nasreen have hardly any role to play in Bangladesh society. Despite the growth in 'NGO-activities' and the proliferation of human rights groups, supposed to be the harbingers of a civil society and secularism, Islam (as understood and interpreted by the conservative *ulama*), is well-entrenched as well.

Consequently it would be over-simplistic to assume that the persecution of women and all discriminatory acts against them are going to disappear from the region in the near future, because along with popular Islam with all its misogynous expositions there is a layer of patriarchy in the body politic of Bangladesh. This study reveals that neither misogyny nor the persecution of women in the region is solely associated with popular Islam. The bulk of the peasant and non-peasant population favour patriarchy and both 'Islamists' and 'secular' Bangladeshi Muslims ardently legitimize the subjection and deprivation of women in the name of Islam. Some of them even invoke God and the Prophet for help and guidance in this regard.

In sum, as the study reveals, patriarchy has been the main stumbling-block towards the empowerment of Bangladeshi women. The marriage of convenience between patriarchy and popular Islam has further aggravated the situation. Unless the 'banyan tree' (or patriarchy, as defined by that poor illiterate Bangladeshi woman) is cut down there is no hope for Bangladeshi women. Only through mass literacy and mutual understanding between the custodians of Islam and the human rights activists and feminists, may Bangladeshi women achieve equal rights and opportunities in every sphere of life.

Notes

1 Introduction

1 See Taj I. Hashmi, 'Islam in Bangladesh Politics', in H. Mutalib and T.I. Hashmi (eds), *Islam, Muslims and the Modern State*, pp. 100–34.
2 The Government of Bangladesh, *The Constitution of the People's Republic of Bangladesh*, Section 28 (1 & 2), Government Printing Press, Dhaka, 1990, p. 19.
3 See Coordinating Council for Human Rights in Bangladesh, (CCHRB) *Bangladesh: State of Human Rights*, 1992, CCHRB, Dhaka; Rabia Bhuiyan, *Aspects of Violence Against Women*, Institute of Democratic Rights, Dhaka, 1991; US Department of State, *Country Reports on Human Rights Practices for 1992*, Government Printing Office, Washington, DC, 1993; Rushdie Begum *et al.*, *Nari Nirjatan: Sangya O Bishleshon* (Bengali), Narigrantha Prabartana, Dhaka, 1992, *passim*.
4 CCHRB Report, 1993, p. 69.
5 Immigration and Refugee Board (Canada), Report, 'Women in Bangladesh', Human Rights Briefs, Ottawa, 1993, pp. 8–9.
6 Ibid, pp. 9–10.
7 *The Daily Star*, 18 January 1998.
8 Rabia Bhuiyan, *Aspects of Violence*, pp. 14–15.
9 Immigration and Refugee Board Report, 'Women in Bangladesh', p. 20.
10 Taj Hashmi, 'Islam in Bangladesh Politics', p. 117.
11 Immigration and Refugee Board Report, 'Women in Bangladesh', p. 6.
12 Tazeen Mahnaz Murshid, 'Women, Islam, and the State: Subordination and Resistance', paper presented at the Bengal Studies Conference (28–30 April 1995), Chicago, pp. 1–2.
13 Ibid, pp. 4–5.
14 U.A.B. Razia Akter Banu, 'Jamaat-i-Islami in Bangladesh: Challenges and Prospects', in Hussin Mutalib and Taj Hashmi (eds), *Islam, Muslim and the Modern State*, pp. 86–93.
15 Lynne Brydon and Sylvia Chant, *Women in the Third World: Gender Issues in Rural and Urban Areas*, p. 39.
16 'Women's Struggle for a Dignified, Place in Society: Bangladesh Scenario', Editorial, *The Independent* (Bangladesh), 5 May 1998.
17 Md. Mahbubar Rahman and Willem van Schendel, 'Gender and the Inheritance of Land: Living Law in Bangladesh', in Jan Brenan *et al.* (eds) *The Village in Asia Revisited*, pp. 248–50.
18 Ibid, pp. 254–74.

2 Women in Islam: a Reappraisal

1 Yvonne Y. Haddad and Jane I. Smith, 'Women in Islam: "The Mother of All Battles"' in Suha Sabbagh (ed), *Arab Women: Between Defiance and Restraint*, Ch. 19.
2 Roy Anderson and *et al.*, *Politics and Change in the Middle East: Sources of Conflict and Accommodation*, Prentice Hall, Englewood Cliffs, N.J., 1990, p. 279.
3 Diane D'souza, 'Women: Status and Comparative Religions', *The Firmest Bond* (Al-Wurwat al-Wusqa), No. 64–65, Special Winter & Spring Issue, 1996–97, pp. 56–7.
4 Ibid, p. 57.
5 Ibid, pp. 36–7; Qamaruddin Khan, *Status of Women in Islam*, pp. 13–15; Moghadam (ed.), *Identity and Politics*, p. 331.
6 Jan Hjarpe, 'The Attitude of Islamic Fundamentalism', in Bo Utas (ed.), *Women in Islamic Societies*, p. 12.
7 Ibid, p. 13.
8 B. Stowasser in F. Hussain, p. 22, *Daily Star*, 26 April 1999.
9 Kari Elisabeth Borresen, 'Women's Studies of the Christian Tradition: New Perspectives', in Ursula King (ed.), *Religion and Gender*, Blackwell, Oxford, 1995, p. 247.
10 Ibid, p. 253.
11 Erin White, 'Religion and the Hermeneutics of Gender: an Examination of the Work of Paul Ricoeur', in Ursula King, pp. 80–81.
12 F. Max Muller (ed.), *The Sacred Books of the East*, Vol. 25, *The Laws of Manu*, translated by G. Buhler, V: 147–8, Motilal Banarsidass, Delhi, 1988 (first published in 1886), p. 195.
13 Ibid, V: 154, p. 196.
14 Ibid, V: 155–64, p. 196–7.
15 Ibid, IX: 14, p. 330.
16 Ibid, IX: 18, p. 330.
17 Ibid, IX: 104–38, pp. 345–54.
18 Humayun Azad, *Nari* [Bengali], Agami Prakashani, Dhaka, 1995, pp. 50–3.
19 Paul Lunde and Justin Wintle, *A Dictionary of Arabic and Islamic Proverbs*, Routledge & Kegan Paul, London, 1984, pp. 5, 85, 87.
20 Leila Ahmed, *Women and Gender in Islam: Historical Roots of a Modern Debate*, Yale University Press, New Haven, 1992, p. 29.
21 Ibid.
22 Philip K. Hitti, *History of the Arabs: From the Earliest Times to the Present*, Macmillan Press London, 1958, p. 432.
23 Madelein Tress, 'Halakha, Zionism and Gender: The Case of Gush Emunim,' in Valentine M. Moghadam (ed.), *Identity, Politics and Women: Cultural Reassertions and Feminisms in International Perspective*, Westview Press, Boulder, 1994, p. 309; Leila Ahmed, *Women and Gender*, pp. 26–35.
24 Leila Ahmed, *Women and Gender*, p. 36.
25 Ibid, pp. 5, 13–26.
26 A BBC (Radio) Feature on Current Affairs, 11 May 1995.

27 *Time*, 17 November 1997, p. 9.
28 Ibn Kathir, *Qisas al-anbiya* [The Stories of the Prophets] cited in Barbara Freyer Stowasser, *Women in the Qur'an, Traditions and Interpretation*, Oxford University Press, New York, 1994, pp. 47 and 147 n. 55.
29 *The Economist*, 25 April 1992, p. 44.
30 Ernst Cassirer, *The Philosophy of the Enlightenment*, Princeton University Press, Princeton 1951, pp. 155–8.
31 Gamal A. Badawi, 'Women in Islam', in Khurshid Ahmad (ed.), *Islam: Its Meaning and Message*, The Islamic Foundation, Leicester, 1988, p. 133.
32 John Stuart Mill, *The Subjection of Women*, Hackett Publishing Company, Indianapolis, 1988 (first published in 1869), p. 32.
33 Summit Sarkar, '"Kaliyuga", "Chakri" and "Bhakti": Ramakrishna and His Times', *Economic and Political Weekly*, 18 July 1992, pp. 1549–51.
34 Frank F. Conlon, 'Hindu Revival and Indian Womenhood: The Image and Status of Women in the Writings of Vishnubawa Brahmachari', *South Asia*, Vol. XVII, No. 2, 1994, pp. 48–53.
35 Naila Minai, *Women in Islam: Tradition and Transition in the Middle East*, John Murray, London, 1981, p. 4.
36 Haleh Afshar, 'Fundamentalism and Women in Iran', in Oliver Mendelsohn and Upendra Baxi (eds), *The Rights of Subordinated Peoples*, Oxford University Press, Delhi, 1994, p. 283.
37 Asghar Ali Engineer, *Islam and Liberation Theology: Essays on Liberative Elements in Islam*, Sterling Publishers, New Delhi, 1990, p. 171.
38 See for details Minai, *Women in Islam*, p. 19, Engineer, *Islam and Liberation Theology*, pp. 171–2; Aishah Lemu & Fatima Heeru, *Women in Islam*, p. 18.
39 Ahmed Ali also feels that the term *wadribu* (which appears in this verse) has been incorrectly translated by others as 'beating up', while the actual meaning would be 'have intercourse'. He cites Raghib's *Lisan al-Arab* and renowned Arab scholar Zamakhshari's works in this regard. He also cites the *hadis*, 'Never beat God's handmaiden', in support of his interpretation. See *Al-Qur'an: a Contemporary Translation by Ahmed Ali*, Princeton University Press, Princeton, 1993, pp. 78–9.
40 A.A. Engineer, *Islam and Liberation Theology*, pp. 172–3.
41 Daniel W. Brown, *Rethinking Tradition in Modern Islamic Thought*, Cambridge University Press, Cambridge, 1996, pp. 24–5.
42 Naila Minai, *Women in Islam*, p. 20
43 Wiebke Walther, *Women in Islam: From Medieval to Modern Times*, Markus Wiener Publishing, New York, 1993, p. 48.
44 A.A. Engineer, *Islam and Liberation Theology*, pp. 173–5.
45 Ibid, pp. 176–7.
46 *Al-Qur'an: A Contemporary Translation by Ahmed Ali*, p. 73.
47 Wiebke Walther, *Women in Islam*, pp. 57–8.
48 Fatima Mernissi, *Beyond the Veil: Male-Female Dynamics in Muslim Society*, Al Saqi Books, London, 1985, p. 70.
49 *Sahih al-Bukhari*, Vol. 7, Translated by Muhammad Muhsin Khan, Islamic University Al-Madina (n.d), pp. 129–30.
50 Ameer Ali, *The Spirit of Islam*, Methuen & Co. Ltd, London, 1964, pp. 227–9.

51 Ibid, pp. 229–30.
52 Ibid, pp. 233–4.
53 Karen Armstrong, *Muhammad: a Western Attempt to Understand Islam*, Victor Gollancz Ltd, London, 1991, p. 145.
54 Ameer Ali, *The Spirit of Islam*, pp. 234–6.
55 Ibid, pp. 234–5.
56 Ibid, p. 237.
57 Ibid, pp. 235–6; Karen Armstrong, *Muhammad*, pp. 196–7.
58 Barbara Freyer Stowasser, *Women in the Qur'an, Traditions and Interpretation*, Oxford University Press, New York, 1994, p. 122.
59 Fatima Mernissi, *Beyond the Veil*, pp. 70–1.
60 Ameer Ali, *The Spirit of Islam*, p. 255.
61 P.K. Hitti, *History of the Arabs*, pp. 237–8.
62 Fatima Mernissi, *Women and Islam: an Historical and Theological Enquiry*, Basil Blackwell, Oxford, 1991, pp. 192–3.
63 P.K. Hitti, *History of the Arabs*, pp. 238–9.
64 Leila Ahmed, *Women and Gender in Islam:* pp. 76–7.
65 Fatima Mernissi, *Beyond the Veil*, pp. 50–2.
66 Aziz Ahmad, *Islamic Modernism in India and Pakistan*, 1857–1964, Oxford University Press, London, 1967, pp. 53, 63, 95; Gail Minault, 'Sayyid Mumtaz Ali and "Huquq un-Niswan": an Advocate of Women's Rights in Islam in the Late Nineteenth Century', *Modern Asian Studies*, Vol. 24, No. 1, 1990, pp. 147–72.
67 Ameer Ali, *The Spirit of Islam*, p. 231.
68 Minou Reeves, *Female Warriors of Allah*, p. 35.
69 Barbara Freyer Stowasser, *Women in the Qur'an*, pp. 6 and 121.
70 Geraldine Brooks, *Nine Parts of Desire: The Hidden World of Islamic Women*, Anchor Books, Sydney, 1996, pp. 109–11; Leila Ahmed, p. 53.
71 Leila Ahmed, *Women and Gender*, 60–1.
72 Fatima Mernissi, *Women and Islam*, pp. 141–4.
73 Leila Ahmed, *Women and Gender*, pp. 73–4.
74 Minou Reeves, *Women and Gender*, pp. 47–50.
75 Wiebke Walther, *Women in Islam: From Medieval to Modern Times*, p. 70.
76 Fatima Mernissi, *Women and Islam*, pp. 85–92.
77 Ibid, p. 92.
78 Barbara Stowasser, *Women in the Qur'an*, pp. 90–1.
79 Ibid, p. 93.
80 Leila Ahmed, *Women and Gender*, pp. 164–8.
81 Zakaria Bashier, *Muslim Women in the Midst of Change*, pp. 13–17.
82 Katy Gardner, 'Purdah, Female Power and Cultural Change: a Sylheti Example', *Journal of Social Studies*, No. 65, July 1994, p. 22.
83 Ibid, p. 1.
84 Ibid, pp. 2–5.
85 Leila Ahmed, *Women and Gender*, p. 236.
86 Ibid, pp. 236–8.
87 Ibid, p. 164; Jacqueline Siapno, 'Gender Relations in Mindanao', in Camillia Fawzi El-Solh and Judy Mabro (eds), *Muslim Women's Choices: Religious Belief and Social Reality*, Berg, Providence/Oxford, 1994, p. 195.
88 Leila Ahmed, *Women and Gender*, p. 164.

89 Barbara Stowasser, *Women in the Qur'an*, p. 129.
90 Abul Ala Mawdudi, *Purdah and the Status of Women in Islam*, Islamic Publications, Lahore, 1972, pp. 39–72, 135–216.
91 Leila Ahmed, *Women and Gender*, pp. 144–64.
92 Fazlur Rahman, *Islam*, University of Chicago Press, Chicago, 1979, p. 232.
93 *The Encyclopaedia Britannia*, Vol. 22, 'Islam', Chicago, 1989 (15th Edition), pp. 33–4.
94 Aisha Lemu and Fatima Heeren, *Women in Islam*, The Islamic Foundation, Leicester, 1992, pp. 22–3, 48–9.
95 Amina Wadud-Muhsin, *Qur'an and Women*, Penerbit Fajar Bakti Sdn, Bhd., Selangor (Malaysia), 1995, p. 87.
96 See Asghar Ali Engineer, *The Rights of Women in Islam*, IBS Buku Sdn. Bhd. Selangor (Malaysia), 1992, p. 73.
97 Ibid, p. 75.
98 Abla Amawi, 'Women and Property Rights in Islam', in Suha Sabbagh (ed.), *Arab Women: Between Defiance and Restraint*, Olive Branch Press, New York, 1996, pp. 156–8.
99 Fatima Mernissi, *Women and Islam*, pp. 49–61.
100 Qamaruddin Khan, *Status of Women*, pp. 14–15.
101 Ibid, p. 15.
102 Shamshad M. Khan, *Why Two Women Witnesses?* Ta–Ha Publishers Ltd, London, 1993, pp. 6–15.
103 Amina Wadud-Muhsin, *Qur'an and Women*, pp. 85–6.
104 Qamaruddin Khan, *Status of Women*, pp. 57–6.
105 Asghar Ali Engineer, *The Rights of Women*, p. 68.
106 Ibid.
107 Ahmad Ibn Hanbal, *Musnad*, cited in Weibke Walther, *Women in Islam*, p. 48.
108 Cited in Fatima Mernissi, *Women and Islam*, pp. 64 and 75.
109 Ibid, p. 79.
110 Ibid, p. 70.
111 Ibid, p. 76.
112 *Sahih Bukhari*, cited in Mernissi, *Women and Islam*, p. 76.
113 The *Encyclopaedia of Islam* (New Edition), Vol. III, E.J. Brill, Leiden, 1971, pp. 24–5.
114 Barbara Stowasser, *Women in the Qur'an*, p. 28.
115 Daniel Brown, *Rethinking Tradition*, pp. 97–9.
116 Ibid.
117 Fazlur Rahman, *Islam*, pp. 74–5.
118 Ibid, p. 251.
119 A.A. Engineer, *The Rights of Women*, p. 11.
120 Ibid, pp. 11–12.
121 Minou Reeves, *Female Warriors of Allah*, p. 54.
122 Fatima Mernissi, *Beyond the Veil*: pp. 32–45, 113.
123 Leila Ahmed, *Women and Gender*, p. 68.
124 Judith Tucker (ed.), *Arab Women: Old Boundaries, New Frontiers*, Indiana University Press, Bloomington 1993, Chs. 8 and 9.
125 Minou Reeves, *Female Warriors of Allah*, pp. 27 and 58.

126 Barbara Stowasser, 'Women's Issues in Modern Islamic Thought', in Judith E. Tucker (ed.), *Arab Women*, p. 4.

127 Margot Badran, *Feminists, Islam and Nation: Gender and the Making of Modern Egypt*, Princeton University Press, Princeton, 1995, pp. 18–21.

128 Kevin Dwyer, *Arab Voices: the Human Rights Debate in the Middle East*, Routledge, London 1991, pp. 184–7, 237.

129 Ibid, pp. 150–2, 182–4.

130 See Geraldine Brooks, *Nine Parts of Desire*, chs. 10 and 11.

131 Fatima Mernisssi, *Women and Islam*, p. 23.

132 *Straits Times*, 8 September 1995.

3 Mullas, Popular Islam and Misogyny

1 Taj I. Hashmi, 'Women and Islam: Taslima Nasreen, Society and Politics in Bangladesh', *South Asia, Vol. XVIII*, No. 2, December 1995, pp. 41–2.

2 See Asim Roy, *Islamic Syncretistic Tradition in Bengal*, Princeton University Press, Princeton, 1983, *passim*.

3 Rafiuddin Ahmed, *The Bengal Muslims, 1871–1906: a Quest for Identity*, Oxford University Press, Delhi, 1981, p. 197 (n. 118); Richard M. Eaton, *The Rise of Islam and the Bengal Frontier, 1204–1760*, University of California Press, Berkeley, 1983, pp. 292–6.

4 Muhammad Abdur Rahim, *Social and Cultural History of Bengal, Vol. 1 (1201–1576)*, Pakistan Historical Society, Karachi, 1963, pp. 269–70.

5 Ibid, p. 270.

6 Rafiuddin Ahmed, *The Bengal Muslims*, p. 29.

7 Muin-ud-Din Ahmad Khan, *History of the Fara'idi Movement*, Islamic Foundation, Dhaka 1984, p. 91.

8 Asim Roy, *Islamic Syncretistic Tradition*, p. 51.

9 Ibid, pp. 159–63, 208–12; Abdul Karim, *Social History of The Muslims in Bengal down to A.D. 1538*, Asiatic Society of Pakistan, Dhaka, 1959, pp. 161–4, 209; Abdul Mannan Talib, *Bangladeshe Islam* [Bengali], Adhunik Prakashani, Dhaka, 1980, p. 228.

10 Katy Gardner, *Global Migrants, Local Lives: Travel and Transformation in Rural Bangladesh*, Clarendon Press, Oxford, 1995, pp. 258–9.

11 Ibid, pp. 259–60.

12 M.A. Khan, *History of the Fara'idi Movement*, pp. 93–4.

13 Barbara D. Metcalf, *Islamic Revival in British India: Deoband, 1860–1900*, Princeton University Press, Princeton, 1982, p. 162.

14 M.A. Rahim, *Social and Cultural History*, pp. 336–40; Asim Roy, *Islamic Syncretistic Tradition*, ch. 6.

15 A.M. Talib, *Bangladeshe Islam*, pp. 234–44; Asim Roy, *Islamic Syncretistic Tradition*, pp. 159–64.

16 See for details, Azizur Rahman Mallick, *British Policy and the Muslims in Bengal, 1757–1856*, Bangla Academy, Dhaka, 1977, chs. III–V; M.A. Khan, *History*, passim; Taj I. Hashmi, 'Karamat Ali and the Muslims in Bengal, 1800–1873', *Dacca University Studies*, Vol. XXIII, June, 1976.

17 K. Gardner, *Global Migrants*, pp. 230–3, 236–8.

18   K.M. Mohsin, 'Tabligh Jama't and the Faith Movement in Bangladesh', in Rafiuddin Ahmed (ed.), *Bangladesh: Society, Religion and Politics*, South Asia Studies Group, Chittagong, 1985, pp. 237–43.

19   K. Gardner, *Global Migrants*, pp. 237–43.

20   B. Metcalf, *Islamic Revival in British India*, p. 163.

21   See Bernard Hours, 'The Work of the Imam, Servant of the Community and Precarious worker in Bangladesh', *Journal of Social Studies*, p. 143.

22   Ibid, pp. 143–52.

23   Ibid, p. 145.

24   Ibid, pp. 153–4.

25   Ibid, p. 143.

26   Ibid, p. 143.

27   See for details Taj I. Hashmi, *Pakistan as a Peasant Utopia: the Communalization of Class Politics in East Bengal, 1920–1947*, Westview Press, Boulder, 1992, *passim*.

28   Taj I. Hashmi, 'Karamat Ali and the Muslims in Bengal'.

29   Rafiuddin Ahmed, *The Bengal Muslims*, pp. 183–6.

30   Asim Roy, *Islamic Syncretistic Tradition*, pp. 249–50.

31   Humayun Azad, *Nari* [Bengali], Agami Prakashani, Dhaka, 1995, pp. 50–4, 72–9.

32   Sumit Sarkar, '"Kaliyuga", "Chakri" and "Bhakti": Ramakrishna and His Times', *Economic and Political Weekly*, 18 July 1992, pp. 1543–4, 1550–51.

33   A.R. Mallick, *British Policy and the Muslims in Bengal*, pp. 39–58; W.W. Hunter, *The Indian Musalmans*, W. Rahman, Dhaka, 1975, pp. 167–71.

34   See Maulana Muhammad Mian Deobandi, *Ulama-i-Hind Ka Shandar Maazi* [Urdu], Vol. 1, Jamiat-ul-Ulama-i-Hind, Delhi, 1942, *passim*.

35   W.W. Hunter, *The Indian Musalmans*, pp. 180–1.

36   Ibid, pp. 186–7.

37   Ibid, p. 186.

38   Barbara Metcalf, *Islamic Revival*, pp. 100–01, 110.

39   Aziz Ahmad, *Islamic Modernism in India and Pakistan, 1857–1964*, Oxford University Press, London, 1967, pp. 49–53.

40   Ibid. pp. 72–6; Gail Minault, 'Sayyid Mumtaz Ali and "Huquq un-Niswan": an Advocate of Women's Rights in Islam in the Late Nineteenth Century', *Modern Asian Studies*, Vol. 24, February 1990.

41   Barbara Metcalf, *Perfecting Women: Maulana Ashraf Ali Thanawi's Bihishti Zewar*, University of California Press, Berkeley, 1990, p. 8.

42   Ibid, p. 8.

43   Ibid, pp. 9–23.

44   Ibid, pp. 14 and 23.

45   See Karamat Ali Jaunpuri, *Miftah ul-Jannat* [Urdu], Jaunpur (n.d), *passim*; *Zakhira-i-Karamat* (his complete works in Urdu), Vols. I–III, Publisher Haji Muhammad Saeed, Calcutta, 1924.

46   Rafiuddin Ahmed, *The Bengal Muslims*, p. 30.

47   Maulvi Muhammad Shamsul Huda, *Neamul Qur'an* [Bengali], the Author, Dhaka, 1961 (tenth edition), p. 96.

48   Ibid, pp. v–vi (Preface).

49   Ibid, pp. 244–6.

50   Ibid, pp. 246–7.
51   Ibid, pp. 252–7.
52   Ibid, p. 258.
53   Ibid, p. 258.
54   Ibid, pp. 297–8.
55   Ibid, pp. 300–01.
56   Ibid, p. 301.
57   Ibid, p. 313.
58   See Bernard Hours, *Islam and Development in Bangladesh*, Centre for Social Studies, Dhaka, 1995, p. 55.
59   Araz Ali Matubbar, *Complete Works* [Bengali], Vol. 1, Ed. Ayub Hossain, Pattok Shomabesh, Dhaka, 1994, p. 11.
60   Maulana Gholam Rahman, *Maksudul Momeneen* [Bengali], Qazi Anisur Rahman, Dhaka, 1994 (45th edition), pp. 81–6.
61   Maulana Abdul Halim Hossaini, *Islami Hukumat* [Bengali], Imanullah Khondkar, Comilla (n.d.), pp. 5–7.
62   *Maksudul Momeneen*, pp. 269–70.
63   Karamat Ali Jaunpuri, *Tazkiat ul-Aqaid*, in *Zakhira-i-Karamat* [Urdu], Vol. I, p. 82.
64   See Maulana Mansurul Haq (ed.), *Mr Maududir New Islam* [Bengali], Jamia Qur'ania Arabia, Lalbagh, Dhaka, 1985, *passim*.
65   Rafiuddin Ahmed, *The Bengal Muslims*, p. 87.
66   *Neamul Qur'an*, p. 255.
67   Ibid, pp. 255–6.
68   Ibid, p. 259.
69   Ibid, pp. 261, 282.
70   Ibid, p. 283.
71   Ibid, p. 294.
72   Ibid, pp. 303–4.
73   Ibid, pp. 304–5.
74   *Maksudul Momeneen*, pp. 366–7.
75   *Neamul Qur'an*, p. 306.
76   Ibid, p. 307.
77   *Maksudul Momeneen*, p. 327.
78   Maulana Muhammad Sakhawatullah, *Hekayat-i-Sahaba* (Bengali), Tablighi Kutub Khana, Dhaka, 1982, pp. 192–4.
79   See Taslima Nasreen, *Nirbachito Column* (Bengali), Inankosh Prakashani, Dhaka, 1993, *passim*; Taj I. Hashmi, 'Women and Islam', pp. 38–40.
80   *Maksudul Momeneen*, p. 378; Maulana Fazlur Rahman Anwari, *Maksudul Momin*, Taj Publishing House, Dhaka, 1981, pp. 331–2.
81   *Maksudul Momeneen*, p. 378.
82   Ibid, pp. 317–18.
83   *Maksudul Momin*, pp. 328–9.
84   *Maksudul Momeneen*, p. 326 and *Maksudul Momin*, p. 335.
85   *Maksudul Momeneen*, p. 329 and *Maksudul Momin*, p. 335.
86   *Maksudul Momeneen*, pp. 327–8, 330–6.
87   Ibid, p. 342.
88   Ibid, pp. 318–19.
89   Ibid, pp. 332, 334.

90 Ibid, pp. 343–57; *Maksudul Momin*, pp. 332–8.
91 *Maksudul Momin*, pp. 336–8; Maulana Ashraf Ali, *Muradul Momeneen* (Bengali), Hamidiya Library, Dhaka, 1993, pp. 302–8.
92 *Maksudul Momeneen*, pp. 379–80.
93 Ibid, pp. 381–3.
94 See for details Taj I. Hashmi, 'Islam in Bangladesh Politics', in H. Mutalib and T.I. Hashmi (eds), *Islam, Muslims and the Modern State*, Macmillan Press, London, 1994, pp. 100–38.
95 'Saidi: New Dealer in the Drug and Pornography Market' [Bengali], Cover story of Weekly *Bichinta*, Dhaka 3 May 1991, p. 12.
96 Ibid, p. 12.
97 Ibid, p. 13.
98 '*Purdah* and Women's Rights in Islam' [Bengali], audiotape, C.H. Products, Dhaka, 1991; *Ain-Shalish Kendro* (Legal-aid Centre), 'The Eclipse' (a videotape on persecution of women in rural Bangladesh at the hands of village elders and *mullas*), [Bengali], Dhaka, 1994.
99 Saidi, 'Purdah and Women's Rights in Islam'.
100 Saidi, 'Rights of Husbands and Wives' [Bengali], audiotape, C.H. Products, Dhaka, 1992.
101 Betsy Hartmann and James K. Boyce, *A Quiet Violence: View from a Bangladesh Village*, University Press Ltd, Dhaka, 1990 (fifth impression).
102 Ibid, pp. 88.
103 Ibid, pp. 88–9.
104 Ibid, p. 89.
105 *Banglabazar Patrika* (Bengali daily), Dhaka, 4 August 1994 (See Reports by Amnesty International, *Bangladesh: Taking the Law in their Own Hands, the Village Salish*, London, October 1993 and *Bangladesh: Fundamental Rights of Women Violated with Virtual Impurity*, London, October 1994, for further details on persecution of women in rural Bangladesh by village elders and *mullas*).
106 Pradip Sinha, *Nineteenth Century Bengal: Aspects of Social History*, Firma K.L. Mukhopadhyay, Calcutta, 1965, p. 124.

4 Women as Victims of the Salish

1 Computed from newspaper reports, editorials, letters and articles published in various newspapers and periodicals in Bangladesh during 1991 and 1995. The Bengali dailies, *Janakantha, Sangbad, Ittefaq, Ajker Kagaj, Bangla Bazaar Patrika* and English dailies, *Bangladesh Observer* and *Daily Star* and English weekly *Holiday* throughout the period (1991–95) contained reports and features on the subjection and persecution of women in Bangladesh, especially in the name of Islam and *Sharia* law.
2 Shapan Adnan, '"Birds in a Cage": Institutional Change and Women's Position in Bangladesh,' *Journal of Social Studies*, No. 46, October 1989, pp. 8–10.
3 R. Carstairs, *The Little World of an Indian District Officer*, Macmillan, London, 1912, p. 26.

4   Cathy A. Frierson, *Peasant Icons: Representations of Rural People in Late Nineteenth-Century Russia*. Oxford University Press, New York, 1993, pp. 156–65.
5   Shapan Adnan, 'Birds in a Cage', p. 2.
6   Ibid, pp. 6–8.
7   Amnesty International, 'Bangladesh: Taking the Law in their hands' (October 1993), pp. 1–2.
8   Sheikh Muhammad Ikram, *Raud-i-Kausar* [in Urdu], Adabi Dunya, Delhi, 1991, p. 591; Rafiuddin Ahmed, *The Bengal Muslims, 1871–1906: a Quest for Identity*, Oxford University Press, Delhi, 1981, p. 45.
9   A.K.M. Sirajul Islam, *'Fatwa Ki ebong Keno?'* (What is Fatwa and Why?), *Janakantha*, 27 April 1994 and 29 April 1994.
10 Amnesty International, 'Taking the law in their hands', (October 1993), pp. 2–3.
11 *Bangla Bazar Patrika*, 21 June 1994.
12 *Bhorer Kagaj*, 5 January 1995.
13 *Sangbad*, 5 April 1995.
14 *Ittefaq*, 3 May 1995; *Ajker Kagaj*, 10 April 1995.
15 Ibid, p. 3.
16 Amnesty International, 'Bangladesh: Fundamental rights of women violated with virtual impunity', London, October 1994, p. 6; Maleka Begum and K.S. Ali (eds), *Fatwa, 1991–1995*, passim.
17 Amnesty International, 'Bangladesh: Taking the law in their hands' pp. 3–4; *Bangla Bazar Patrika*, 23 February 1994; 'The Eclipse,' Video-tape, *Ain-Shalish Kendro*, Dhaka, 1995.
18 *Bangla Bazar Patrika*, 23 February 1994: Amnesty International, 'Fundamental rights of women violated' (October 1994), p. 7.
19 *Sangbad*, 20 May 1993; Amnesty International, 'Bangladesh: taking the law in their hands' (October 1993), p. 4 and 'Fundamental rights of women violated . . .'(October 1994), p. 7; *Janakantha*, June 7, 1994.
20 *Bangla Bazar Patrika*, 5 October 1993; *Bhorer Kagaj*, 16 June 1994.
21 Amnesty International, 'Bangladesh: taking the law in their hands', p. 5.
22 Amnesty International, 'Fundamental rights of women violated' . . ., p. 7.
23 Ibid.
24 Ibid.
25 Ibid, pp. 7–8; *Bhorer Kagaj*, 8 June 1994; *Janakantha*, 13 July 1994.
26 *Sangbad, Ajker Kagaj, Bangla Bazar Patrika*, 30 September 1994; Amnesty International, 'Fundamental rights of women', p. 8.
27 Firoze Mahmud and Sayeedar Rahman, *'Savare ek nashta mahilar Kando'* [The activities of an unchaste woman at Savar], *Chitrabangla* [Bengali Cine-weekly], 13 October 1994, pp. 19–22.
28 *Bangla Bazar Patrika*, 1 May 1994.
29 Ibid.
30 Amnesty International, 'Fundamental Rights of Women Violated' (1994), p. 8.
31 Ibid.; *Bangla Bazar Patrika*, 4 August 1994.
32 *Janakantha*, 28 November 1994; *Sangbad*, 29 November 1994.
33 *Sangbad*, 10 April 1995.
34 *Ajker Kagaj*, 6 June 1994; *Janakantha*, 7 June 1994.

35 *Janakantha* and *Bangla Bazar Patrika*, 20 June 1994; *Bhorer Kagaj*, 10 May 1994; Amnesty International, 'Fundamental Rights of Women Violated', pp. 8–9.
36 See my article, 'Women and Islam: Taslima Nasreen, Society and Politics in Bangladesh', *South Asia*, Vol. XVIII, No. 2, December 1995, pp. 23–48.
37 See my chapter, 'Islam in Bangladesh Politics', in Hussin Mutalib and Taj I. Hashmi (eds), *Islam, Muslims and the Modern State*, Macmillan, London and St. Martin's Press, New York, 1994, pp. 128–34.
38 Ibid.
39 Syed M. Hashemi, 'State, Politics and Civil Society in the Context of Donor Hegemony: Bangladesh at 25', paper presented at 'Bangladesh at 25' Conference, New York, 5–7 December 1996, pp. 12–13.
40 Amnesty International, 'Fundamental Rights of Women' . . ., p. 9.
41 Ibid.
42 *Janakantha*, 1 April 1994.
43 Rajni Kothari, Keynote lecture delivered at a workshop on 'Sources of Conflict in South Asia: Ethnicity, Refugees, Environment', held at Kandy, Sri lanka, 6–16 March 1997, cited in *Newsletter* of the Regional Centre for Strategic Studies, Colombo, April 1997, pp. 2–3.
44 Ibid.
45 Zillur Rahman Siddiqi, 'Why Fundamentalists are Opposed to NGOs', *Sangbad* [Bengali daily], 3 April 1994.
46 Amnesty International, 'Fundamental Rights of Women Violated', p. 10.
47 Ibid; *Ajker Kagaj*, 6 June 1994.
48 'What is the real motive of the *fatwabaz*?' [Bengali], *Janakantha*, 28 February 1994.
49 Ibid, 28 February and 17 April 1994; Amnesty International, 'Fundamental Rights of Women Violated', p. 10.
50 *Ajker Kagaj*, 6 June 1994.
51 *Janakantha*, 7 June 1994; Amnesty International, 'Fundamental Rights of Women Violated', pp. 10–11.
52 Amnesty International, 'Fundamental Rights of Women Violated', p. 11.
53 *Janakantha*, 7 June 1994.
54 Ibid, 4 June 1994.
55 *Bhorer Kagaj*, 7 June 1994.
56 *Inqilab*, 4 April 1994.
57 See Taslima Nasreen, *Lajja* [Bengali], Pearl Publications, Dhaka 1993, pp. 27–31; Mahmudur Rahman Manna, *Samprodayikota O Jamaat* [Communalism and the Jamaat], Ananya, Dhaka, 1993, *passim*.
58 My interview with Colonel (retired) Nuruzzaman, Dhaka, 22 June 1995.
59 Ahmed Sharif, 'The Government and the *Fatwabaz Muftis*' [Bengali], *Ajker Kagaj*, 16 May 1994.
60 *Janakantha*, 18 May 1995.
61 My interviews with villagers in Rangpur, Bogra, Dhaka, Manikganj and Mymensingh in 1995 and 1996; See M. Rashiduzzaman, 'The Dichotomy of Islam and Development: NGOs, Women's Development and *fatawa* in Bangladesh', *Contemporary South Asia*, Vol. 6, No. 3, November 1997, pp. 240–6.

62 Najmul Haq Haqqani, 'Swajatir Torey Biplabi Ahban' [Revolutionary Message for Fellow Countrymen], *Janakantha*, 6 June 1994.
63 Joe Klein, 'Mothers vs. Mullahs', *Newsweek*, 17 April 1995, p. 17.
64 Ibid.
65 *Time*, 21 April 1997, p. 42.
66 S.M. Nurul Alam, NGOs Under Attack: a Study of the Socio-Cultural and Political Dynamics of the 'NGO Operations in Bangladesh' (Mimeo), Study Commissioned by PACT-PRIP (USAID Sponsored Project), Chs. 6 & 7, Dhaka, 1995.
67 W.W. Rostow, *The Stages of Economic Growth: a Non-Communist Manifesto*, Cambridge University Press, Cambridge 1960, *passim*.
68 Talcot Parsons, *Societies: Evolutionary and Comparative Perspectives*, Prentice-Hall, Englewood Cliffs, 1966, *passim*.
69 B.C. Smith, *Understanding Third World Politics: Theories of Political Change and Development*, Indiana University Press, Bloomington, 1996, pp. 79–81.
70 Ibid, p. 81.
71 See Taj I. Hashmi, *Pakistan as a Peasant Utopia The Communalization of Class Politics in East Bengal 1920–1947*, Westview Press, Boulder 1992, Chs. 5 & 7.
72 Shelley Feldman and Florence E. McCarthy, *Rural Women and Development in Bangladesh: Selected Issues*, NORAD, Ministry of Development Cooperations, Oslo, 1984, p. 360.
73 Ibid, pp. 95–6.
74 Robert Redfield, 'The Folk Society', *American Journal of Sociology*, Vol. 52, January 1947, p. 295.
75 Ferdinand Tonnies, *Community and Society (Gemeinschaft und Gesellschaft)*, translated and edited by Charles P. Loomis, Michigan State University Press, East Lansing 1964, p. 34.
76 Ibid, pp. 42–4, 163.
77 Ibid, p. 166.
78 Ibid, p. 159.
79 See Cathy Frierson, *Peasant Icons*, pp. 32–53 for *narod* culture.
80 Ibid, pp. 68–70.
81 Anisul Haq, 'There is nothing to be worried about *fatwas*' [in Bengali], *Bhorer Kagaj*, 23 July 1994. It is noteworthy that due to the concerted efforts of various human rights groups and individuals, both within and outside Bangladesh, there had been a considerable abatement in the number of cases of victimization of a rural women through the *salish* during 1995 and early 1997. However, according to a report in early September 1997, one 15-year-old girl named Ayesha received 100 lashes in accordance with a *salish* verdict at Gazipur, not far from the capital city, for having 'illicit relationship' with 60-year-old Nasu Mia, before she was 'allowed' to marry the man. No action was taken against the man ['Lashing Womenkind', a letter to the Editor, weekly *Holiday*, 26 September 1997].
82 BBC (Bengali) Radio, 25 September 1999: *Daily Star*, 26 September 1999.

5 NGOs and Empowerment of Women

1   I.C. Moser, 'Gender Planning in the Third World': Meeting Practical and Strategic Gender Needs', *World Development*, Vol. 17, No. 11, 1989, p. 1815.
2   Sarah C. White, *Arguing with the Crocodile: Gender and Class in Bangladesh*, University Press Ltd, Dhaka, 1992, pp. 14–15.
3   Harry Blair, 'Civil Society, Democratic Development and International Donors in Bangladesh', paper presented at the 'Bangladesh at 25' Conference Columbia University, New York, 5–7 December 1996.
4   Martha Alter Chen, *A Quiet Revolution: Women in Transition in Rural Bangladesh*, BRAC Prokashana, Dhaka, 1993, pp. 72–3.
5   Ibid, pp. 166–7.
6   Ibid, pp. 171–2.
7   Ibid, pp. 172–5.
8   Ibid, pp. 175–83.
9   Ibid, p. 184.
10 Ibid.
11 Ibid.
12 Ibid, pp. 185–93; Kristen Westergaard, 'People's Empowerment in Bangladesh: NGO Strategies', *Journal of Social Studies*, No. 72, April 1996, pp. 34, 38–40, 43.
13 Ibid, pp. 33–4.
14 Ibid, pp. 37–42.
15 Kamal Siddiqui, 'Strengthening Local Democracy', *Grameen Poverty Research*, Vol. 4, No. 1, February, 1998, p. 5.
16 Ibid.
17 Hameeda Hossain, 'Women Enter the Union Councils', Ibid, pp. 6–7.
18 Mirza M. Hassan, 'Democratizing Local Government: Current Reforms and Future Agenda', Ibid, p. 4.
19 Mirza M. Hassan and Zakir Hossain, 'Rural Poor and Electoral Democracy: Reflections on the Parliamentary Elections of 1996', *Grameen Poverty Research*, Vol. 2, No. 4, October 1996, p. 11.
20 Rezaul Hoque and Noore Alam Siddiquee, 'Grassroots Democratisation in Bangladesh: the NGO Experience', *Journal of Social Studies*, No. 79, January 1998, p. 62.
21 Ibid, p. 51.
22 Corine Lesnes, 'Bangladeshi Women Begin to Fight Back', *Guardian Weekly*, 23 July 1995, p. 15.
23 Ibid.
24 Syed M. Hashemi and Sidney Ruth Schuler, 'Sustainable Banking with the Poor: a Case Study of Grameen Bank', JSI Research and Training Institute, Arlington, Virginia, 8 January 1997, mimeo, pp. 15–44.
25 Willem van Schendel, *Three Deltas: Accumulation and Poverty in Rural Burma, Bengal and South India*, Sage Publications, New Delhi, 1991, pp. 282–3.
26 Ibid, pp. 285–7, 291–7.
27 Ibid, p. 287.
28 Taj I. Hashmi, *Pakistan as a Peasant Utopia:* Westview Press, Boulder, 1992, passim.

Notes 223

29 Betsy Hartmann and James K. Boyce, *A Quiet Violence: View from a Bangladesh Village*, University Press Ltd, Dhaka, 1990, p. 95.
30 Ibid, p. 98.
31 Tahrunnessa A. Abdullan and Sondra A. Zeidenstein, *Village Women of Bangladesh: Prospects for Change*, Pergamon Press, Oxford, 1982, pp. 75–7.
32 See for details, Willem van Schendel, *Peasant Mobility – The Odds of Life in Rural Bangladesh*, Van Goreum, Assen (Holland), 1981, *passim*; Shapan Adnan, *et al.*, 'Land, Power and Violence in Barisal Villages', the Village Study Group, Dhaka, 1976, mimeo; Hartmann and Boyce, *A Quiet Violence*, pp. 194–209; Edward J. Clay, 'Institutional change and Agricultural Wages in Bangladesh', *Bangladesh Development Studies*, Vol. 4, No. 4, November 1976; Eric G. Jensen, *Rural Bangladesh: Competition for Scarce Resources*, Norwegian University Press, Oslo, 1986, Chs. 4–7; M. Ameerul Huq (ed.), *Exploitation of the Rural Poor*, Bangladesh Academy for Rural Development, Comilla, 1976, passim; Mohiuddin Alamgir, *Bangladesh: a Case of Below Poverty Level Equilibrium*, BIDS, Dhaka, 1978, pp. 94–101.
33 Muhammad Yunus (ed.), *Jorimon and Others: Faces of Poverty*, Grameen Bank, Dhaka, 1991, pp. 2–4.
34 Ibid, pp. 7–14.
35 Kirsten Westergaard, *Pauperization and Rural Women in Bangladesh: a Case Study*, BARD, Comilla, 1983, pp. 10–11, 75–81, 112–21.
36 Kirsten Westergaard, 'People's Empowerment in Bangladesh: NGO Strategies', p. 33.
37 Ibid, p. 34.
38 Ibid, p. 36.
39 Ibid, pp. 42, 50, 52–4.
40 Ibid, pp. 34.
41 Ibid, p. 50.
42 Thomas W. Dichter, 'Questioning the Future of NGOs in Microfinance', *Journal of International Development*, Vol. 8 No. 2, 1996, p. 260.
43 Ibid, p. 261.
44 Moshrefa Mishu, 'NGO: Bampanthider Karoniyo' (NGOs and the Responsibility of the Left), *Forum* [Bengali], Vol. 16, Dhaka, May–June, 1994, pp. 6–8.
45 *Holiday*, 7 February 1997, p. 8.
46 *New Nation*, 26 October 1996.
47 Saira Rahman and Adilur Rahman Khan, 'Emerging NGO culture in Bangladesh', *Holiday*, 10 January 1997.
48 Syed M. Hashemi, 'State, Politics and Civil Society in the Context of Donor Hegemony: Bangladesh at 25', paper presented at 'Bangladesh at 25' Conference Columbia University, New York, 5–7 December 1996, pp. 12–13.
49 Ibid; Shelley Feldman, '(Re) presenting Islam: Manipulating Gender, Shifting State Practices and Class Frustrations', and Harry Blair, 'Civil Society Democratic Development and International Donors in Bangladesh', papers presented at the 'Bangladesh at 25' Conference, New York, 5–7 December 1996.

50   Syed M. Hashemi, 'State, Politics and Civil Society'; *Dhaka Courier*, 'ADAB is beyond Government Control: NGOs Defeating the Bureau', 28 August 1992; *Bhorer Kagaj*, 29 July 1992; and Ishtiaq Jamil and Manzurul Mannan, 'A Study of Government-NGO Relations in Bangladish in the Period 1992 and 1993: Collaborations or Confrontations', mimeograph, Dhaka, March 1994.
51   Kirsten Westergaard, 'Boringram: a Restudy of a Village in Northern Bangladesh: How to Live Better on Less Land'; Roushan Jahan, 'Gender Roles and Relations: a Changing Context', papers presented at 'Bangladesh at 25' Conference, New York, 5–7 December 1996.
52   Ciba-Geigy Foundation for Cooperation with Developing Countries, 'The Political Economy of Rural Underdevelopment', Internet: http://www.ciba.com/cgf/cgf home.html, 29 February 1996, p. 1.
53   Ibid, pp. 2–3.
54   Sarah C. White, *Arguing with the Crocodile: Gender and Class in Bangladesh*, University Press Ltd, Dhaka, 1992, pp. 14–15.
55   Ibid, p. 16.
56   'BRAC at a Glance: Objectives: Poverty Alleviation and Empowerment of the Poor', *Holiday*, 30 August 1996, p. 14.
57   Ibid.
58   'BRAC celebrates 25 years', *Holiday*, 21 February 1997, p. 7.
59   BRAC, *Desh-Kal-Samaj* [Bengali], BRAC Printers, Dhaka, 1990, pp. 57–66.
60   Ibid, pp. 66–8, 84–5, 233–5.
61   Ibid, p. 236.
62   Ibid, pp. 212–28.
63   Ibid, pp. 275–83, 290–7.
64   Shamim Hamid, *Why Women Count: Essays on Women in Development in Bangladesh*, University Press Ltd, Dhaka, 1996, pp. 115–16.
65   I talked to various garment-factory owners and female employees of *Aarong* outlets in Dhaka and elsewhere during December 1995 and December 1996.
66   T.W. Dichter, 'Questioning the Future..', pp. 261–2.
67   Richard Montgomery, 'Disciplining or Protecting the Poor? Avoiding the Social Cost of Peer Pressure in Micro-Credit Schemes', *Journal of International Development*, Vol. 8, No. 2, 1996, pp. 290–1.
68   Ibid, pp. 291–9.
69   Interview with a former BRAC executive who does not want to reveal his identity for personal reasons; see *BRAC Report, 1997*, 'BRAC at a Glance', pp. 6–7, Dhaka 1997.
70   Ibid.
71   Cynthia Guttman, *In Our Own Hands: the Story of Saptagram: a Women's Self-Reliance and Education Movement in Bangladesh*, UNESCO, Paris 1994, p. 4.
72   Ibid, p. 5.
73   Ibid, p. 8–9, 2–5.
74   Ibid, pp. 9–11, 2–7.
75   Ibid, pp. 14–16.
76   Ibid, pp. 20–2.
77   Ibid, pp. 29–32.

78 Shelley Feldman and Florence E. McCarthy, *Rural Women and Development in Bangladesh: Selected Issues*, NORAD, Ministry of Development Cooperations, Oslo, 1984, p. 100.
79 Ibid., pp. 216–20.
80 See Shamin Hamid, *Why Women Count*, p. 117; Abu N.M. Wahid (ed.), *The Grameen Bank: Poverty Relief in Bangladesh*, Westview Press, Boulder 1993, Chs. 1 & 2; David Bornstein, *The Price of a Dream: the Story of the Grameen Bank*, University Press Ltd, Dhaka 1996, pp. 19–61; *Asia Week*, 2 June 1995, p. 58.
81 Shamim Hamid, *Why Women Count*, pp. 117–18.
82 Ibid, p. 118.
83 Ainon Nahar Mizan, *In Quest of Empowerment: the Grameen Bank Impact on Women's Power and Status*, University Press Ltd, Dhaka, 1994, pp. 128–139.
84 Ibid, pp. 144, 148.
85 Ibid, p. 152.
86 Para Teare, 'Grameen Woman Blues', reproduced from *Living Marxism*, No. 90, May 1996, Internet:http://www.junius.co.uk/lm90/lm90-grameen.html, p. 1.
87 Professor Muhammad Yunus, 'Towards a Poverty-Free World', paper presented at the Bangladesh: Democracy and Development Conference, Melbourne, 22–23 March 1997; Professor M. Yunus, 'What is the Microcredit Summit?', *Grameen Poverty Research* (Newsletter of the Grameen Trust), Vol. 3, No. 2, April 1997, p. 1.
88 Ibid.
89 Jeffrey Tucker, 'The Micro-Credit Cult', Internet: *http://www.soc.titech.ac.jp/titso...Chi- ab/cim/negative-grameen.html*, pp. 1–3. (04/12/97)
90 Ibid.
91 Prabhu Ghate, *et al.*, 'Poverty Alleviation and Enterprise Development: The need for a Differentiated Approach', *Journal of International Development*, vol. 8, No. 2, 1996, pp. 176–7.
92 T.W. Dichter, *Questioning the Future . . .*, p. 263.
93 S.R. Osmani, 'Limits to the Alleviation of Poverty Through Non-farm Credit', *Bangladesh Development Studies*, Vol. 17, pp. 1–18.
94 David Hulme and Paul Mosley, *Finance Against Poverty*, Vol. 2, Routledge, London, 1996, p. 114.
95 Habib Ahmed, 'Microfinance Institutions in Bangladesh: Virtuous Circles or Vicious Cycles?', Department of Economics, National University of Singapore, Mimeo, April 1997, pp. 15–16.
96 Professor Yunus's speech at the 'Workshop on Microfinance', Bangladesh: Democracy and Development Conference, Melbourne, 23 March 1997.
97 J. Allister McGregor, 'Government Failures and NGO Success: Credit, Banking and the Poor in Rural Bangladesh, 1970–90', in Tim Lloyd and Oliver Morissey (eds), *Poverty, Inequality and Rural Development* (Vol. 3), St. Martin's Press, New York, 1994, p. 112.
98 David Bornstein, *The Price of a Dream*, pp. 149–51.
99 Ibid, p. 139, Ataus Samad, 'Downslide is accelerating', *Holiday*, 1 May 1997, p. 1.

100 Professor Yunus, 'Workshop on Microfinance' speech, Melbourne, 23 March 1997.
101 Syed, M. Hashemi and Sidney Ruth Schuler, 'Sustainable Banking with the Poor . . .', p. 53.
102 Para Teare, 'Grameen Women Blues', pp. 3–4.
103 Badruddin Umar, 'Grameen Bank: Ekti Samrajyabadi Chakranto' [Grameen Bank: an Imperialist Conspiracy], Seba [Bengali Weekly], Dhaka, 30 March 1997, p. 3.
104 Aminur Rahman, 'Micro-Credit for Women in Rural Bangladesh: Retrenchment of Patriarchal Hegemony as a Consequence', Chicago Anthropology Exchange, Vol. XXIII, Spring 1996, p. 6.
105 Ibid, pp. 10–14.
106 Sarah C. White, 'Men, Maseulinities, and the Politics of Development', Gender and Development, Vol. 5, No. 2, June 1997, p. 20.
107 Tasneen Siddiqui, 'Gender Dimensions of Government and NGO Relations in Bangladeshk' (Mineo), p. 17, Dhaka, 1996 (Working Paper).
108 Ibid, p. 11.
109 Ibid, pp. 12–13.
110 J.A. McGregor, 'Government Failures and NGO Success', p. 119; Manzurul Mannan, 'Culture, Cash and Credit: the Morality of Money Circulation', Paper Presented at European Network of Bangladesh Studies Workshop, University of Bath, UK, 16–18 April 1998.
111 Howard Jones, Social Welfare in Third World Development, Macmillan, London, 1990, p. 234.
112 Ibid.
113 Philip Gayin, Bangladeshe Poshak Shilpe Nari Sramik [Bengali], Bangladesh Human Rights Coordination Council, Dhaka, 1990, pp. 7–15, 86–7; Government of Bangladesh, Women in Bangladesh: Equality Development and Peace (National Report to the Fourth World Conference on Women, Beijing 1995), Ministry of Women and Children Affairs, Dhaka, 1995, p. 22.
114 Bangladesh Observer, 1 August, and 7 September 1997.
115 Immigration and Refugee Board, Canada, Human Rights Brief: Women in Bangladesh, Ottawa, 1993, pp. 15–16.
116 Ibid, p. 16.
117 Hameeda Hossain et al., No Better Option? Industrial Women Workers in Bangladesh, University Press Ltd, Dhaka, 1990, pp. 99–100, 105; Philip Gayin, op. cit., p. 87.
118 Peter Custers, Capital Accumulation and Women's Labour in Asian Economies, Zed Books, London, 1997, pp. 133–63.
119 Hameeda Hossain, No Better Option?, pp. 98, 108.
120 Marilyn Rock, 'The Garment Export Workers of Bangladesh: From Passive Victims to Active Agents of Change', paper presented at the 'Bangladesh: Democracy and Development' Conference, Melbourne 22–23 March 1997, p. 24.
121 Ibid.
122 Naila Kabeer, 'Women's Labour in the Bangladesh Garment Industry: Choice and Constraints' in Camillia Fawzi El-Solh and Judy Mabro (eds), Muslim Women's Choices: Religious Belief and Social Reality, Berg Publications, Oxford, 1994, pp. 165–6, 172–7.

123 Cynthia Guttman, *In Our Hands*, p. 28; David Bornstein, op. cit., pp. 161–2.

124 Hedayetul Huq, 'Aspects of Christian NGO work in a Muslim Society: Challenges and Response in Bangladesh', Paper presented at the ASAA Conference, Melbourne, 8–11 July 1996; Joe O Klein, 'Mothers vs. Mullahs: A program favoured by Hillary Clinton meets Islamic resistance', *Newsweek*, 17 April 1995, p. 17; *Financial Express* (Dhaka), 11 April 1994; *Ajker Kagaj* (Bengali Daily), 5 April 1994; *Banglabazar Patrika* (Bengali Daily), 6 April 1994; *Inqilab* (Bengali Daily), 10 & 11 April 1994.

125 See for details Taj I. Hashmi, 'Islam in Bangladesh Politics', in H. Mutalib and T.I. Hashmi (eds), *Islam, Muslim and the Modern State*, Macmillan Press, London, 1994, pp. 127–34.

126 An amorphous group of 'leftist/secular' supporters of the Awami League Party (also known as 'pro-India' among its opponents), who are opposed to the concept of 'Bangladeshi Nationalism' of the 'liberal nationalist' Bangladesh Naionalist Party or BNP (also known as 'pro-Islamic' and 'anti-Indian').

127 'Credit: Where It's Due', TV Transcript of World View International Foundation (WIF), Bangladesh (1995), Internet: http://carryon.one world.org/guides/women/yunus.html.

128 Lubna Tabassum Khan, 'Marital Instability in Dhaka, Bangladesh: With Special Reference to Dual-earner Couples', Internet:http://www.lib.uchicago.edu/libinfo/southasia 4 November 1996.

129 Durgadas Bhattacharjee and M.A. Gaffer, 'Early Implementation Projects on Flood Control, Drainage Improvement and Irrigation (Baseline Survey of Shakpaldia Project, Faridpur)', Mimeograph, Bangladesh Water Development Board, Dhaka, 1991, pp. 679–82, 696–7, 758–67.

130 Antonio Gramsci, *Selections from the Prison Notebooks*, pp. 12, 326 and 333.

131 Michel Foucault, *Power/Knowledge: Selected Interviews and Other Writings* (Colin Gordon, ed.), Pantheon Books, New York, 1980, pp. 119, 141.

132 Ibid., pp. 81–2.

133 Ibid., pp. 83, 89.

134 Peter Custers, *Capital Accumulation*, pp. 31–50, 201–24.

6 Militant Feminism, Islam and Patriarchy

1 See Razia Akter Banu, *Islam in Bangladesh*, E.J. Brill, Leiden, 1991, *passim*; Taj ul-Islam Hashmi, 'Islam in Bangladesh Politics' in H. Mutalib & T.I. Hashmi (eds), *Islam, Muslims and the Modern State*, Macmillan Press, London, 1994.

2 T.I. Hashmi, 'Islam in Bangladesh Politics', 116–17.

3 Taslima Nasreen, *Nirbachito Column* (Bengali) Jnan Kosh, Dhaka, 1993, *passim*.

4 Moudud Ahmed, Bangladesh: *Era of Sheikh Mujibur Rahman* University Press Ltd, Dhaka, 1991, *passim*.

5 M. Abul Kalam, 'Status of Women and Mortality', *Bangladesh Quarterly* (June, 1993), p. 62.

6   See for details Rahnuma Ahmed, 'Women's Movement in Bangladesh
    and the left's Understanding of the Women Question', *Journal of Social
    Studies*, No. 30 (1985), pp. 41–56. Naila Kabeer, 'The Question for National
    Identity: Women, Islam and the State in Bangladesh', Discussion Paper
    268, Institute of Development Studies, Sussex University (Oct. 1989),
    pp. 8–9.
7   *The Constitution of the People's Republic of Bangladesh* (1972), Clause 3,
    Article 29.
8   See Mohiuddin Alamgir, *The Experience of Rural Works Programme in Bang-
    ladesh* (Bangkok, 1977): p. 86, and Shelley Feldman and Florence E.
    McCarthy, *Rural Women and Development in Bangladesh*: Selected Issues,
    Oslo, 1984, pp. 146–54.
9   Naila Kabeer, 'The Question for National Identity', pp. 16 and 19.
10 Ibid, p. 30.
11 N. Kabeer, *Reversed Realities: Gender Hierarchies in Development Thought*,
    University Press Ltd, Dhaka, 1995, pp. 242–5, 257.
12 Fatema Rashid Hasan, 'Limits and Possibilities of Law and Legal Literacy:
    Experience of Bangladesh Women', *Economic and Political Weekly*, 29
    October 1994, pp. WS69–76.
13 See for details B.K. Jahangir and Zarina Rahman Khan (eds), *Bangladeshe
    Nari Nirjatan* (Persecution of Women in Bangladesh) Centre for Social Studies,
    Dhaka, 1993; Zarina Rahman Khan, *Women, Work and Values: Contradic-
    tions in the Prevailing Notions and Realities of Women's Lives in Rural
    Bangladesh*, Centre for Social Studies, Dhaka, 1992; Meghna Guthakurta
    and Suraiya Begum (eds), *Nari, Rashtra, Unnayan O Matadarsha* (Women,
    State, Development and Ideology), Centre for Social Studies, Dhaka, 1990.
14 *Bangladeshe Observer*, 23 June 1994; Telephone interview with Prof. Ahmed
    Sharif, 24 June 1994.
15 *Janakantha*, 12 May 1994.
16 *Morning Star*, 9 June 1994.
17 *Bangladesh Observer*, 27 June 1994.
18 See Taj I. Hashmi, 'Islam in Bangladesh Politics', pp. 111–26.
19 Maulana Delwar Hossain Saidi, '*Purdah* and Women's Rights in Islam'
    [Bengali], Audiotape, C.H. Products, Dhalza, 1991.
20 My interview with Maulana Abbas Ali Khan, acting *amir*, Jamaat-I-Islami,
    Bangladesh, 21 May 1991; *Jamaat-i-Islami's* Programme and Election
    Manifesto (Dhaka, 1991); Razia Akter Banu, 'Jamaat-i-Islami in Bangla-
    desh: Challenges and Prospects', H. Mutalib and T.I. Hashmi (eds), *Islam,
    Muslims and the Modern State*, Macmillan Press, London 1994, pp. 83–4.
21 The Bangladesh Election Commission, *Elections* of 1991.
22 R.A. Banu, *Islam in Bangladesh*, Chapters 9 and 10.
23 See for details about the stages in the development of Muslim women's
    liberation in Bengal, Matahar Hussain Sufi, *Begum Rokeya: Jiban O Sahitya*
    (Bengali), University Press Ltd, Dhaka, 1986; Begum Shaista Ikramullah,
    'From *Purdah to Parliament*, the Cresset Press Ltd; London, 1963,
24 T. Nasreen, *Nirbachito Column, passim*; Farukh Faisal, 'Tarko-Bitarko Ebong
    Taslima Nasreen', *Anannya*, 1–15 November 1993, pp. 26–7.
25 Ahmed Safa's Interview with *Anannya* (1–15 November 1993), pp. 30–1;
    Farukh Faisal, 'Tarko-Bitarko Ebong Taslima Nasreen', p. 28.

26 Farukh Faisal, 'Tarko-Bitarko Ebong Taslima Nasreen', p. 29.
27 T. Nasreen, *Nirbachito Column*, pp. 9–154 and *Jabona Keno Jabo, Vidvya Prakash*, Dhaka, 1992; also her column 'Nashto Column', *Jaye Jaye Din*, 26 October 1993, p. 11.
28 My interview with Enayetullah Khan, editor of *Holiday*, 20 November 1993.
29 *Holiday*, 22 October 1993.
30 F. Faisal, 'Tarko-Bitarko Ebong Taslima Nasreen', p. 28; Ahmad Rafique (writer), Badruddin Umar (leftist writer), Rashed Khan Khan Menon (leftist politician) have also condemned Nasreen for her counter-productive writings. See *Bhorer Kagaj* (Bengali Daily), 11 December 1993, *Janakantha*, 7 June 1994; *Holiday*, 26 August 1994.
31 T. Nasreen, *Nirbachito Column*, p. 70.
32 See Fatima Mernissi, *Women and Islam*, Blackwell, Oxford 1991; and *Beyond the Veil: Male-Female Dynamics in Modern Muslim Society*, Al Saqi Books, London, 1985; Chapters 1, 2 and Conclusion.
33 Abu Faisal, 'Nasreen's Endemic Academic Dishonesty' in Mesbahuddin Ahmed (ed.), *Taslima Nasreener Bipakshe* (Bengali), AnkurPrakashoni, Dhaka, 1993, pp. 87–8, *Sura: Al-Nisa*, verse 19.
34 *Inqilab* (Bengali daily), 8 October 1991.
35 Abu Faisal and Ahmed Mansur, *Taslima Nasreener Islam Biddesh O Apobakkha* (Bengali) Aman Prakashoni, Faridpur 1993, pp. 20–1. *Sura: Al-Baqarah*, verse 228. [The *ayat* continues: 'But men have a degree (of advantage) over them. And God is Exalted in Power.']
36 *Lajja* (Bengali), Pearl Publications Dhaka, 1993, *passim*.
37 See *Bangladesh Observer, Sangbad, Jankantha & Inqilab* (October 1993).
38 *New York Times*, 'Sentenced to Death', 30 November 1993; Meredith Tax, 'Taslima Nasrin: A Background Paper', *Bulletin of Concerned Asian Scholars*, Vol. 24, no. 4 (1993), pp. 72–4; Amnesty International, *Bangladesh: Fundamental Rights of Women Violated with Virtual Impurity*, London, October 1994, p. 14.
39 Interviews with A Sharif and E. Khan.
40 Interview with Taslima Nasreen, Dhaka, 16 November 1993.
41 See *Statesman* (Calcutta), 9 May 1994; *Sangbad* (Bengali daily), 5 June 1995; *Inqilab*, 1 June–31 June 1994; *Straits Times*, 12 August 1994.
42 *Straits Times*, 11 August 1994.
43 *Far Easten Economic Review*, 18 August 1994, p. 23; *Asiaweek*, 17 August 1994, p. 31; *Sangbad*, 1 August–31 August 1994.
44 *Independent*, 1 August 1994; *Newsweek*, 22 August 1994, p. 13; Meredith Tax, *op. cit.*, pp. 72–4.
45 See her signed interview with *Savvy* (Bombay), November 1993, p. 33; T. Nasreen, *Jabona Keno Jabo* pp. 65–6; *Robbar*, 13 February 1994, p. 38.
46 *Janakantha* (Bengali Daily), 4 August 1994.
47 Mary Anne Weaver, 'A Fugitive from Injustice', *The New Yorker*, 12 September 1994, p. 7.
48 Ibid.
49 Ibid, p. 6.
50 Ibid, pp. 5–6.
51 Ibid, p. 5.

52   Taslima Nasreen, 'The Perils of Free Speech', paper presented at the Radcliffe College, Cambridge, Massachusetts, 26 April 1996, cited in the *Journal of South Asia Women Studies*, Vol. 3, No. 1, 1997, web-page: *jsaws@shore.net.*

53   Enrica Garzilli, 'An Unconventional Woman: Two Evenings with Taslima Nasrin', *Journal of South Asia Women Studies* Vol. 2, No. 3, 1996, web-page: *garzilli@shore.net.*

Bibliography

Published and unpublished reports

Alam, S.M. Nurul, 'NGOs Under Attack: a Study of the Socio-Cultural and Political Dynamics of the NGO operations in Bangladesh', Mimeograph, Study Commissioned by PACT-PRIP [sponsored by the USAID], Dhaka 1995.

Amnesty International, 'Bangladesh: Taking the Law in their Own Hands, the Village Salish', Report, London, October 1993.

Amnesty International, 'Bangladesh: Fundamental Rights of Women Violated with Virtual Impunity', Report, London, October 1993.

Bhattacharjee, Durgadas and M.A. Gaffer, 'Early Implementation Projects on Flood Control, Drainage Improvement and Irrigation (Baseline Survey of Shakpaldia Project, Faridpur)' Mimeograph, Bangladesh Water Development Board, Dhaka 1991.

Coordinating Council for Human Rights in Bangladesh (CCHRB), *Bangladesh: State of Human Rights, 1992*, CCHRB, Dhaka, 1993.

Feldman, Shelley and Florence E. McCarthy, *Rural Women and Development in Bangladesh: Selected Issues*, NORAD, Ministry of Development Cooperations, Oslo, 1984.

Government of Bangladesh, *Women in Bangladesh: Equality, Development and Peace*, National Report to the Fourth World Conference on Women, Beijing 1995, Ministry of Women and Children Affairs, Dhaka, 1995.

Government of Bangladesh, *The Constitution of the People's Republic of Bangladesh*, Government Printing Press, Dhaka, 1988.

Government of Bangladesh, Bangladesh Election Commission's Parliamentary Elections Results, 1991 and 1996.

Bangladesh Rural Advancement Committee (BRAC), *BRAC Report, 1997*, BRAC Publications, Dhaka, 1997.

Immigration and Refugee Board, Canada, 'Human Rights Brief: Women in Bangladesh', Report, Ottawa, 1993.

US Department of State, *Country Reports on Human Rights Practices for 1992*, Government Printing Office, Washington DC, 1993.

Newspapers and periodicals

Bengali   *Ajker Kagaj, Anannya* (fortnightly)
          Bangla Bazar Patrika, Bhorer Kagaj, Bichitra (weekly),
          Chitrabangla (weekly)
          Dainik Bangla, Forum (bi-monthly)
          Inqilab, Janakantha, Jaye Jaye Din (weekly)
          Robbar (weekly)
          Sangbad, Sangram
English   *Asia Week*

Bangladesh Observer
Dhaka Courier (weekly)
Economist
Far Eastern Economic Review
Guardian
Holiday (Bangladeshi weekly)
Independent (Bangladeshi daily)
International Herald Tribune
Daily Star (Bangladeshi daily)
New York Times
Statesman (Calcutta)
Straits Times (Singapore)
The Times
New Yorker

Interviews

Maulana Abbas Ali Khan, acting *Ameer* (chief) of the Jamaat-i-Islami (Bangladesh), Dhaka, 21 May 1991;
Professor Ahmed Sharif, Dhaka, 6 and 24 June 1994;
Enayetullah Khan, Editor, *Holiday*, 20 November 1993;
Professor Abul Kasem Fazlul Haq, Dhaka University, 20 May 1991;
Professor Musa Ansari, Dhaka University, 20 May 1991;
Professor Sirajul Islam Chowdhury, Dhaka University, 20 May 1991;
Barrister Ishtiaq Ahmed, Dhaka, 25 May 1991;
Ajay Ray and Saifuddin Manik of the Communist Party of Bangladesh, Dhaka, 26 May 1991;
Professor Maniruzzaman Miah, Vice-Chancellor, Dhaka University, 15 April 1992;
Maulana Matiur Rahman Nizami, Secretary General, Jamaat-i-Islami (Bangladesh), Dhaka, 21 May 1991;
Mohiuddin Ahmed, MP, Dhaka, 17 May 1991;
Taslima Nasreen, Dhaka, 16 November 1993;
Colonel (retired) Nuruzzaman, Dhaka, 22 June 1995;
Dr Tasneem Siddiqui, Dhaka University, 20 September 1997.

Videos and audiotapes

Maulana Delwar Hossain Saidi (Jamaat-i-Islami leader and MP, elected in June 1996 elections), Speech at Chittagong Parade Ground, January 1989 (Video).
Maulana Delwar Hossain Saidi's Audiotapes: '*Purdah* and Women's Rights in Islam' [Bengali], C.H. Products, Dhaka, 1991, 'Rights of Husbands and Wives' [Bengali], C.H. Products, Dhaka, 1992.
Ain-Shalish Kendro (Legal-aid Centre), 'The Eclipse', Documentary videotape on persecution of women in rural Bangladesh [Bengali], Dhaka, 1994.

Books, periodicals and journal articles

Abdullah, Tahrunnessa A. and Sondra Zeidenstein, *Village Women of Bangladesh: Prospects for Change*, Pergamon Press, Oxford, 1982.

Adnan, Shapan, 'Land, Power and Violence in Barisal Villages', Mimeograph, The Village Study Group, Dhaka, 1976.

Adnan, Shapan, '"Birds in a Cage": Institutional Change and Women's Position in Bangladesh', *Journal of Social Studies*, No. 46, October 1989.

Afshar, Haleh, 'Fundamentalism and Women in Iran', in Oliver Mandelsohn and Upendra Baxi (eds), *The Rights of Subordinated Peoples*, Oxford University Press, Delhi, 1994.

Afshar, Haleh, *Women and Empowerment*, Macmillan Press, London, 1998.

Ahmad, Aziz, *Islamic Modernism in India and Pakistan, 1857–1964*, Oxford University Press, London, 1967.

Ahmad, Moudud, *Bangladesh: Era of Sheikh Mujibur Rahman*, University Press Ltd, Dhaka, 1991.

Ahmed, Habib, 'Microfinance Institutions in Bangladesh: Virtuous Circles or Vicious Cycles?' Mimeograph, Department of Economics, National University of Singapore, 1997.

Ahmed, Leila, *Women and Gender in Islam: Historical Roots of a Modern Debate*, Yale University Press, New Haven, 1992.

Ahmed, Rafiuddin, *The Bengal Muslims, 1871–1906: a Quest for Identity*, Oxford University Press, Delhi, 1981.

Ahmed, Rahnuma, 'Women's Movement in Bangladesh and the Left's Understanding of the Women's Question', *Journal of Social Studies*, No. 30, 1985.

Alamgir, Mohiuddin, *The Experience of Rural Works Programme in Bangladesh*, Bangkok, 1977.

Alamgir, Mohiuddin, *Bangladesh: a Case of Below Poverty Level Equilibrium*, BIDS, Dhaka, 1978.

Ali, Ahmed, *Al-Qu'ran: a Contemporary Translation by Ahmed Ali*, Princeton University Press, Princeton, 1993.

Ali, Ameer, *The Spirit of Islam*, Methuen and Co. Ltd, London, 1964.

Ali, Maulana Ashraf, *Muradul Momeneen* [Bengali], Hamidiya Library, Dhaka, 1993.

Amawi, Abla, 'Women and Property Rights in Islam', in Suha Sabbagh (ed.), *Arab Women: Between Defiance and Restraint*, Olive Branch Press, New York, 1996.

Amin, Sonia Nishat, *The World of Muslim Women in Colonial Bengal, 1876–1939*, E.J. Brill, Leiden, 1996.

Anderson, Roy, Amin, Sonia Nishat, *Politics and Change in the Middle East: Sources of Conflict and Accommodation*, Prentice Hall, Englewood Cliffs, N.J., 1990.

Anwari, Maulana Fazlur Rahman, *Maksudul Momin* [Bengali], Taj Publishing House, Dhaka, 1981.

Arens, Jenneke and Jos van Beurden, *Jhagrapur: Poor Peasants and Women in a Village in Bangladesh*, Arens and van Beurden, Amsterdam, 1977.

Armstrong, Karen, *Muhammad: a Western Attempt to Understand Islam*, Victor Gollancz Ltd, London, 1991.

Azad, Humayun, *Nari* [Bengali], Agami Prakashani, Dhaka, 1995.

Badawi, Gamal A., 'Women in Islam', in Khurshid Ahmad (ed.), *Islam: its Meaning and Message*, the Islamic Foundation, Leicester, 1988.

Badran, Margot, *Feminists, Islam and Nation: Gender and the Making of Modern Egypt*, Princeton University Press, Princeton, 1995.

Banu, U.A.B. Razia Akter, *Islam in Bangladesh*, E.J. Brill, Leiden, 1992.

Banu, U.A.B. Razia Akter, 'Jamaat-i-Islam in Bangladesh: Challenges and Prospects', in Hussin Mutalib and T.I. Hashmi (eds), *Islam, Muslims and the Modern State*, Macmillan, Basingtoke and St. Martin's Press, New York, 1994.

Barman, Dalem Chandra, *Emerging Leadership Pattern in Rural Bangladesh*, Centre for Social Studies, Dhaka, 1988.

Bashier, Zakaria, *Muslim Women in the Midst of Change*, The Islamic Foundation, Leicester, 1990.

Begum, Maleka and Khondkar Sakhawat Ali (eds), *Fatwa, 1991–1995* [Bengali], Shiksha O. Sanskriti Charcha Kendra, Dhaka, 1997.

Begum, Rushida, *Nari Nirjatan: Sangya O Bishleshon* [Bengali], Narigrantha Prabartana, Dhaka, 1992.

Bhuiyan, Rabia, *Aspects of Violence Against Women*, Institute of Democratic Rights, Dhaka, 1991.

Blair, Harry, 'Civil Society, Democratic Development and International Donors in Bangladesh', paper presented at the 'Bangladesh at 25' Conference, Columbia University, New York, 5–7 December 1996.

Bornstein, David, *The Price of a Dream: the Story of the Grameen Bank*, University Press Ltd, Dhaka, 1996.

Borresen, Kari Elisabeth, 'Women's Studies of the Christian Tradition: New Perspectives', in Ursula King (ed.), *Religion and Gender*, Blackwell, Oxford, 1995.

BRAC, *Desh-Kal-Samaj* [Bengali], BRAC Printers, Dhaka, 1990.

Brooks, Geraldine, *Nine Parts of Desire: the Hidden World of Islamic Women*, Anchor Books, Sydney, 1996.

Brown, Daniel W., *Rethinking Tradition in Modern Islamic Thought*, Cambridge University Press, Cambridge, 1996.

Brydon, Lynne and Sylvia Chant, *Women in the Third World: Gender Issues in Rural and Urban Areas*, Aldershot, London, 1989.

Carstairs, Robert, *The Little World of an Indian District Officer*, Macmillan Press, London, 1912.

Cassirer, Ernst, *The Philosophy of the Enlightenment*, Princeton University Press, Princeton, 1951.

Chen, Martha Alter, *A Quiet Revolution: Women in Transition in Rural Bangladesh*, BRAC Prokashona, Dhaka, 1993.

Chowdhury, Aditee Nag, *Let Grassroots Speak: People's Participation, Self-Help Groups and NGOs in Bangladesh*, University Press Ltd, Dhaka, 1990.

Clay, Edward J., 'Institutional Changes and Agricultural Wages in Bangladesh', *Bangladesh Development Studies*, Vol. 4. No. 4, November 1976.

Conlon, Frank F., 'Hindu Revival and Indian Womanhood: the Image and Status of Women in the Writings of Vishnubawa Brahmachari', *South Asia*, Vol. XVII, No. 2, 1994.

Custers, Peter, *Capital Accumulation and Women's Labour in Asian Economies*, Zed Books, London, 1977.

Deobandi, Maulana Muhammad Mian, *Ulama-i -Hind Ka Shaandar Maazi [Urdu]*, Vol. 1, *Jamiat-ul-Ulama-i-Hind*, Delhi, 1942.

Dichter, Thomas W., 'Questioning the Future of NGOs in Microfinance', *Journal of International Development*, Vol. 8, No. 2, 1996.

D'souza, Diane, 'Women: Status and Comparative Religions', *Al-Wurwat al-Wusqa (The Firmest Bond)*, No. 64–65, Special Winter & Spring Issue, 1996–97.

Dwyer, Kevin, *Arab Voices: the Human Rights Debate in the Middle East*, Routledge, London, 1991.

Eaton, Richard, *The Rise of Islam and the Bengal Frontier, 1204–1760*, University of California Press, Berkeley, 1993.

Engineer, Asghar Ali, *Islam and Liberation Theology: Essays on Liberative Elements in Islam*, Sterling Publishers, New Delhi, 1990.

Engineer, Asghar Ali, *The Rights of Women in Islam*, IBS Buku Sdn. Bhd. Selangor (Malaysia), 1992.

Faisal, Abu, 'Nasreen's Endemic Academic Dishonesty', in Mesbahuddin Ahmed (ed.), *Taslima Nasreen Pakshe Bipakshe* [Bengali], Ankur Prakashoni, Dhaka, 1993.

Faisal, Abu and Ahmed Mansur, *Taslima Nasreen Islam Biddesh O Apobakkha* [Bengali], Aman Prakashoni, Faridpur, 1993.

Faisal, Farukh, 'Tarko-Bitarko Ebong Taslima Nasreen', *Anannya*, 1–15 November 1993.

Feldman, Shelley, '(Re) presenting Islam: Manipulating Gender, Shifting State Practices and Class Frustrations', Paper presented at the 'Bangladesh at 25' Conference, Columbia University, New York, 5–7 December 1996.

Fisher, Julie, *Nongovernments: NGOs and the Political Development of the Third World*, Kumarian Press, West Hartford (CT), 1998.

Frierson, Cathy A., *Peasant Icons: Representations of Rural People in Nineteenth-Century Russia*, Oxford University Press, New York, 1993.

Foucault, Michel, *Power/Knowledge: Selected Interviews and Other Writings*, ed. Colin Gordon, Pantheon Books, New York, 1980.

Gardner, Katy, 'Purdah, Female Power and Cultural Change: a Sylheti Experience', *Journal of Social Studies*, No. 65, July 1994.

Gardner, Katy, *Global Migrants, Local Lives: Travel and Transformation in Rural Bangladesh*, Clarendon Press, Oxford, 1995.

Gayin, Philip, *Bangladeshe Poshak Shilpe Nari Sramik* [Bengali], Bangladesh Human Rights Coordination Council, Dhaka, 1990.

Ghate, Prabhu, 'Poverty Alleviation and Enterprise Development: the Need for a Differentiated Approach', *Journal of International Development*, Vol. 8, No. 2, 1996.

Gramsci, Antonio, *Selections from the Prison Notebooks of Antonio Gramsci*, ed. and translated by Quintin Hoare and Geoffrey Smith, London, 1971.

Guhathakurta, Meghna and Suraiya Begum (eds), *Nari, Rashtra, Unnayan O Matadarsha* [Bengali], Centre for Social Studies, Dhaka, 1990.

Guttman, Cynthia, *In Our Own Hands: the Story of Saptagram: a Women's Self-Reliance and Education Movement in Bangladesh*, UNESCO, Paris, 1994.

Haddad, Yvonne Y. and Jane I. Smith, 'Women in Islam: "the Mother of All Battles"', in Suha Sabbagh (ed.), *Arab Women: Between Defiance and Restraint*, Olive Branch Press New York, 1996.

Hamid, Shamim, *Why Women Count: Essays on Women in Development in Bangladesh*, University Press Ltd, Dhaka, 1996.

Haq, Anisul, 'There is nothing to be worried about *fatwas*' [Bengali] *Bhorer Kagaj*, 23 July 1994.

Haq, Maulana Mansurul (ed.), *Mr Maududir New Islam* [Bengali], Jamia Qurania Arabia, Lalbagh, Dhaka, 1985.

Haqqani, Najmul Haq, 'Swajatir Tarey Biplabi Ahban' [Bengali], *Janakantha*, 6 June 1994.

Hartmann, Betsy and James Boyce, *A Quiet Violence: View From a Bangladesh Village*, University Press Ltd, Dhaka, 1990.

Hasan, Fatema Rashid, 'Limits and Possibilities of Law and Legal Literacy: Experience of Bangladesh Women', *Economic and Political Weekly*, 29 October 1994.

Hashemi, Syed M., 'NGO Accountability in Bangladesh: Beneficiaries, Donors and the State' in Michael Edwards and David Hulme (eds), *Non-Governmental Organisations – Performance and Accountability: Beyond the Magic Bullet*, Earthscan Publications Ltd, London, 1995.

Hashemi, Syed M., 'State, Politics and Civil Society in the Context of Donor Hegemony: Bangladesh 25', paper presented at 'Bangladesh at 25' Conference, Columbia University, New York, 5–7 December 1996.

Hashemi, Syed M. and Sydney Schuler, 'Sustainable Banking with the Poor: a Case Study of Grameen Bank', JSI Research and Training Institute, Arlington, Virginia, January 8, 1997, Mimeograph.

Hashmi, Taj I., 'Karamat Ali and the Muslims in Bengal, 1800–1873', *Dacca University Studies*, Vol. XXIII, June 1976.

Hashmi, Taj I., *Pakistan as a Peasant Utopia: the Communalization of Class Politics in East Bengal, 1920–1947*, Westview Press, Boulder, 1992.

Hashmi, Taj I., 'Islam in Bangladesh Politics', in Hussin Mutalib and Taj I. Hashmi (eds), *Islam, Muslims and the Modern State*, Macmillan and St. Martin's Press, New York, 1994.

Hashmi, Taj I., 'Women and Islam: Taslima Nasreen, Society and Politics in Bangladesh', *South Asia*, Vol. XVIII, No. 2, December 1995.

Hassan, Mirza M., 'Democratizing Local Government: Current Reforms and Future Agenda', *Grameen Poverty Research*, vol. 4, No. 1, February 1998.

Hassan, Mirza M. and Zakir Hossain, 'Rural Poor and Electoral Democracy: Reflections on the Parliamentary Elections of 1996', *Grameen Poverty Research*, Vol. 2, No. 4, October 1996.

Hitti, Philip K., *History of the Arabs: From the Earliest Times to the Present*, Macmillan Press, London, 1958.

Hjarpe, Jan, 'The Attitude of Islamic Fundamentalism', in Bo Utas (ed.), *Women in Islamic Societies: Social Attitudes and Historical Perspectives*, Curzon Press, London, 1988.

Hoque, Rezaul and Noore Alam Siddiquee, 'Grassroots, Democratisation in Bangladesh: the NGO Experience', *Journal of Social Studies*, No. 79, January 1998.

Hossain, Hamida, *No Better Option? Industrial Women Workers in Bangladesh*, University Press, Ltd, Dhaka, 1990.

Hossain, Hamida, 'Women Enter the Union Councils', *Grameen Poverty Research*, Vol. 4, No. 1, February 1998.

Hossaini, Maulana Abdul Halim, *Islami Hukumat* [Bengali], Imanullah Khondkar, Comilla (n.d.).

Hours, Bernard, 'The Work of the Imam, Servant of the Community and Precarious Worker in Bangladesh', *Journal of Social Studies*, No. 54, October 1991.

Hours, Bernard, *Islam and Development in Bangladesh*, Centre for Social Studies, Dhaka, 1995.

Huda, Maulvi Muhammad Shamsul, *Neamul Quran* [Bengali], The Author, Dhaka, 1961.

Hulme, David and Paul Mosley, *Finance Against Poverty*, Vol. 2, Routledge, London, 1996.

Hunter, W.W., *The Indian Musalmans*, W. Rahman, Dhaka, 1975 (reprint).

Huq, Hedayetul, 'Aspects of Christian NGO Work in a Muslim Society: Challenges and Response in Bangladesh', Paper presented at the ASAA Conference, Melbourne, 8–11 July 1996.

Huq, M. Amirul (ed.), *Exploitation of the Rural Poor*, Bangladesh Academy for Rural Development, Comilla, 1976.

Hussain, Freda (ed.), *Muslim Women*, Croom Helm, London, 1984.

Ikram, Sheikh Muhammad, *Raud-i-Kausar* [Urdu], Adabi Duniya, Delhi, 1991.

Ikramullah, Shaista, *From Purdah to Parliament*, the Crescent Press Ltd, London, 1963.

Islam, A.K.M. Sirajul, 'Fatwa Ki Ebong Keno?' [Bengali], *Janakantha*, 27 April 1994.

Islam, Syed Serajul, 'Impacts of Technology and NGOs on Social Development: The Case of Bangladesh', *Journal of South Asian and Middle Eastern Studies*, Vol. XXI, No. 2, Winter 1998.

Jahan, Roushan, 'Gender Roles and Relations: a Changing Context', paper presented at 'Bangladesh at 25' Conference, Columbia University, New York, 5–7 December 1996.

Jahangir, B.K. and Zarina Rahman Khan (eds), *Bangladeshe Nari Nirjatan* [Bengali], Centre for Social Studies, Dhaka, 1993.

Jamil, Ishtiaq and Manzurul Mannan, 'A Study of Government-NGO Relations in Bangladesh in the Period 1992 and 1993: Collaborations or Confrontations?', Mimeograph, Dhaka, March 1994.

Jaunpuri, Maulana Karamat Ali, *Miftah-ul-Jamnat* [Urdu], Jaunpur, (n.d.)

Jaunpuri, Maulana Karamat Ali, *Zakhira-i-Karamat*, Vols. I-III, Haji Muhammad Saeed, Calcutta, 1924.

Jones, Howard, *Social Welfare in Third World Development*, Macmillan Press, London, 1990.

Kabeer, Naila, 'The Question for National Identity: Women, Islam and the State in Bangladesh', Discussion Paper 268, IDS, Sussex University, October 1989.

Kabeer, Naila, 'Women's Labour in the Bangladesh Garment Industry: Choice and Constraints' in Camillia Fawzi El-Solh and Judy Mabro (eds), *Muslim Women's Choices: Religious Beliefs and Social Reality*, Berg, Oxford, 1994.

Kabeer, Naila, *Reversed Realities: Gender Hierarchies in Development Thought*, University Press Ltd, Dhaka, 1995.

Kalam, M. Abul, 'Status of Women and Morality', *Bangladesh Quarterly*, June 1993.

Karim, Abdul, *Social History of the Muslims in Bengal down to A.D. 1538*, Asiatic Society of Pakistan, Dhaka, 1959.

238 *Bibliography*

Khan, Muin-ud-Din Ahmad, *History of the Fara'idi Movement*, Islamic Foundation, Dhaka, 1984.
Khan, Qamaruddin, *Status of Women in Islam,* Sterling Publishers Ltd, Delhi, 1990.
Khan, Shamsul M., *Why Two Women Witnesses?* Ta-Ha Publishers Ltd, London, 1993.
Khan, Zarina Rahman, *Women, Work and Values: Contradictions in the Prevailing Notions and Realities of Women's Lives in Rural Bangladesh*, Centre for Social Studies, Dhaka, 1992.
King, Ursula, (ed.), *Religion and Gender*, Blackwell, Oxford, 1995.
Klein, Joe O., 'Mothers vs Mullahs: a Program Favored by Hillary Clinton meets Islamic resistance', Newsweek, 17 April 1995.
Kothari, Rajni, 'Sources of Conflict in South Asia: Ethnicity, Refugees, Environment', cited in *Newsletter*, the Regional Centre for Strategic Studies, Colombo, April 1997.
Lemu, Aisha and Fatima Heeren, *Women in Islam*, the Islamic Foundation, Leicester, 1992.
Lesnes, Corine, 'Bangladeshi Women Begin to Fight Back', *Guardian Weekly*, 23 July 1995.
Lunde, Paul and Justin Wintle, *A Dictionary of Arabic and Islamic Proverbs*, Routledge & Kegan Paul, London, 1984.
Mahmud, Firoze and Sayeedur Rahman, 'Savare Ek Nashto Mahilar Kando', *Chitrabangla* [Bengali weekly], 13 October 1994.
Mallick, Aizur Rahman, *British Policy and the Muslims in Bengal, 1757–1856*, Bangla Academy, Dhaka, 1977.
Manna, Mahmudur Rahman, *Samprodayikota O Jamaat* [Bengali], Ananya, Dhaka, 1993.
Mannan, Manzurul, 'Culture, Cash and Credit: The Morality of Money Circulation', Paper Presented at European Network of Bangladesh Studies Workshop', University of Bath, UK, 16–18 April 1998.
Matubbar, Araz Ali, *Complete Works*, [Bengali], Vol. 1, Pathok Samabesh, Dhaka, 1994.
Mawdudi, Abul Ala, *Purdah and the Status of Women in Islam*, Islamic Publications, Lahore, 1972.
Max Muler, F. (ed.), *The Sacred Books of the East: the Laws of Manu*, Vol. 25, translated by G. Buhler, Motilal Banarsidars, Delhi 1988 (first edition 1886).
McGregor, J. Allister, 'Government Failures, and NGO Success: Credit, Banking and the Poor in Rural Bangladesh', 1970–90, in Tim Lloyd and Oliver Morissey (eds), *Poverty, Inequality and Rural Development* (Vol. 3), St. Martin's Press, New York, 1994.
Mernissi, Fatima, *Beyond the Veil: Male-Female Dynamics in Muslim Society*, Al Saqi Books, London, 1985.
Mernissi, Fatima, *Women and Islam: an Historical and Theological Enquiry*, Blackwell, Oxford, 1991.
Mernissi, Fatima, *Islam and Democracy: Fear of the Modern World*, Addison-Wesley Publishing Company, New York, 1993.
Metcalf, Barbara D., *Islamic Revival in British India: Deoband, 1860–1900*, Princeton University Press, Princeton, 1982.
Metcalf, Barbara D., *Perfecting Women: Maulana Ashraf Ali Thanawi's Bishisti Zewar*, University of California Press, Berkeley, 1990.

Mill, John Stuart, *The Subjection of Women*, Hackett Publishing Company, Indianapolis, 1988 (first edition 1869).

Minai, Naila, *Women in Islam: Tradition and Transition in the Middle East*, John Murray, London, 1981.

Minault, Gail, 'Sayyid Mumtaz Ali and *"Huquq un-Niswan"*: An Advocate of Women's Rights in Islam in the Late Nineteenth Century', *Modern Asian Studies*, Vol. 24, No. 1, 1990.

Mishu, Moshrefa, 'NGO: Bampanthider Karoniyo', *Forum* [Bengali], Vol. 16, Dhaka, May–June 1994.

Mizan, Ainon Nahar, *In Quest of Empowerment: the Grameen Bank Impact on Women's Power and Status*, University Press Ltd, Dhaka, 1994.

Moghadan, Valentine M. (ed.), *Identity, Politics and Women: Cultural Reassertions and Feminisms in International Perspective*, Westview Press, Boulder, 1994.

Mohsin, K.M., 'Tabligh Jama't and the Faith Movement in Bangladesh', in Rafiuddin Ahmed (ed.), *Bangladesh: Society, Religion and Politics*, South Asia Studies Group, Chittagong, 1985.

Montgomery, Richard, 'Disciplining or Protecting the Poor? Avoiding the Social Cost of Peer Pressure in Micro-Credit Schemes', *Journal of International Development*, Vol. 8, No. 2, 1996.

Moser, C., 'Gender Planning in the Third World: Meeting Practical and Strategic Gender Needs', *World Development*, Vol. 1, No. 11, 1989.

Murshid, Tazeen Mahnaz, 'Women, Islam, and the State: Subordination and Resistance', paper presented at the Bengal Studies Conference, 28–30 April 1995, Chicago.

Nasreen, Taslima, *Nirbachito Column* [Bengali], Jnan Kosh, Dhaka, 1993.

Nasreen, Taslima, *Lajja* [Bengali], Pearl Publications, Dhaka, 1993.

Nasreen, Taslima, *Jabona Keno Jabo* [Bengali], Vidya Prakash, Dhaka, 1992.

Nasreen, Taslima, 'The Perils of Free Speech', paper presented at the Radcliffe College, Cambridge, Mass., 26 April 1996, cited in the *Journal of South Asia Women Studies*, Vol. 3, No. 1, 1997, web-page: *jsaws@shore.net*.

Osmani, S.R., 'Limits to the Alleviation of Poverty through Non-farm Credit', *Bangladesh Development Studies*, Vol. 17, 1988.

Parsons, Talcot, *Societies: Evolutionary and Comparative Perspectives*, Prentice-Hall, Englewood Cliffs, 1966.

Rahim, Muhammad Abdur, *Social and Cultural History of Bengal, Vol. 1 (1201–1576)*, Pakistan Historical Society, Karachi, 1963.

Rahman, Aminur, 'Micro-Credit for Women in Rural Bangladesh: Retrenchment of Patriarchal Hegemony as a Consequence', *Chicago Anthropology Exchange*, Vol. XXII, Spring, 1996.

Rahman, Fazlur, *Islam*, University of Chicago Press, Chicago, 1979.

Rahman, Maulana Gholam, *Maksudul Momeneen* [Bengali], Qazi Anisur Rahman, Dhaka, 1994 (45th edition).

Rahman, Md. Mahbubur and Willem van Schendel, 'Gender and the Inheritance of Land: Living Law in Bangladesh', in Jan Breman, Rahman, Md. Mahbubur and Willem van Schendel, (eds), *The Village in Asia Revisited*, Oxford University Press, Delhi, 1997.

Rahman, Saira and Adilur Rahman Khan, 'Emerging NGO Culture in Bangladesh', *Holiday*, 10 January 1997.

Rashiduzzaman, M., The Dichotomy of Islam and Development: NGOs, Women's Development and *Fatawa* in Bangladesh', *Contemporary South Asia*, Vol. 6, No. 3, November 1997.

Redfield, Robert, 'The Folk Society', *American Journal of Sociology*, Vol. 52, January 1947.

Redfield, Robert, *The Little Community and Peasant Society and Culture*, Chicago University Press, Chicago, 1962.

Reeves, Minou, *Female Warriors of Allah: Women and the Islamic Revolution*, E.P. Dutton, New York, 1989.

Rock, Marilyn, 'The Garment Export Workers of Bangladesh: From Passive Victims to Active Agents of Change', paper presented at the 'Bangladesh: Democracy and Development', Conference, Melbourne, 22–23 March 1997.

Rostow, W.W., *The Stages of Economic Growth: a Non-Communist Manifesto*, Cambridge University Press, Cambridge 1960.

Roy, Asim, *Islamic Syncretistic Tradition in Bengal*, Princeton University Press, Princeton, 1983.

Sakhawatullah, Maulana Muhammad, *Hekayat-i-Sahaba* [Bengali], Tablighi Kutub Khana, Dhaka, 1982.

Samad, Ataus, 'Downslide is Accelerating', *Holiday*, 1 May 1997.

Sarkar, Sumit, '"Kaliyuga", "Chakri" and "Bhakti": Ramakrishna and His Times', *Economic and Political Weekly*, 18 July 1992.

Sharif, Ahmed, 'The Government and the *Fatwabaz Muftis*', *Ajker Kagaj* [Bengali], 16 May 1994.

Siapno, Jacqueline, 'Gender Relations in Mindanao', in Camillia Fawzi El-Solh and Judy Mabro (eds), *Muslim Women's Choices: Religious Belief and Social Reality*, Berg, Oxford, 1994.

Siddiqui, Kamal, 'Strengthening Local Democracy', *Grameen Poverty Research*, Vol. 4, no. 1, February 1998.

Siddiqui, Tasneem, 'Gender Dimensions of Government and NGO relations in Bangladesh', Dhaka, 1996. (Mimeograph)

Siddiqi, Zillur Rahman, 'Why Fundamentalists are Opposed to NGOs', *Sangbad* [Bengali], 3 April 1994.

Sinha, Pradip, *Nineteenth Century Bengal: Aspects of Social History*, Firma K.L. Mukhopadhyay, Calcutta, 1965.

Smith, B.C., *Understanding Third World Politics, Theories of Political Change and Development*, Indiana University Press, Bloomington, 1996.

Stowasser, Barbara Freyer, *Women in the Quran, Traditions and Interpretations*, Oxford University Press, New York, 1994.

Stowasser, Barbara Freyer, 'Women's Issues in Modern Islamic Thought', in Judith E. Tucker (ed.), *Arab Women: Old Boundaries, New Frontiers*, Indiana University Press, Bloomington, 1993.

Sufi, Motahar Hossain, *Begum Rokeya: Jivan O Sahitya* [Bengali], University Press Ltd, Dhaka, 1986.

Talib, Abdul Mannan, *Bangladeshe Islam* [Bengali], Adhunik Prakashani, Dhaka, 1980.

Tax, Meredit, 'Taslima Nasrin: a Background Paper, *Bulletin of Concerned Asian Scholars*, Vol. 24, No. 4 (1993).

Todd, Helen, *Women at the Centre: Grameen Bank Borrowers after One Decade*, Westview Press, Boulder, Colorado, 1996.

Tonnies, Ferdinand, *Community and Society (Gemeinschaft und Gesellschaft)*, Michigan University Press, East Lansing, 1964.

Tress, Madelein, 'Halakha, Zionism and Gender: the Case of Gush Emunim', in Valentine M. Moghadam (ed.), *Identity, Politics and Women: Cultural Reassertions and Feminisms in International Perspectives*, Westview Press, Boulder, 1994.

Tucker, Judith (ed.) *Arab Women: Old Boundaries, New Frontiers*, Indiana University Press, Bloomington, 1993.

Umar, Badruddin, 'Grameen Bank: Ekti Samrajyabadi Chakranto', *Seba* [Bengali weekly], Dhaka, 30 March 1997.

Van Schendel, Willem, *Peasant Mobility – the Odds of Life in Rural Bangladesh*, Van Goreum, Assen (Holland), 1981.

Van Schendel, Willem, *Three Deltas: Accumulation and Poverty in Rural Burma, Bengal and South India*, Sage Publications, New Delhi, 1991.

Wadud-Muhsin, Amina, *Qur'an and Women*, Penerbit Fajar Bakti Sdn. Bhd., Selangor (Malaysia), 1995.

Wahid, Abu. N.M. (ed.), *The Grameen Bank: Poverty Relief in Bangladesh*, Westview Press, Boulder, 1993.

Walther, Wiebke, *Women in Islam: From Medieval to Modern Times*, Markus Wiener Publishing, New York, 1993.

Weaver, Mary Anne, 'A Fugitive from Injustice', *New Yorker*, September 12, 1994.

Westergaard, Kirsten, *Pauperization and Rural Women in Bangladesh: a Case Study*, BARD, Comilla, 1983.

Westergaard, Kirsten, 'People's Empowerment in Bangladesh: NGO Strategies', *Journal of Social Studies*, No. 72, April 1996.

Westergaard, Kirsten, 'Boringram: A Restudy of a Village in Northern Bangladesh: How to Live Better on Less Land', paper presented at 'Bangladesh at 25' Conference, Columbia University, New York, 5–7 December 1996.

White, Erin, 'Religion and the Hermeneutics of Gender: An Examination of the Work of Paul Ricoeur', in Ursula King (ed.), *Religion and Gender*, Blackwell, Oxford, 1995.

White, Sarah C., *Arguing with the Crocodile: Gender and Class in Bangladesh*, University Press Ltd, Dhaka, 1992.

White, Sarah C., 'Men, Masculinities and the Politics of Development', *Gender and Development*, Vol. 5, No. 2, June 1997.

Wiebke, Walther, *Women in Islam: From Medieval to Modern Times*, Markus Wiener Publishing, New York, 1993.

Yunus, Muhammad (ed.), *Jorimon and Others: Faces of Poverty*, Grameen Bank, Dhaka, 1991.

Yunus, Muhammad, 'Towards a Poverty-Free World', paper presented at the 'Bangladesh: Democracy and Development' Conference, Melbourne, 22–23 March 1997.

Yunus, Muhammad, 'What is the Microcredit Summit?', *Grameen Poverty Research*, Vol. 3, No. 2, April 1997.

Index

Aarong (BRAC Department Stores)   152, 155, 160
Abbasid (Caliphate, 750–1258)   19, 20, 26, 34, 43–4
Abduh, Sheikh Muhammad (1854–1905)   38–9, 45–6, 58, 62
Abdul Aziz, Maulana Shah (1746–1823), of Delhi,
    issued *fatwa* declaring British India *Dar-ul-Harb* (abode of war)   104
Abdullah, ibn Umar   53
Abdur Rahman, a villager from Savar (Dhaka)   110
Abdur Razzak, a villager from Savar (Dhaka)   110
Abdul Mannan, a villager from Sirajganj district   105
Abraham   23
Abu Bakr, the first Caliph of Islam   35, 37, 40
Abu Bakara, narrator of controversial *hadis*   50
Abu Hurayra, Companion of the Prophet, and narrator of *hadises*   52–3
Abu Lahab, uncle and arch-enemy of the Prophet   44
Abu Sufyan, Makkan adversary of the Prophet, later embraced Islam   35
Abyssinia   35
ADAB (Association of Development Agencies of Bangladesh)   116,
    150–1
Adam   16–17, 20–2, 28, 54, 87
Adnan, Shapan   101
Afghani, Jamal-al-din (1838–97), Pan-Islamic writer and activist   38,
    45–6, 62
Afghanistan   2, 16, 24–5, 39, 44, 57, 62, 180, 194
Agra   73
Ahmed Ali, English translator of Quran with radical views and
    interpretations   29, 32
Ahmed, Rafiuddin   68
Aishah al-Taymariyah (d. 1902), Egyptian feminist   59
Aishah bint Talha, independent granddaughter of Caliph Abu Bakr   37
Ajker Kagaj, Bengali daily   120
Akali Begum, village woman (Thakurgaon district)   121
Al-Abbas, founder of Abbasid dynasty   37
Aleya, Grameen Bank borrower   165
Al-Ashari, Aul Hasan (died 935), restorer of orthodoxy and scholasticism
    in Islam   20, 56
Al-Azhar University   20, 70
Al-Marah-al Jadidah (The New Women), by Qasim Amin of Egypt
    (1900)   58
Al-Qurutubi, liberal Muslim scholar of early Islamic period   51
Al-Tabari (died 923), commentator of the Quran, sceptical of many
    hadises   51, 54
Algeria   25, 39, 45, 57
Ali, the fourth Caliph of Islam   33, 37, 39, 41, 43, 50–1

244 *Index*

Ali, Chiragh, liberal Muslim thinker from north India, follower of Sir
Sayyid Ahmed Khan 38, 71
Ali, Maulana Mumtaz, liberal nineteenth-century north Indian Muslim
writer, who favoured women's liberation 38, 58, 71–3
Ali, Shariati, Iranian Islamic thinker and scholar (1960s–70s) 46
Ali, Syed Ameer (1849–1928) Muslim Modernist, justice and historian
from Calcutta 38
Aligarh Movement, for 'Islamic Modernism', nineteenth and twentieth
centuries 71
Alimunnesa, a village woman (Jessore district) 111
Aligarh 73
Amin, Qasim, Egyptian Muslim writer, advocated liberation of women in
late nineteenth and early twentieth centuries 46, 58
Amin, Samir 45
Amina, 'independent' great-granddaughter of the Prophet 37
Amini, Mufti Fazlul Haq, anti-NGO and conservative Bangladeshi Muslim
cleric 125–6
Amnesty International, on persecution of women in the name of Islam
through *salish* courts 107–9 & 114–15; on NGO-Islamist conflicts
116, 199–200
Amr ibn al-Aas, early Muslim general 37
Ananda Bazar, Bengali daily (Calcutta) 195
Ananda Award, Taslima Nasreen's receiving the award and the
controversy 195
'Anglo-Mohammedan', pro-British and conservative Muslim from the
sub-continent 183–5
Anjali Karmakar, a woman from Rajshahi district 112
Anjuman-I-Mahisunnah, traditional Islamist and misogynist
association 120
Anwari, Maulana Fazlur Rahman, a misogynist *mulla*, author of *Maksudul
Momin* in Bengali 73, 80, 83
Aristotle, his misogyny 19, 21
Armstrong, Karen 35
Ashrobullah, father of Nurjahan, *salish* victim from a village in
Sylhet 107
Asma bint al-Numan, repudiated her marriage with the Prophet 38
Asma bint Yazid, female Muslim soldier, killed nine enemy soldiers at the
Battle of Yarmouk (636) 39
Assyrian 21
Arkoun, Mohammad 66
Arthashastra (of Katilya), promotion of misogyny 69
Augustine, his misogyny 20
Australian Broadcasting Corporation, anti Islamic bias 200
Awami League (Bangladeshi political party) 115–16, 122, 129, 132,
190–2
Ayat Ali, villager from Savar (Dhaka) 110
Ayesha, wife of the Prophet 35, 39, 40–1, 44, 50, 52–3, 85
Azad, Humayun 204

Bangladesh Academy of Rural Development (BARD), at Comilla 146
Bangla Academy 195
Babri Mosque at Ayodhya (India) 198, 202
Bangladesh Anti-Christian Organization 119–20
Bangladesh *Mahila Parishad* 109
Bangladesh Nationalist Party (BNP) 115–16, 119, 123, 129, 132–3, 190–2
Bangladesh Women's Lawyers' Association 188
BJP (Bharatiya Janata Party) 197, 199, 201
'Bangladeshi' nationalism 116
'Bengali' nationalism 116, 175
BRAC (Bangladesh Rural Advancement Committee), exploitation of
    female employers and borrowers and profit oriented policies 116–25;
    village women becoming self-reliant 135–47; critical of government
    servants and corruption in every layers of the society 152–8; vs *mullas*
    and others critical of NGOs 116–25
Ben Bella (of Algeria) 57
Beauty Khatun (of Sirajgang) 105
Bhashani, Maulana (1880–1976) 183
Bhorer Kagaj (Bengali daily) 120
Bhutto, Zulfikar Ali (1925–79) 191
Blair, Harry 150
'Blasphemy Law', Jammat-i-Islami's and *mullas'* demand for introduction
    in Bangladesh 200, 204
Bihishti Zewar 72, 80
Bokkor Ali, a poor villager 159
Bukhari, Imam (817–70), collector of *hadises* 50, 53, 56
Burqa (niqab) or veil worn by South Asian women 44, 75
Bourgiba, Habib (of Tunisia) 57
Bornstein, David (author, admirer of Grameen Bank) 165
Byzantine (Greek) rule and their influences on Arab (Muslim) rulers,
    subjection of women and introduction of *harem* 20–1, 44
Brahmachari, Vishnubawa, his misogynous ideas 24

Canadian International Development Agency (CIDA), its promotion of
    feminism in Bangladesh 149
Calcutta Madrasah (1781) 70–1
Chen, Martha 136
'Care-taker government', formed in 1996 122, 190
'CIA agent' 201
'Clash of civilizations 207
Clinton, Hillary 162, 168
Clinton, President 200
Child Marriage Restraint Act, 1929 2
Code Hammurabi 21
Ciba-Geigy Foundation Report on NGOs in Bangladesh (their
    ineffectiveness) 151–2
Clive, Robert 75
Chatterjee, Maitreyi 195
Code of Criminal Procedure, 1898 103

Coordinating Council of Human Rights, Bangladesh,
  on persecution of women by *salish* 112; on NGO-*mulla*
  conflict 117
Council of Disputes (Municipal Areas) Ordinance, 1983 103
Cruelty to Women Act, 1983 3

Dalim Begum (Saptagram member), village woman 159
Dar ul-Harb 104
Dars-I-Nizamiyah 71, 92
Dowry Prohabitation Act, 1980 2
D'souza, Diane 13
Deoband Madrasah 65–6, 71–3
Dulali, village women (Noakhali) 109
Durkheim, Emile 130
Desh-Kal-Samaj (BRAC publication) 153, 155
Dichter, T.W. (Critic of Grameen Bank) 164

Egypt 19, 22–3, 38–9, 41, 46, 58–9, 67, 70
El-Saadawi 45
East India Company 75, 125, 206
Engineer, Asghar Ali 30, 48, 54
Ershad, General 4, 5, 10, 150, 181, 187–8, 190, 192
Eve (Hawwa) 16–17, 20, 22, 28, 54

Fatima (daughter of the Prophet) 33, 90
Fatima bint al-Dahhak, repudiated her marriage with the Prophet 38
Fatima of Nishapur (died 849), *Sufi* 56
Firdausi (medieval Persian poet), his misogyny 41
Feldman, Shelley 150
Fanon, Frantz 45
Faraizi 65, 70, 77
Firingi Mahal Madrasah 71, 73
Friends in Village Development, Bangladesh (Habiganj) 121
Food for Work Programme 140, 154
Factory Act, 1965 172
Foucault, Michel 177
'female circumcision' (genital mutilation) 22–3
'*fatwa* to kill' (Taslima Nasreen) 199
'fatwabaz *mulla*' 97, 119–24, 132, 189

Gad al-Haq, Sheikh (Egyptian), defended 'female circumcision' 22
Gangopadhyay, Sunil 195
Ganoshangathon 138, 140
Gano Sahajya Sangstha (GSS) 157
Gano Shastho Kendro 160
Gardner, Katy 45
General Union of Palestinian Women (Pro-PLO) 58
Ghazzali, Imam (1058–1111) 20;
  his misogynous expositions, 56–7

Ghulam Azam (Professor), Chief of the Jamat-i-Islami, Bangladesh, 122,
   190; his 'public trial' in 1992 for alleged war crimes 116, 132, 189;
Ghatak-Dalal Nirmul Committee (Killer-Collaborator Elimination
   Committee) 123
Grameen Bank 8–9, 100–3, 105, 115–20, 125–6, 128–30, 133, 135–6,
   142, 146, 158, 161–71, 174–5, 178, 189
Gramsci, Antonio 177

Hafsa 35, 40
Hafizjee Huzur Sangsad 199
Hagar 23
Haque, Kazi Imdadul (1882–1926) 185
Hartmann and Boyce 89, 144
Hasan (son of Ali) 56, 90
Hasan al-Turabi (Dr) 44–5
Hashemi, Syed 142, 150, 165
Hasina, Sheikh (Prime Minister 1996–) 115, 122, 133, 190–1
Hidden Face of Eve 59
Hind Umm Salma 35, 37
Hindutva 201
Hitti, P.K. 37
Hjarpes, Jan 15
Hoda Lutfi 59
Holiday (English weekly) 197
Hossain, Kamal (Dr) 202
Hours, Bernard 67
Huda Sharawi (1879–1947) 59
Hudud Law 180–1
Husayn (Son of Ali) 37, 90

Ibn Abbas 36
Ibn Battuta 41
Ibn Hanbal 56
Ibn Ishaq (died 767) 43
Ibn-Khallikan 37
Iman Desh Bachao Andolon (Movement for the Protection of Faith and
   Motherland) 120
IMF 118
Inquilab (Bengali daily) 120
Iran 2, 16, 24–5, 45–6, 58, 60, 62, 180
'Islam in danger' 130, 203
'Islam-loving' (Islam-oriented political parties and individuals) 129,
   192–3
Islami Oikko Jote (Islamic United Front) 133
'Islamic Feminism' 14
'Islamic Modernism' 14–16, 38–9, 45–8, 50–1, 54–5, 58, 62, 71–2
Islamism ('fundamentalism', 'militancy' and 'political Islam') 1–2, 4–5,
   57, 67–8, 103, 114–17, 119, 123, 125, 129, 132, 149, 180–3, 184,
   189–4, 202–3, 207, 209

'Islamic micro-credit' 122
Islamic Revolution (Iran) 25, 58
Islamization (of Bangladesh) 2, 7, 10, 63, 78, 88, 97, 105, 187, 190–2, 194

Jamaat-i-Islami 4–6, 87, 116, 122–3, 132–3, 141, 175, 181, 183–4, 189–93, 200
Janakantha (Bengali daily) 120, 189
Jataka Tales 17, 69
Jatiya Party 191
Jatiya Mahila Sangstha (National Women's Organization) 186
Jaunpur 73
Jaunpuri, Maulana Karamat Ali (1800–73) 65, 67, 71–3, 80
Jaunpuri *pirs* 65
Jaye Jaye Din (Bengali weekly) 197, 203
Jihan (Anwer Sadat's wife) 59
Jilani, Abdul Qadir (medieval Iraqi *sufi*) 74
Jilbab (cloak) 42–3
Jorimon, poor village woman (Tangail) 145–6
Jorimon and Others: Faces of Poverty 145
Judeo-Christian 18, 21

Kabeer, Naila 173, 187
Kabeer, Rokeya Rahman (Professor), founder of Saptagram (NGO) 157–8
Kamal Ataturk 58
Kamal, Begum Sufia (poet) 203–4
Karika (NGO-run handicraft shop) 160
Kartabhaja 69
Kasem Bhuiyan, villager from Savar (Dhaka) 110
Kathamrita 69
Kenyatta, Jomu (of Kenya), defended 'female circumcision' 23
Khabarer Kagaj (Bengali daily) 194
Khadija (first wife of the Prophet) 34–5
Khalid bin Walid 36
Khan, Ayub (President) 4, 39, 59, 187
Khan, Enayetullah (Editor, *Holiday*) 197
Khan, Sir Sayyid Ahmad 38, 54, 58, 62, 71
Khatibullah, villager from Dinajpur district 113
Khawla bint al-Azwar (female warrior on the side of the Prophet) 39
Khomeini, Ayatollah 58, 200
Khwaz Khizr 75
Kothari, Rajni 117
Kudderza Bibi, an 'independent' Muslim village woman from Sylhet district 45

Lajja (Shame), controversial book by Taslima Nasreen 198–9
Liberation War (1971, Bangladesh) 4, 115–16, 123, 181, 184, 196
Lily Begum (Saptagram member), village woman 157
Lovely of village Kellai (Manikganj) 113

Madina   15, 26, 33, 37, 40, 42–4, 47
Mahabharata   18, 68–9
Mahila Parishad (Council of Women)   186–7
Maimuna (wife of the Prophet, related to Khalid bin Walid)   35
Majlis-i-Shura (Jamat-i-Islami)   87
Makka   19, 26, 35, 40–3, 46–7, 49, 50
Maksudul Momin (misogynous Bengali book by a *mulla*)   80–1
Maksudul Momeneen (misogynous Bengali book by a *mulla*)   80–1, 83
Manu's Law (*Manusanghita*)   17–18, 68
Married Women's Property Act, 1870 (Britain)   23
Marx, Karl   172, 177
matbar (matabbar), village headman   98, 112, 206, 208
Maulana Abdur Rahim (Satkania, Chittagong), *local mulla*   108
Maulana Fazlul Haq (Kasba, Brahmanbaria), *local mulla*   109
Maulana Idris (Savar, Dhaka), local *mulla*   110
Maulana Gholam Mustafa (Jessore), local *mulla*   111
Maulana Mannan (Chatakchara village, Sylhet), village *mulla* and
   misogynist *salish* judge   107
Maulana Muhammad Ismail (Chhagalnayya, Feni), local *mulla*   114
Maulana Muzzammil Haq (Feni)   114
Maulana Ibrahim (Bogra), local *mulla*   119, 121–2
Mawdudi, Maualna (1903–1979), founder of the Jamat-i-Islami   44, 77–8
mehr (dower in Muslim marriage)   31, 85
member-matbar-mulla triumvirate   98, 100–2, 111–13, 118, 124, 136–9,
   143, 175, 178, 207
Menon, Rashed Khan   150
Metcalf, Barbara   72
Mernissi, Fatima (Moroccan feminist scholar)   38, 60
Miftah ul-Jannat (by Karamat Ali Jaunpuri)   72, 80
milad   65
Mill, John Stuart   23–4
Ministry of Women's Affairs, created by President Ziaur Rahman   186
'mini Khomeini'   10, 97
Mofis Mulla, a villager in Hartmann and Boyce's book   89–90
Motaleb, a villager from Sylhet   107
Mughal   19, 70
Mulaika bint Kaab, repudiated her marriage with the Prophet   38
mullas   3, 8–11, 24, 44, 56, 62, 97–9, 101, 128–9, 136–8, 153, 158, 173–4,
   177, 181, 185–6, 193, 197–8, 201, 206–8; *ulama* or 'urban *mullas*'
   [*maulanas, pirs, sufis, sheikhs, muftis* etc.] representing the 'great'
   traditions of Islam   61–73, 78, 87, 94, 98–9, 104, 113–14, 117, 120,
   124–6,186, 200, 204, 209; *maulvi, munshi* and rustic-rural *mullas,*
   representing the 'little' tradition of Islam   61–4, 66–70, 73–94, 97–8,
   104–6, 108–13, 115, 117–21, 123–5, 129–32, 174, 176, 182, 192
Musharraf, a villager from Jessore   111
Muslim Brotherhood   49, 67
'Muslim Bengali'   78
Muslim League   183
muta (temporary marriage)   26, 34

Mutawakkil, Caliph ('the bigot')   34
(Sepoy) Mutiny (1857–8)   70
Mutazila (Mutazilite), opposed polygamy   34
Muhammad, the Prophet   15, 25, 32–45, 51–3, 58, 62, 74, 76, 79–87, 89, 120, 199, 209

Nabawiah Musa (Egyptian feminist)   59
Nadwa (north India, famous for its *madrasah*)   73
Nafisa (female *sufi,* early Islam)   56
nafs (soul of feminine noun)   28
Naila (wife of the third Caliph Usman)   51
Naripokkho   186
Napoleon   70
Nari (by Humayun Azad)   204
Narod culture   131
Nasreen, Taslima   4, 6, 10, 63, 80, 96, 115, 117, 123, 132, 142, 149, 180–2, 184–6, 190, 192–9, 200–4, 209
Nari Unnayan Shakti   186
Nasser (of Egypt)   59
Nath cult (Hindu)   65
Nawal Saadawi (Egyptian feminist), author of *The Hidden Face Of Eve* (1980)   59
Naziban Bibi, village woman (Bogra)   120
Nazrul Islam, Qazi (1899(?)–1976), Bengali poet   185
Neamul Quran (misogynous Bengali book by Maulvi Shamsul Huda)   74
'NGO-Culture'   11; NGOs, limitations, mostly help middle peasants not the poorest   147–8; both leftists and Islamists critical of   148; lack of accountability to the Government   149; 'NGO-Business'   149–50; 'Islamic NGOs'   150; Ciba-Geigy Foundation's disenchantment with   151–2; NGOs' gender bias for more funding from Western donors   152; 'agents of neo-imperialism' and 'enemies of Islam'   175
NGO Forum in Beijing (1995)   60
NGO-Grameen Lobby (Grameen-NGO Lobby)   100–1, 125–6, 128, 132–3, 275, 178
NGO-Grameen Activities (Grameen-NGO Activities)   118, 123–5, 129, 175
'NGO-*Wallas*' (promoters of NGOs, pejorative)   206
Nietzsche (German philosopher)   75
Nijera Kori (NGO)   116, 136, 142, 160, 188
Nirbachito Column (by Taslima Nasreen)   194–7
Nizam-i-Islami (Islami-oriented political party)   183
NORAD (Norwegian Agency for Development Cooperation)   158
Nurjahan of Chatakchara village (Sylhet)   107–8
Nurjahan of Dokhin Sripur village (Faridpur)   108
Nuruzzaman, Colonel (retired)   123
Nusaybah bint Kaab (female Muslim warrior during the period of the Prophet)   39

Origen (medieval church-father)   20
Ottoman   19–20

'Orientalist' prejudice against Islam 12–13, 26
Oxfam 158

Pakistani 98, 104, 115, 123, 186, 189; military junta (1971) 175, 181, 183–4, 189
Panchatantra 69
Pach Pir 65
Panch Pandit 65
Para Teare (of Genderwatch), critic of the Grameen Bank 162, 168
Persian 21, 34, 41, 64, 68, 79
Plato 8, 21
Plassey (battle of) 75
PLO (Palestine Liberation Organization) 57
Post-*Taliban* Afghanistan 130
Protestant Revolt 20
Puranas 68
purdah (seclusion) 45, 75, 79, 83, 88–90, 101–3, 114, 121, 130, 137, 146, 153, 158–9, 173–4, 193

Qajar dynasty 19
Queen Sheba (Bilqees) 49
Quraysh 37

Rabiah Basri (717–801) 56
Rahima Begum (Saptagram member) 159
Rahman, Anisur (Professor) 118
Rahman, Farida (BNP leader) 192
Rahman, Fazlur (author, *Islam*) 47, 54–5
Rahman, M. Mahbubur 7
Rahman, Maulana Gholam (author, *Maksudul Momeneen*) 73, 80–3
Rahman Shafik (editor *Jaye Jaye Din*) 203
Rahman, Shamsur (poet) 204
Rahman, Sheikh Mujibur (Mujib), died 1975 5, 115, 183, 190
raman 22, 68
ramani 22, 68
Ramakrishna Paramahansa 24, 69
Ramayana 68–9
Rangpur-Dinajpur Rural Service Programme (RDRS) 138
Rashid al-Din 41
Razia Begum, village woman (Pirojpur) 106
Razia Khatun, village woman of Bara Chaimata (Kishoreganj) 112
Razia Khatun, village woman (Kishoreganj) 93
'Resumption Proceedings' (1820s–1850s) 69
Reza Shah, Muhammad (Iran) 58
Rock, Marilyn 173
Rokeya, Begum (1880–1932), feminist author 59, 185
Roqaiya, village woman (Feni) 109
Rousseau 23
Rostow's Model (of the stages of economic growth) 127

Roy, Asim (Dr)   64, 68
Rozia Akhter Rina, village woman (Feni)   106
Rumpelstiltskin, the evil dwarf of the story, compared with Grameen
   Bank   163
Rushdie, Salman   200; 'Female Salman Rushdie'   203

Sadat, Anwer   59
Safavid (dynasty)   19
Safiya (Jewish wife of the Prophet)   35
Safiyah (aunt of the Prophet)   39
Sahaba Sainik Parishad (The Council of the Companions of the
   Prophet)   199
Sahajiya   65, 69
Sahabdhani   69
Saidi, Maulan Delwar Hossain, Jamat-i-Islami MP, misogynous *mulla*   73,
   87–9, 192
Sakina (Sukaynah)   36–7, 41, 43
salish courts   7–9, 61, 63, 93, 96–9, 101, 103–14, 116, 123, 129–31, 137–9
Sammilito Sangskritic Jote (Alliance of Cultural Forum)   190
Sangbad (Bengali daily)   108
Sapnahar, a village woman (Brahmanbaria)   109
Saptagram (NGO run by women)   157–60, 188
Sara   23
Sassanid (Persian), influence on Islam and subjection of women   21,
   41, 44
Satya Pir   65
Sati   24, 68
Saudi Arabia   2, 16, 19, 24, 39, 59, 62, 66
Sawda, Prophet's wife   35
Schuler, Sidney Ruth   142, 165
Scott, James (Professor)   125
Sen, Keshabchandra   94
Shafi, Imam   81
Shah Waliullah Smriti Sangsad   199
Shahida, a village woman from Savar (Dhaka)   110–11
Shahida, a village woman from Jesssore   111–12
Shakta   69
Shamsuddin, author of controversial newspaper article in *Janakantha*
   (1994)   189
Shamsul Huda, Maulvi (author, *Neamul Quran*)   74–80
Sharia (Muslim law)   2, 4, 7, 9, 14–15, 28, 30, 39, 46–52, 54–6, 58, 60,
   62, 64–6, 91, 93, 97–8, 103–4, 112–14, 129, 137, 154, 181, 184, 186,
   192–3, 206
Sharif, Ahmed (Professor) (d. February 1999)   123, 154, 204
Shefali, village woman (Sirajganj)   105
Sheikh Saadi, medieval Persian (misogynous) poet   41, 79
Shree Chaitanya (1486–1533)   65
Shetuli (NGO-run handicraft shop)   160
Shukur Ali, poor villager from Sirajganj   105

SIDA (Swedish International Development Agency) 158
Siddiqi, Zillur Rahman (Professor) 118
Siraju ud-Dawla, Nawab 75
'Sixteen Decisions' (Gameen Bank) 161, 178
Sophia, Queen of Spain 168
Statesman (Calcutta daily) 200
'State Religion' 4, 181
Stowasser, Barbara 36
'Spirit of the Freedom Struggle (1971)' 4
Sudan Communist Party 57
Sufia Begum, village woman from Dinajpur 113
Suhayl, relative of Sawdah, wife of the Prophet 35
Suppression of Violence against Women and Children Act, 1998 3
Sura al-Ahzab 32, 42, 75
Sura al-Falaq 57
Sura al-Nisa 29
Swartz, Oswald (Dr) 79

Tabligh movement 66, 77, 183, 192
Tahirr al-Mara'h (by Qasim Amin) 58
Taha, Muhammad 46
Taif 37
Taijul Islam, *matbar* from Jessore 112
Taliban 2, 24–5
Tantric (*Tantra*) 68–9
Tariqa-i-Muhammadiya (nineteenth-century Islamic movement) 65
'Taslima Nasreen Suppression Committee' 195
Tayuni (nineteenth-century Islamic movement) 65
Tertullian 20–1
Thanawi, Maulana Ashraf Ali 71–4, 80
'Thirty five Commandments' (of a *mulla*) 83–6
Time 126
Tonnies, Ferdinand 130–1
Tota Mia, villager from Brahmanbaria 109
Toronto Star 172
Tucker, Jeffrey 163
Tunisia 39, 59
Turkey (Turkish) 21, 25, 39, 58
'Two-Nation Theory' of Jinnah 182

Umar (the second Caliph) 35, 37, 40, 43, 52
Umar, Badruddin 118, 167
Umayyad (dynasty) 19–20, 26, 34, 37, 43
Umm Habiba, Prophet's wife, daughter of Abu Sufyan 35
Umm Kulthum, wife of Amr ibn al-Aas 37
Umm Waraka, female *imam* (prayer leader) during the time of the Prophet 40
Umm Salma, wife of al-Abbas, founder of the Abbasid dynasty 37
Umm Salma, wife of the Prophet 40

Usman (the third Caliph)   40, 51
UNESCO   160

Van Schendel, Willem (Professor)   7, 143
Village Courts Ordinance, 1976   103
Vivekananda, Swami   24, 69

Wahhabi   70
Walther, Wiebke   33
Waliullah, Shah (1702–62)   30, 55
waz mahfil   87–9
Westergaard, Kirsten   141, 147
World Bank   118, 170
Women's Development Forum   186
Women's Rehabilitation Foundation   186
Women in Development Project, promoted by General Ershad   187

Yahya bin Said   54
Yamen   49
Yunus, Professor Muhammad (founder of the Grameen Bank)   119, 125,
    145, 163, 168, 175
Yusef al-Badry, Sheikh, defends 'female circumcision'   23

Zaid   36
Zainab bint Jahash   36, 43
Zainab bint Khuzayma   35
Zaynab Fawwaz, Egyptian feminist (d. 1914)   59
Zia, Khaleda (Prime Minister of Bangladesh, 1991–6)   111, 115–16, 120,
    150, 181, 190–1
Ziaur Rahman (Zia), President (d. 1981)   4, 5, 115, 135, 184, 186, 190,
    192
Zia-ul-Haq, (Pakistani military ruler, 1977–88)   181
zawj (spouse)   28
Zohra, poor village woman (Dhaka)   106
Zoroastrian (women as men's property)   21
Zubayr, Hazrat Shah   75